PUT ON YOUR BOOTS AND PARACHUTES!

This book is dedicated to the memory of

ANDREW F. 'ANDY' KILCULLEN
1921-1987

Twice President and for many years the Treasurer of the C-47 Club, who was the organiser of reunions and overseas visits. One of the original members of B Company, 505th Parachute Infantry Regiment who, after the war, served for thirty years with the New York City Police. He retired as a First Grade Detective in the 10th Precinct's Homicide Squad. He was Airborne's greatest ambassador and a generous friend.

PUT ON YOUR BOOTS AND PARACHUTES!

PERSONAL STORIES OF THE VETERANS

OF THE

UNITED STATES 82nd AIRBORNE DIVISION

FROM THE SECOND WORLD WAR

IN THE

EUROPEAN THEATRE OF OPERATIONS

including

A SUMMARY OF THE WAR DIARY OF

WILLIAM H. TUCKER

I COMPANY, THIRD BATTALION,

505th PARACHUTE INFANTRY REGIMENT

WRITTEN AND EDITED BY

DERYK WILLS

First published, March 1992

Published by Deryk Wills, 70 Hidcote Road, Oadby, Leicester LE2 5PF

Copyright: Deryk Wills and William H. Tucker

ISBN 0 9518451 0 1

Printed by AB Printers Limited, Cannock Street, Leicester

Part One

A COLLECTION OF PERSONAL STORIES FROM THE

VETERANS OF THE 82nd AIRBORNE DIVISION

INCLUDING THE DIARY OF JAMES J. COYLE,

E COMPANY, 505TH PARACHUTE INFANTRY REGIMENT

COMPILED AND WRITTEN BY

DERYK WILLS

Introduction

For many years I have sat enthralled at 82nd Airborne Reunions listening to war stories. The characters and the situations recalled were, I found, fascinating, and in the end I decided that they should be recorded as an historical document.

My collection grew and I began to realise that these stories all dovetailed together, linking themselves in a remarkable way. I have not set out to write the Division's war history, but just to record these personal stories that would have been lost forever in a few years time.

The names of these men will be unknown to many of you, but we do owe them our gratitude. These men came from across the Atlantic Ocean and helped fight Hitler's army to bring about peace in Europe. Some of them were first and second generation Germans. Many had eastern European names. All knew what the word 'freedom' meant. When the war was over they returned to civilian life and became stalwart members of their local communities.

The usual veteran's comment has been, ''Please don't make me out to be a hero when telling my story.'' I must state that I have been dealing in facts and have researched these stories thoroughly.

I have not set out to make any man a hero, but as I progressed one fact became perfectly obvious to me. Every man who served in the United States 82nd Airborne Division during World War Two, whether a paratrooper or a Gliderman, was a hero in his own right. Of that there is no doubt in my mind.

After Normandy the 505th Parachute Infantry Regiment gained the reputation of being a pack of jackals, the toughest, the most resourceful infantry in Europe.

It was while I was visiting Dennis Force at his home at Bremerton, Washington, in 1990, I read Bill Tucker's War Diary for the first time which he had privately printed for his friends. Bill had told me about it on several occasions but this was my first chance to read it. Needless to say, I was very impressed.

I immediately wrote to Bill and explained the content of my proposed book and asked him to let me include an edited version of his Diary. After some consideration he thankfully agreed.

These are not stories from Generals, but the ordinary front line soldiers' view of combat which is rare and so important.

The question will be asked, ''Why has an Englishman written this book about the men of a famous United States Division?''

Well, I felt that I was far enough removed to have an objective eye on the subject. This book has been a labour of love in making sure the world knows of these veterans and their dedication and the sacrifice they made in cause of freedom in Europe. I have the greatest love and respect for these men who I have got to know so well.

It has not been a case of wondering where do I start in writing this book. The problem has been, when do I stop.

Many veterans have given me encouragement right from the start. I would like to mention a few; Ed Dugan, Don McKeage, Jim Coyle, Delbert Humpston, Dennis Force, Richard Tedeschi, Robert Franco and Bill Tucker.

I also would like to acknowledge the great help I have had from my son, David, in collecting these stories. On many of his visits to the Reunions as a guest jumper with the 82nd Old Tymers Parachute Club he carried with him a list of questions and a tape recorder.

I have been able to double check these stories with excellent books written on the subject of the U.S. 82nd Airborne Division. One, *Ready*, is a detailed Regimental history written by Allen Langdon, a wartime member of the 505th Parachute Infantry Regiment. He didn't finish it until 1986, four years before he died. He left us with a masterpiece. Allen was also a paratrooper to the end. He made a parachute jump with Bill Tucker and Elmo Jones into the Drop Zone at Groesbeek, Holland, in 1984 to commemorate the 40th Anniversary of Market Garden.

Another was written by General James M. Gavin: titled *On To Berlin*, it is another classic in its field.

I would like to point out that in writing these stories I have used the true English spelling developed over a period of a thousand years on the East side of the Atlantic Ocean. What you guys have done with it on the West side in the last two hundred years is your problem.

Deryk Wills,
Oadby, Leicester.
1st November 1991.

The 82nd Airborne Division

The 82nd was formed as an Infantry Division at Camp Gordon, Georgia, on 25th August 1917. The nickname 'All Americans' came when it was discovered that there were men in this unit from each State of the Union. This was reflected in the shoulder flash with the initials 'AA' in a design of red, white and blue.

During the First World War the Division participated in three major campaigns. They spent more consecutive days in the front line than any other American unit. During the Meuse-Argonne offensive alone they suffered in excess of 7,400 casualties.

Their actions earned two of the men the Congressional Medal of Honor; Lt. Colonel Emory J. Pike and Corporal Alvin C. York.

On 27th May, 1919, the Division was disbanded.

After the outbreak of the Second World War the 82nd. was reactivated on 25th March, 1942, as an Infantry Division under the command of Major General Omar N. Bradley. Brigadier General Matthew B. Ridgway was appointed his second-in-command. Their base was Camp Claiborne, Louisiana.

They were about three quarters of the way through their basic training when Bradley was transferred to rescue an ailing National Guard Division. Ridgway was given the command of the 82nd Division and the change over was effected on June 26.

At the end of the training schedule a full-dress review for this Infantry Division was staged on August 15. Sixteen thousand men were on parade when Ridgway broke the news that they were going to be reorganised into Glider Regiments as a new Airborne Division.

As reported in the book 'Ridgway's Paratroopers', "The next morning we had 4,500 men Absent-without-leave (AWOL)."

"What in the world made them do that?" Ridgway questioned his Aide.

"Sir, you scared the pants off them." was the reply. "But don't worry, they will be back." And come back they did over the next three or four days and training started afresh.

In mid-September the new airborne division moved to Fort Bragg, North Carolina, which became its permanent home right up to the present day. At first, Glider Infantry regiments were formed and later, in January 1943, they were joined by the 504th Parachute Infantry Regiment. A month later their sister unit, the 505 arrived.

Ridgway had already met Colonel James Gavin and he knew that under Gavin's leadership the 505 was possibly the best trained of all the parachute regiments.

As the 82nd Airborne Division left the United States to engage the enemy in Europe it comprised of these units:-
Division Headquarters and Headquarters Company
82nd Airborne Military Police Platoon
504th Parachute Infantry Regiment
505th Parachute Infantry Regiment
325th Glider Infantry Regiment
Headquarters and Headquarters Battery Divisional Artillery
319th Glider Field Artillery Battalion
320th Glider Field Artillery Battalion
376th Parachute Field Artillery Battalion
456th Parachute Field Artillery Battalion
80th Airborne Anti-Tank Battalion
307th Airborne Engineer Battalion
407th Airborne Quartermasters Company
307th Airborne Medical Company
821th Airborne Signal Company
782nd Airborne Ordnance Maintenance Company
82nd Airborne Reconnaissance Platoon
82nd Parachute Maintenance Company.

During periods of combat other units were attached at various times and were considered a vital part of the Division:
508th Parachute Infantry Regiment
507th Parachute Infantry Regiment
401th Glider Infantry, Second Battalion.

The States to North Africa

The 505th Parachute Infantry Regiment had been 'born' on 6th July 1942, at Fort Benning, Georgia. A programme of hard physical training was a matter of course for everyone, including the Medics and Chaplains, and it carried the rule, 'If you fall out, you ship out.' Three out of four volunteers failed the tough competition, especially in the southern heat.

Each selected man then went to a Jump School and completed five parachute jumps before earning those silver wings and the right to wear the distinctive jump boots.

The Chaplain was Rev. George 'Chappie' Wood and he became the first Chaplain in the United States history to make a combat parachute jump. 'Chappie' joined the Chaplains Corp in June 1942 and when they didn't get around to activating his outfit — the 100th Bomber Group — he volunteered for airborne duty.

Chaplin Wood reported to Colonel James Gavin at Fort Benning on 6th October, 1942. "Gavin asked me if I knew what I was doing, and when I said 'Yes', he sent me to a young Lieutenant for jump training."

On his second training jump, 'Chappie' badly sprained his ankle, and to complete his five jumps had to be helped out of the airplane's door each time.

On 12th February, 1943, the 505th Parachute Infantry Regiment joined the 82nd Airborne Division at Fort Bragg, North Carolina.

The fiercely independent 505 didn't want to join up with anybody and took a longtime to settle down in the Division. When addressed as the 82nd, the paratroopers would shout back, "We're the Five-O-Five!"

They were from all walks of life, all volunteers attracted by the extra $50 a month jump pay and the chance to wear the famous jump boots. Their ages averaged about 24 years old, a little older than the British Airborne. A lot of them were farm boys from the South, sometimes known as the 'barefooted shit kickers'. By joining the Army they could spend an extra hour in bed and get up 5.30am, better than their farming days. They were able to eat three square meals a day, have uniforms and even proper boots to wear. For some of them, having lived through the depression, the United States Army was sheer luxury.

Some of the Staff Officers had not undergone parachute training and therefore were not entitled to wear jumpboots. To placate everybody, General Ridgway issued an order saying that if any Staff Officer made one parachute jump he could wear the boots.

Even the most timid officers queued up to throw themselves out of the door of a C-47 just to get the chance to wear the complete 'airborne' uniform, some suffering dire results.

Staff Sergeant Harry Anderson, E Company, 505, remembers the early days of the Regiment and the training back in the States of the 505.

One story Harry tells is of the regular Absent-without-leave problem amongst the men. Major Edward Krause was furious at this practice and had his men lined up to have their 'ears chewed off'. Krause was shaking with rage and said that he could lick any man in the outfit. One of the tough bar room fighters stepped forward for the challenge but Krause brushed him aside with, "I'll see you later soldier."

The AWOL's continued and one day a picture appeared in one of the newspapers of a crowd of 505 paratroopers surrounded by girls taken in Orlando. The caption referred to 'Our paratroopers relax and enjoy themselves.' They were all AWOL.

A Squad was sent to bring them back, but they went missing for three days as well.

One day, Harry Anderson was in the outer office of Major James A. Gray, the Second Battalion Commanding Officer, when a trooper came in to see the officer on a personal matter. Harry opened the sliding trap between the offices and announced that Private Prescott wanted to see the Major. "Wants?" shouted Gray. Harry hurriedly changed it to "Private Prescott wishes to see the Major on a personal matter." The Private was admitted.

A little later the sliding trap opened and the voice of Major Gray came through, "Anderson, do you have a round of ammunition out there? Prescott here wants to leave the service!".

It was James Gray, then a Captain, while in California came into possession of a large brutish Boxer dog answering to the name of Max. When Gray joined the 505 the dog came too. The fighting men enjoyed having the dog around and the riggers made him a special parachute and harness.

Max was taken up for his first flight and when Lieutenant Clyde Russell jumped, the battling boxer followed him out of the door, gyrated gracefully earthwards and landed in far better shape than most of his fellow jumpers.

The story goes that he didn't like sitting down on the metal floor of the C-47 as it vibrated his private parts and so he was especially anxious to leave the plane as soon as he could.

Max made a total of ten jumps from a plane in flight. He became so famous that Paramount and Movietone News wanted to make a 'short' of him. The day he was to become a film star the battling Boxer took on a two ton truck and Max came off second best, but he did recover from his injuries.

While in Alabama one of the nearby roadhouses was called 'Cotton's Fish Camp'. One night a fight started with the local hillbillies and six paratroopers. Tommy Thompson and Gasper Lucero were two in the party who were in the thick of it. Lucero was badly hurt with knife wounds in his back and needed hospital treatment.

The word got around the Regiment and plans were made for a raiding party to tear the Roadhouse apart and burn it down. The gossip leaked out and Colonel James Gavin put Cotton's Fish Camp 'off limits'. The attacking force was met by the Military Police and the State Troopers.

The next night at Retreat, Gavin announced, "Yesterday I put out an order that Cotton's Fish Camp was 'off limits'. About three parts of this command disobeyed that order, so I am going to take some steam out of you."

That night the men were ordered on parade with full equipment and weapons and Gavin hiked them around for a day and a night. As Sergeant John Rabig recalled, "We were never more than fifteen miles from the camp at any one time, but he walked the shit out of us."

The badly injured Private Gasper Lucero recovered in time to go overseas. He was killed in action in Italy.

Sergeant Charles Kaiser remembers the humour very well. The first leave after training was preceded by a parade taken by Major Edward Krause. He ordered, "Nobody leaves this camp until he has a haircut like mine." He took his hat off to show that he had no hair at all.

The 505th Parachute Infantry Regiment sailed from New York harbour aboard the S.S. Monterey on 28th April, 1943. The destination, a closely guarded secret, was revealed when they arrived in Casablanca, French Morocco, in North Africa on 10th May. For them the war had really begun.

The 325th Glider Infantry sailed a day later, the 29th, on the converted luxury liner Santa Rosa. It was very overcrowded with a double load of soldiers on board. It was necessary to spend three nights sleeping in a regular bunk, and then three nights on deck, wherever there was room to spread a blanket. The sea was very rough so many preferred to stay on deck every night because of seasickness.

Meals were served continuously from morning to night. Because of the numbers on board, meals had to be eaten standing up, the men moving slowly along the tables so that no time was lost.

Water was very limited, even to drink, and the few showers that were taken were in salt water which left everyone feeling rather sticky.

Del Humpston remembers the movies that were shown to break the monotony. He went one night with his close buddy, Al Gardner, to see Humphrey Bogart in Casablanca. Nobody could have guessed that this was their destination, but somebody in the know had a sense of humour.

Staff Sergeant Harry Anderson remembers the secrecy. "We had to cover our Divisional insignias on our uniforms and wear our trousers over our jump boots so nobody would know that the 82nd Airborne Division was in North Africa."

"That is until we walked down the gang-plank at Casablanca and the waiting military band struck up with our march, 'The All-American Soldier'. That night 'Axis Sally' was welcoming the Division to Africa on her radio programme from Italy."

Even in wartime there are amusing incidents which stick in the memory for years. As the 325th Glider Infantry left the docks after disembarking, Del Humpston noticed an Arab dressed in baggy pants made from a GI's barrack bag. The soldier's name and serial number were still visible, stencilled across his backside.

The Arabs stole everything they could lay their hands on. Guards had to be posted around the camps, day and night, to stop the thieving. On one train journey, which lasted ten days, the barrack bags were all stacked on a flat car and as the train slowly crawled up a steep gradient two Arabs grabbed one of the bags. The guards on this particular night were Private Woots Chaffins, of Yellow Mountain, Kentucky, and Private Henry Williams of Martinsberg, West Virginia.

Firing two shots with his M-1 rifle, Chaffins hit one of the Arabs. It was dark so he didn't know how bad the Arab was wounded, but he did hear him groan. The bag was never recovered.

While in North Africa the Division was put through endless days and nights of training. Dysentery became the norm and tablets of Atabrine were the order of the day to prevent malaria. On many days the temperature soared to 120 degrees F.

It was discovered later that the cause of the widespread dysentery was the dung-laden dust in the area which was whipped up by the wind.

Harry Anderson, 505, was never far from his bottle of booze, even in North Africa he had a private supply. Robert Bales came to him one day and asked if he could buy a bottle. Harry asked what was wrong. Bales had just had a 'Dear John' letter from his girl in the States, she had found the Navy more attractive. "You don't drink alone with me around," said Harry, and they went off into the desert with a bottle and various things like substitute lemon scrounged from the cookhouse and they both got uproariously drunk.

It was Robert Bales who made history back at Fort Benning when he accidently made the highest parachute jump on record. In November 1942 he was taking photographs from a plane flying at 13,500 feet when he lost his balance in holding the heavy camera and fell out of the door.

After several hours searching he was located, uninjured, twenty miles away. He had fallen about three thousand feet before his chute opened and then several panels were blown. The fate of the camera was not recorded at the time.

Every Company had a Company Fund where $5 a month from everybody paid for extra food bought in the local market, or items for the good of the men. E Company had such a fund and everybody was kept guessing on what goodies would be purchased.

One day at Kairouan a large box arrived at E Company, 505. Excitement was intense until they saw the contents. It was full of condoms.

That night Bob Hope, Jerry Colonna and Frances Langford put on a show for the 82nd Airborne. E Company were there in force with the contents of their box. They proceeded to blow the condoms up like balloons. Throughout the show large balloon type objects floated across the audience much to the amusement of the paratroopers and to the bewilderment of singing star Frances Langford.

As a special to this show, the 505 made a parachute jump over the open air auditorium. One of the jumpers, Bill Tucker, recalls the night. "We boarded the plane and as it rose into the twilight I pleasantly noticed the surroundings and how much cooler the night air was higher up, away from the filth, disease and rotten food."

"That particular night Bob Hope and Frances Langford were entertaining the troops below and perhaps our jump was something of a show off for their benefit. We overflew the show and could see the lighted platform eight hundred feet below. At any rate I wheeled into line and jumped lustily out the door, not paying much attention to anything.''

''I gathered in my chute when I hit and tramped on back to sit down and catch the end of the Frances Langford Bob Hope Show.''

''In 1978 I met and had a brief talk with Bob Hope, telling him that the first time I had seen him was from the vertical distance of eight hundred feet — he remembered the night.''

In a letter to the C-47 Flyer, Lt. Colonel Mark Alexander, then a Major and Commanding Officer of the Second Battalion, 505, recalls some unusual parachuting experiments. In planning the invasion of Sicily it was decided that mules would be useful in the rough terrain. Some ideas were tried out to fly them in CG-4A Gliders, and another suggestion was to drop them by parachute.

Mark Alexander takes up the story. ''Few people know the story but in North Africa, near Kairouan, we jumped a mule from a C-47. I do not know where the order came from but I was assigned to round up a jump team consisting of one mule, Corporal Robert Bales, Corporal Fred Freeland, Sergeant Jack Gavin and myself.''

''I talked to the 64th Group Troop Carriers' Executive Officer, Tommy Thompson into flying us. We secured a 48 foot supply chute, blindfolded the mule and somehow got him into the plane with the big door off. As we approached the Drop Zone the mule got smart and lay down on the floor. We had to slide him out of the door.''

''We were pushing so hard that I fell out on top of the mule and watched him fall below me until my chute opened. Well, the mule broke two legs and we decided that the operation was not practical.''

''The idea originated somewhere in the command above me. Ironically it illustrates how poor our intelligence information was regarding our pending jump in Sicily. There were more mules in Sicily per square mile than in about any other part of the world.''

''With that same team of Bales, Freeland and Gavin, we conducted another experiment. At that time we were dropping blood plasma in canvas bundles and breaking about half the bottles. I learned that the British had some aluminum bundles about six foot long and eighteen inches in diameter. We stole a couple of them and packed the plasma therein. The results were almost 100 per cent better.''

''However, after persuading Tommy Thompson to fly us again, we took off with just the small door open and proceeded to the Drop Zone. Just before the drop we pushed the end of the bundle out about three feet, the air stream knocked the bundle back against the edge of the door. The big door popped off, flew back and wrapped itself around the tail of the plane.''

''The plane was shaking all over the place and the pilot, Thompson, came running back and screamed, 'What the hell are you bastards doing to my plane now?' I told him not to worry about it because it was just that the big door had wrapped itself around his tailplane — and we jumped out of the door.''

Sergeant Fred Freeland of the Second Battalion, 505, who was killed in action in the Ardennes.

"Thompson told me later that he had a hell of a time landing the C-47."

Jack Gavin was killed in action in Holland and Fred Freeland met the same fate in the Ardennes. Mark Alexander was seriously wounded in Normandy.

It was Fred Freeland who came up with the idea of a black panther for the regimental crest and he did the first drawings which were adopted. Since then there have been several changes in the design.

Fred was a very talented young man whose interest in draughtsmanship, photography and design became of great value to the Regiment. Sergeant Tommy Gore remembers the drawings of swing wing aircraft — now fifty years on a reality — and Fred's hair raising experiments of jet propulsion using the propellant from bazooka shells.

The one thing about Africa that sticks in the mind of veteran 504 trooper Albert 'Big Al' Resko was the flies. Millions and millions of flies that got everywhere. He explained, "You could always tell the new boys. They would fish out the flies from their chow with a spoon before they ate it. The old sweats would just press them into the gravy until they stopped struggling and then swallowed them down with the food. We were past caring."

Al was later wounded in Italy and returned to the States after hospitalisation and became a parachute instructor at Fort Benning.

SECOND LIEUTENANT JAMES J. COYLE
E COMPANY, 505

While I was attending the Officer's Infantry School, I used to see paratroopers jumping on the nearby Drop Zone almost daily and realised that they must be some of the best troops in the Army. When I received my commission, I volunteered and went directly to Parachute School in March of 1943.

On completion of the course at the Parachute School I was assigned to an officers pool attached to the 513th Regiment. Within a week or so orders came sending most of the officers — including Theodore 'Pete' Peterson, Howard Jensen, Sal Palisano and myself, all later members of E Company 505 — to a unit called EGB 447. We were never told what kind of a unit this was supposed to be. It turned out to be very unorganised, with enlisted men assigned to various provisional Companies with no service records or equipment. One week after the unit was formed we were shipped to the New York Port of Embarkation, Camp Shanks.

We spent a few days being issued with equipment, getting shots, writing up our wills, etc., and then in the middle of the night took a short troop train ride to a dock on Staten Island. There we boarded an old beat-up liner, the *SS George Washington* and sailed out of New York Harbour on 29th April, 1943.

As it turned out, the 504th Parachute Infantry Regiment, 82nd Airborne Division, was on the ship as well as Major General Matthew B. Ridgway, although we never saw him. We did see Colonel Reuben Tucker who was the troop commander of the *George Washington*. He gave us a particularly hard time as orphans. The *George Washington* was so crowded with troops that we had to take turns sleeping, one night in a bunk and one night laying on the open deck.

Maintaining control of the men was difficult in those circumstances, especially making sure that they got fed and a bunk when it was their turn. About halfway across the Atlantic, the old tub's engines broke down and the other ship in the convoy (which I later learned was the *Monterey*, carrying E Company, 505th Parachute Infantry Regiment) sailed away and left us bobbing about in the sea like a sitting duck.

A destroyer stayed with us, and during the night it kept dropping depth charges (on what I don't know — there was no alert on our ship). This was a little unnerving as I was about two decks below the water line with my men and the explosions sounded as though they were going to split open the hull. By the morning the engines were repaired and we were on our way again.

A few days later we landed at Casablanca, French Morocco, and were transported about ten miles to a Replacement Depot at Fort Lyautey. After a week, during which we tried to get the group better organised and being issued with more equipment (we were still unaware of the mission of EGB 447), we boarded 40 and 8 cattle cars for Oujda.

Upon arrival the officers and men were broken up into small groups and assigned to various units of the 82nd Airborne Division. Lieutenant 'Pete' Peterson and I and some of the men were assigned to E Company, 505th Parachute Infantry Regiment and moved by truck to the desert where the Company was camped.

We arrived in the middle of the night, it was 24th May. The Company was out on a night problem and Pete and I were assigned a tent as our quarters. The Company returned a few hours later and Lieutenant Bill Meddaugh came to meet us. We introduced ourselves and asked questions about the Company, the name of the Company Commander was Lieutenant Talton W. Long. Pete and I had finally realised that EGB 447 was nothing more than a group of replacements sent overseas with the Division until we landed.

The next morning I reported to Lieutenant Long and was assigned to the First Platoon as Lieutenant Waverly W. Wray's Assistant Platoon Leader.

For two months we trained in the desert primarily on night manoeuvres. Oujda was an extremely hot, dry, dusty, flyridden area and in a very short time we were all suffering from dysentery.

I discovered early on that the officers and men of E Company were of a superior calibre compared to any with whom I had served in my two years in the army. I maintained a low profile while I learnt the names of the men as quickly as I could, and tried to pick up as much information as possible on airborne equipment, tactics, etc. It was fortunate that I was not aware that I would be in combat in two months. I'd had two years of training in the regular infantry but I was a green Lieutenant in this parachute outfit with only five jumps to my credit.

Fortunately, I was picked to be part of a training operation as a test for the pilots and navigators of the C-47 airplanes at the airport near our camp. Each plane was assigned one paratroop officer to jump after a long three-hour flight in which the crew flew various headings which eventually would bring them to our Drop Zone. Each jumper was to plot his landing point on a map and the results would indicate the accuracy of the air crew's navigation. I did not know at the time, if it hadn't been for this aircrew test my first night jump with full combat equipment would have been in the invasion of Sicily.

I must admit that I was a little nervous flying around alone in the back of the C-47 for hours. When, at last, the crew chief came back and the red warning light glowed, I acted as though I did this every night of the week, and when the green light flashed on I nonchalantly said 'So long', and jumped out the door.

I later learned that one of my fellow jumpers had gone out of a plane on one of the headings over the Mediterranean and was never recovered.

The desert where I landed was full of rocks and I was lucky not to break a leg when I hit because there was no one around to help me if I were injured. After about twenty minutes of wandering in the dark, I heard a fellow wanderer nearby who turned out to be Lieutenant Bill Meddaugh. The Battalion was supposed to be near the Drop Zone but Bill and I were alone in a very silent desert, so we made ourselves comfortable and went to sleep for a few hours.

At daybreak, we spotted some parked trucks about two miles away and hiked over to them and located E Company nearby. The jumpers had been scattered all over the desert and landed everywhere but on the DZ. This was pointed out to the aircrews very firmly, but politely, by Colonel James M. Gavin, the Regimental Commander, at the critique of the problem that afternoon.

After two months at Oujda we broke camp and flew to another unbearably hot area outside the city of Kairouan in Tunisia. The crew chief on my plane said that the controller at the airfield told him it was 120 degrees F. on the field when we landed.

We bivouacked in pup tents and within a few days briefings began for what we knew as a combat jump. We were never told exactly where we were going during the briefings but the maps that were issued had Italian names on them. Just before we boarded the planes in the late afternoon of 9 July, 1943, we were told it was to be the invasion of Sicily.

We took off from the field at Enfidaville in a cloud of dust and after what seemed like an hour of circling to get in formation the C-47's flew out over the Mediterranean Sea.

The Regimental Commanders being presented to King George VI in 1944 by General James Gavin. Left to right in the line are; General Andy March (Artillery), Colonel Roy Lindquist (508), Colonel Reuben Tucker (504), Colonel William Ekman (505) and Colonel Charles Billingslea (325). (U.S. Army photograph)

Sicily

Very clear in the memory of Edward Dugan, 505th Parachute Infantry Regiment, were the events leading to his first combat jump on the 9th July 1943. This was going to be the Army's first and Gavin gave orders that every jumper and every piece of equipment would be dropped on Sicily. No one would return by air.

"The North African sun at Kairouan was still shining with a brightness and the heat was in evidence as the sweat began to show through our jump suits. Little time was lost in securing the equipment bundles beneath the fuselage of the aircraft under the supervision of the flight crews."

"The troopers then began the tedious job of putting on their main and reserve parachutes along with equipment and weapons. We never could understand why we carried a reserve chute since the altitude we jumped at would certainly not permit an opening of the reserve in time to be of much help. The weight of the chutes, equipment and weapons which each of us was required to carry into combat was burdensome, and after lifting one's self into the C-47 and settling in a bucket seat it felt as though we had just finished a ten mile march."

"It was 10pm and I remember the heat inside the plane was almost unbearable, the perspiration poured down over our faces as the engines, one at a time, turned over until a full crescendo developed in unison. It was at this point that the overwhelming feeling of apprehension crept over us as the aircraft taxied for take-off. As we roared down the runway at full throttle the prop blast threw cool air into the cabin as we lifted off for our first airborne operation."

"Many of the paratroopers were suffering from dysentry caught in North Africa and this caused one hell of a problem. Portable toilets, or 'honey buckets', were installed in the C-47's to help the afflicted. Some of the men did not put their chutes on until the last minute, as trying to take your pants down with all that equipment strapped to you was almost impossible. Others just suffered in silence."

One of the most harrowing reports of the jump into Sicily came from First Lieutenant C. A. Drew of F Company, 504. There had been a foul up on the ground as to the arrival of the C-47 troop carriers. Another problem was that each Division seemed to have its own password.

"I was the jumpmaster in Plane 531. This plane was leading a formation of three planes and was No. 7 in our Company. The pilot gave me a warning twenty minutes out from the DZ. After the red light came on he had to give me a green light a minute later due to the plane being on fire."

"We jumped into a steady stream of anti-aircraft fire, and not knowing it was from friendly troops. There were four men killed and four wounded from my platoon. Three of these men were hit coming down and one was killed on the ground because he had the wrong password. After landing we found out that this had been changed to 'Think'—'Quickly'."

"The anti-aircraft fire we jumped into was from the 180th Infantry of the 45th Division. They were not told that we were coming. Later we found out that the 45th Division had been informed, but the word never got to the 180th Infantry."

"We tried to reorganise but found we only had 44 men and 3 officers. We searched all night for the rest. After accounting we took care of our dead and wounded and started towards our objective. We arrived at the 504 Command Post at 2 o'clock on 12th July."

"About 75 yards from where I landed, Plane No. 915 was hit and burned. To my knowledge only the pilot and three men got out, the pilot being thrown through the window. One plane was shot down on the beach and another was down, burning on the beach about a 1,000 yards to my front. Altogether there were three planes I know of shot down."

That jump was also recalled in a letter written by Sergeant Maynard Wade of I Company, 505. Many years later he wrote this.

"It was the 9th July in 1943, and about 8pm when we got on the C-47's. When we got off the ground the Lieutenant opened a sealed envelope and read to us what we were going to do. The orders were to jump ten miles behind the German lines at the city of Gela. We were supposed to jump at 200 feet so that we would assemble quickly."

"It took the planes four hours to get over there. In the meantime I told the Lieutenant that I was going to take off my emergency chute because jumping that low, if our main chutes didn't open then it would be too late for our emergency chute. So I took mine off, leaned back in my seat and dosed off to sleep."

"When I woke up something told me to put my emergency chute back on, so I did. There had been twenty three C-47's shot down so our pilot took us up to 2000 feet and dumped us out. I had my mind on the Germans and I didn't realise that my main chute had failed to open. I couldn't see because there was no moon, but when it came to me that I was falling too fast, I pulled my emergency chute."

"That saved me. Seconds later I hit the ground. I landed on the top of a steep hill and I rolled back several times, finishing up with my chute strings wrapped all around me. After cutting myself loose, I picked up my gun and tried to get back up the hill but it was too steep at that point."

"When I got back up to the top I tripped over something. It happened to be my mortar. So I put it together and collected three or four shells and went in search of my Company. I walked and walked for three hours. It took time because I didn't want to step on a booby trap. I was snapping my cricket, and then suddenly I heard a bug snapping back. It was my own Company. You know I could have kissed them." [The cricket was a child's toy which clicked and was used as a means of identification at night. One click-click would be answered by two click-clicks.]

In September while back in North Africa, Sergeant Wade was badly injured in a mortar training accident and was shipped back to the States. For him the war was over.

Lieutenant Carl Clawson of B Company, 505, parachuted into Sicily ahead of the British Eighth Army and next day met two British soldiers relaxing and brewing their tea. Invited to join them, he sat down. Every now and again there was a burst of firing from a sniper nearby which did not seem to worry his hosts at all.

A few shots came near and then one of the British, with some annoyance, picked up his Lee Enfield rifle and crept out of sight. Later there was a burst of firing and all went quiet. The soldier came back, put down his rifle and picked up his mug of tea without a word.

"I didn't like to ask him what had happened and he didn't offer any explanation, but we weren't troubled any more by snipers after that," said Carl later. "As I remember it the tea was so strong you could stand the spoon upright in it."

Robert 'Doc' Franco, the Assistant 505 Regimental Surgeon remembers: "A moment after my chute opened there was a light around us. I thought it could be an enemy flare, and as I turned my head, there behind me were two huge fire-balls falling slowly. They had to be an airplane, but I have never heard this memtioned, nor could I explain why a plane should be hit so far from our projected Drop Zone."

"We were really scattered. My Jumpmaster and I, I was No. 2, went out the door simultaneously and I never saw him again for a week."

"As a regimental officer I had dozens of articles, such as a map case, binoculars, entrenching tool, canteen, compass and 'rescue kit', slung from various parts of my cotton webbing. In addition, a load of surgical instruments weighing fifteen or twenty pounds was strapped tightly around my abdomen in a specially designed container: it lay just below my reserve chute."

"The moon had set an hour before and visibility was close to nil. I landed in the middle of what sounded like, but did not feel like, a great explosion. I believe that I had been oscillating and had hit a roof, probably tiled, at the apex of one of my swings. I bounced two or three times on the roof, then hit the ground. I had a fleeting glance of a building and a cross-roads, and my memory of the sand-table said that this could easily be an enemy pill-box camouflaged as a house."

"When I stopped bouncing and rolling I looked back and identified the structure as a house, and I told myself to prepare for the end. (It was one of my fellow Medical Officers, Lieutenant Kurt Klee who, I later learnt, landed on the barbed wire in front of an Italian pill-box and was killed before he could get out of his harness.) Instead, a door opened and a man rushed out and stared at me, then he turned towards the house yelling something in Italian, and went back in the house. I never saw him again, but a small scraggy dog which had emerged with him stood two feet from me barking his silly head off."

"After I detached the chute and stood up I felt strangely light, almost weightless. I thought at first it was the elation we always felt on being on the ground again. Then I soon realised that every single article that had been suspended by small steel hooks from the webbing belt had gone. Everything! The only explanation I could think of was that as I went skidding across the tiles all these things were 'rubbed off'. Whatever happened, everything that was not strapped to my body was gone.''

''I started walking, by the Polar Star, towards the north, with that fool dog following me, still barking at my heels. Almost immediately I fell waist deep into the water of an irrigation ditch. Later I began to find troopers, first one, then another, until there were about fifteen of us. They were all enlisted men, all privates as I remember, and all looking bewildered and a little scared. I told myself to act like an officer and led the way. It was a little hazardous to be in front of these inexperienced lads with their rifles at the ready and probably their safety catches off.''

''I led the way over hill after hill, we hiked all day on July 10th, slept that night, and kept on the next day. We finally came to what looked like a formal olive grove and off into the distance I could see water with fighter planes above it, and some sort of activity. Leaving the men to rest I walked towards the water and found myself in the town of Gela and in the midst of the intense activity of a beach-head.''

''As I watched and wondered what to do I heard a voice; it came from a man standing in a tiny porch near the corner of a small building. I walked towards the man and stopped short and saluted when I saw three stars on his helmet. He returned the salute and put out his hand for a hand-shake, and said, 'I'm General Bradley.' He asked if I had any men with me and continued, 'Jim Gavin is in a hell of a fight up the road and he needs every man he can get. Come in, get an overlay of the area, get your men and catch up with your outfit.'''

''He introduced me to his Aide, arranged for a overlay to be prepared, and told me to hurry back. When I returned with my men, his little office was filled with people. He looked up, 'Come in Captain Franco.' The conference stopped for a few moments while the Aide went over the map overlay with me. General Bradley started to say good-bye but he stopped and asked if I had transportation. Without waiting for the obvious answer he said, 'Come with me!' He took our group out to where the road and the beach met and flagged down a DUKW, talked to the driver and told him where to drop us, shook hands and wished us well.''

''I was impressed, it simply showed that this General knew exactly what was going on.''

Twenty year old Herbert Buffalo Boy Canoe, D Company, 505, landed on a piece of rocky ground. When he got his bearings he realised that he was in the middle of an enemy strong point. His carbine jammed so all he had to fight with was a trench knife and some grenades.

Buffalo Boy crawled away to safety with tracer bullets flying over his head. About half a mile away he came across a farmhouse and through a window spotted three Germans drinking wine and having a party.

One of the Germans came outside to relieve himself and while in the act the American Indian crept up behind and killed him with his knife. The other two Germans were despatched with a grenade.

Richard Tedeschi, F Company, 505, was in a hangar of an airfield checking to see if there were any souvenirs worth having when he heard an aircraft and firing. Looking out he saw two Airborne Troopers running across open ground with a German Me109 fighter machine-gunning them. ''They just kept running when those sons-of-bitches should have been hitting the dirt. Luckily a British Spitfire came on the scene and chased the Kraut away. When the guys finally arrived at the hangar I found one of them was my brother, Jack, from the 307 Engineers.''

Richard was one of a family of fourteen children. Eight were boys, with four of them serving in the forces.

Another member of F Company, 505, Platoon Sergeant John Gore felt that he had a lucky escape to come out of North Africa in one piece. He had accidently burned down his pup tent in Oujda, Algeria, by falling asleep while smoking, but would never admit it.

After twenty-two years with it on his conscience he finally admitted his crime to his Captain, Neal Lane McRoberts, at the Convention in Atlantic City in 1966. John felt better, but McRoberts had guessed what had happened all along.

Richard Tedeschi with Dr. Robert 'Doc' Franco (right) photographed in Nijmegen in 1984.

A wartime photograph of James J. Coyle.

Staff Sergeant John Rabig recalls one incident which cheered up D Company, 505, one day. The whole Battalion was one the move, marching down a long dusty road when they fell out for a ten minute break.

Much to the concern of Rabig, one of his men, Eugene 'Big Lew' Lewallen, pulled a motorcycle out of the ditch and started tinkering with it. Rabig chewed him off because it could have been booby-trapped.

'Big Lew' in no time at all had the machine running and proceeded to ride it up and down the road. The march continued, but with the motorcycle being ridden alongside D Company. "He would wheel her around in expert fashion. 'Look at that son-of-a-bitch,' the guys would say. Then he got reckless — up to the front of the column and down to the back."

"In the evening they pulled us off the road and we bedded down in an olive grove. That night a runner arrived from Battalion Headquarters. They wanted to know who had the motorcycle and the order was that it must be handed over to Battalion HQ the next morning."

"Big Lew was beside himself with anger at the proposed loss of his plaything and began to think of ways how he could sabotage the machine. In the ration packs there were several pieces of lump sugar, so he went round every God damn guy he could find and collected about 25 pieces. The sugar was put into the gasoline tank."

"The motorcycle was duly collected the next morning. Later the familiar noise of its engine was heard coming up the road, alongside the column of men. The rider was no other than Captain Hubert Bass riding up and down, making sure the Battalion was altogether."

"Much to the amusement of D Company the engine was purring away like a kitten without any sign that the sugar in the gasoline tank was having its desired effect."

"The more Lewallen got mad the more the guys needled him — he got no sympathy. Everytime it passed, Big Lew's buddies shouted, 'Hey Lew, how about that motorcycle, give it another lump of sugar!' Just like it was a horse. 'Big Lew' Lewallen never got his machine back."

SECOND LIEUTENANT JAMES J. COYLE
E COMPANY, 505

The flight to Sicily was a rough one. The planes flew low over the water and seemed to bump around more than usual. Most of the men in my plane became air sick but I believe it was more a result of eating their D-ration (which was similar to a very hard bar of milk chocolate) than it was to the turbulence. In any event, I spent the flight in a seat by the open door, throwing out paper bags which a smart crew chief had provided to prevent the men from throwing up all over his plane.

I was not aware of any navigational problems. If the flight crew were off track, they did not inform me. The formation seemed to be holding together which made me feel that everything was going well. The red light came on. I was barely able to get the men's static lines hooked up to the cable in the plane and get an equipment check before we crossed the coast of Sicily. The green light came on and we jumped out into the dark.

It seemed that my chute had only been deployed about ten seconds before I hit the ground. While it is difficult to judge altitude at night, I am certain that my plane-load jumped at no more than 400 feet. No one in the First Platoon was injured however, and we were able to assemble and locate our equipment bundles quickly.

The mission of the First Platoon was to set up a roadblock about two miles north of the DZ to prevent the enemy from moving to the beach at Gela where the 1st Division were landing in the morning. We moved out with Lieutenant Wray in the lead and myself bringing up the rear, which was where Wray always placed me. In this case it was fortunate that he did.

We had observed a beacon light which we assumed was on an airfield indicated on our maps as north of Gela. This would be an aid in moving across country as there were no roads which would take us to our objective.

The moon was now bright but it was rough going at times because we seemed to hit a stone wall, which we had to climb over, every two hundred yards or so. After an hour the column halted and the men sat down for a short break. It was a welcome rest, and when more than fifteen minutes had passed and we had not moved out again, I began to worry. I went to the head of the column — or what was left of it! When Wray had moved off after the break only half the platoon had moved out with him. Halfway back in the column a couple of men had fallen asleep and never saw the front half go.

I got the men awake and on their feet and started after the rest of the platoon. I led the men for another half hour over the stone walls and was finally becoming really concerned about locating Wray and the rest of the platoon. Suddenly I was challenged and found them covering us with their weapons from behind a stone wall. Lieutenant Wray had reached a road which appeared to be the objective and we set up our roadblock and waited until dawn.

No Germans or Italian soldiers showed up. There were no houses or civilians around to question as to our exact location, but everything indicated that we were in the right spot or close to it.

At about 9am, a runner from Company Headquarters arrived to inform us that we had been dropped at Marina Di Ragusa, about 20 miles east of Gela! Wray and I couldn't believe it as everything looked so right. We found out later that the beacon we had seen was the Comiso airfield, not the airfield north of Gela as we had thought.

We rejoined the Company outside of Marina Di Ragusa. The rest of E Company were on a hill overlooking the harbour and while we were forming up to enter the town, a U.S. Navy cruiser hoved into sight offshore. As we watched it, it opened fire with one of its big guns and a tracer shell just cleared the top of the hill which we had occupied. The first shot fired at me in combat came from our own navy! Lieutenant Talton Long quickly ordered an orange identification panel to be run up the flagpole in front of a nearby building and no further fire was received.

There was no sign of enemy troops in the town and we entered Marina Di

Ragusa unopposed. The Company was then ordered to attack a position of Italian troops which had been spotted nearby. As we moved up, a single shot was fired at us, hitting no one. It was apparently a 'Shot of Honour' which the Italians fired before surrendering. There was no further resistance and we took about 200 prisoners.

When I examined the enemy fortifications, I discovered that they were made of granite and mortar with pill boxes connected by stone lined trenches. Had the Italian troops wanted to fight, it would not have been an easy job to blast them out of this position. While we were assembling the prisoners, the Italian Commander came out of his fortified headquarters with his suitcase packed and carried by his orderly. He had been ready for a trip to America for some time.

We rejoined the Second Battalion on the road and began the march to Gela. Italians were coming out of the surrounding fields with their hands raised, but at this point Lieutenant Long just moved them to the rear. We had no means of guarding or feeding prisoners. I felt sorry for them. They knew that in effect their country had been betrayed by Mussolini and occupied by the Germans. They had nothing to fight for.

A few German soldiers in our sector of Sicily retreated, taking all their equipment with them, and eventually escaped across the Straits of Messina. To the best of my knowledge, Sergeant Julius Axman and his squad were the only ones in E Company to engage in a firefight with Germans, a type of Marine unit, in which Pfc. Harry C. Downey was killed.

That night, 10 July, as we were hiking up the road, we saw in the distance a tremendous sustained volley of anti-aircraft fire fill the sky. We took this to be an attack by German bombers on Gela. At about the same time several planes flew in from the sea directly over our heads. No one fired on them; in fact, the men were calling out up and down the line ''C-47's!, C-47's!'' even before they were able to spot a plane or two against the moon. I never knew a paratrooper who couldn't identify a C-47 just by the sound of its engines.

Months later we were to learn that we had witnessed the shooting down of twenty-three planeloads of paratroopers from the 504th Parachute Infantry Regiment by friendly naval and shore anti-aircraft fire!

After bivouacking for the night, we boarded trucks for Gela. Along the way we were caught by two fighter aircraft which came over the crest of a low hill and were on us before we saw them. Had they strafed up the road they would have hit the entire convoy and would have caused many casualties, but for some reason they flew diagonally across the road from our right rear to our left front.

As a result they only hit one truck, the one immediately in front of me. Three men in the truck were wounded. The convoy halted and the men scattered, but the planes did not return for further strafing.

Many E Company men insisted the planes were German. In some respects they did resemble Focke-Wulf 190's, but as the second plane flew by my truck I got a close view of the insignia on the tail. It was an Italian symbol: the fasces, a bundle of reeds with a battle axe stuck through the centre.

From this point on we leap-frogged up the southern Sicilian coast road, sometimes in trucks but mostly by hiking, carrying all our weapons and equipment on our backs. One of the hikes, which took us through the town of Santa Mararita, was one of the longest in my five years in the army. It was certainly the most difficult for me as I was now very ill with dysentery, as were many of the men of E Company.

On one of the nightly bivouacs we moved off the road in complete darkness to a nearby hill. We never pitched pup tents — I do not recall it ever raining while we were in Sicily. We just ate our K-ration, covered our heads with a pocket mosquito netting which we all carried, lay down on the ground and went to sleep.

By this time we did not dig slit trenches and provided only minimal security. Early on the 2nd Armoured Division had passed us by and were now far out to our front. When I awoke the next morning, I found myself practically on the front steps of the Temple of Juno which I discovered later was a famous temple from the period of the ancient Greek occupation of Sicily.

In another bivouac area I had the only 'close call' I had in Sicily. We were just getting organised into platoon areas and had removed our packs and equipment. It was still daylight and I was standing watching the men get ready for the night when a shot rang out right behind me. I felt a sharp blow on my left shoulder and right buttocks simultaneously. My first thought was that someone had accidently set off a hand grenade.

When I turned around I saw our First Platoon Medic standing a few feet away with an M-1 rifle in his hands. He appeared to be in a state of shock waiting for me to fall down. I later learned that he liked to fool around with the men's rifles and had picked one up and had accidently discharged a round.

Fortunately the bullet struck a rock behind me and had ricocheted before it hit me in the butt. A piece of rock hit me on the shoulder. The poor Medic came rushing over, pushed me down to the ground before giving me a shot of morphine. Captain Robert 'Doc' Franco, the Battalion Surgeon, came up, cleared out the wounds and patched me up. Because of the ricochet it was a slight wound and, I'm sure, a source of amusement to the men, but I had to sleep on my stomach for the following week. My first wound in action and no Purple Heart!

We continued moving west for several weeks and eventually reached the town of Trapani. This was the end of E Company's operations in Sicily. Sometime in late August we were flown back in C-47s to Kairouan in North Africa.

While E Company had seen little action, enough troops of the First Battalion had landed on the proper DZ, engaged units of the German Herman Goering Division, and prevented them from attacking the troops landing by sea at Gela. The 505th Regiment's mission had been accomplished.

We remained in the Kairouan area until early September when E Company boarded C-47's once again and flew back to Sicily with the Second Battalion. We bivouacked in pup tents adjacent to the airport at Comiso.

Lieutenant Waverly W. Wray had been transferred to D Company while we were in North Africa. The First Platoon had a new leader, Lieutenant Dave Packard. The Company Commander, Lieutenant Talton Long, must have known that I had hoped to take over the Platoon because he took the trouble to explain to me that Packard was an original 505 man who had missed the jump in Sicily because he was in hospital as a result of an accidental explosion during a demolition demonstration. I could understand Long's position and appreciated his explanation to me. It wasn't something that he was required to do. Dave Packard and I soon became good friends.

We were alerted for a mission and prepared our equipment bundles ready to load the planes when the mission was cancelled. Much later we learned that the mission was to jump on an airfield in Rome. Whoever dreamed up that mission did not understand the capabilities of airborne troops. The Fifth Army did not get to Rome until six months later. We were good, but not that good. The 82nd Airborne Division would have been wiped out.

I had contracted malaria while in Sicily and still had the constant dysentry that I had picked up within weeks after arriving in North Africa. At Comiso I developed jaundice and with all three diseases at once, was in a bad way with a high fever.

I went to Lieutenant Long and told him that I had to turn myself in to the Medics, but would be back as soon as I could make it. I told him that I would get in touch with him when I found out which hospital I was being sent to. I expected to be back before E Company left Comiso, but I wanted to be sure that if they moved I would know where to locate them. Several men on leaving hospital had been sent to other units and could not get back to the 505. I wanted to be certain that I could return to E Company. As it happened, I almost didn't make it back.

I was in the hospital for six weeks and was on intravenous feeding and drugs for the first two. About the third day, a troop carrier pilot in the next cot spotted my paratrooper boots under my cot and asked what outfit I was from. When I said, he told me that he had dropped the 505 at Salerno, Italy, the night before. At that point I thought that I would never get back to my Company, but I was in no shape then to leave hospital.

After I had been in the hospital for about a month and almost recovered but still weak, a 'Sirocco', a violent wind storm, came in from the Mediterranean. This field hospital was entirely housed in tents near the coast at Castellamare. The storm brought every tent down. Those of us who were able did our best to help the men who were in casts or wounded, but it was chaos until they got a unit of engineers in to get the tents off us and enough ambulances to transfer us to a large civilian hospital in Palermo.

Within a day or two after arriving in Palermo, I took off with two other 505 men and we got a ride in a truck going to Comiso airfield. The rear echelon of the 505 were still there. I talked to the officer in charge into letting me try to get back to the Company in Italy. He wanted me to stay and train a newly arrived group of replacements, but my persistence paid off and I went in search of a C-47 heading in the direction of Italy.

Captain Neal Lane McRoberts in 1944.

Italy

Several times the paratroopers were keyed up for another combat jump. For days there had been secret negotiations with the Italian Government by General Maxwell Taylor.

One idea was to drop the 82nd Airborne Division at an airfield near Rome, way behind the German front line. The plans were made and the paratroopers were sitting in the C-47's waiting to take off from Sicily. Luckily the operation was cancelled at the last minute.

Sergeant Charles Kaiser of the Third Battalion Headquarters Company, 505, well remembers the comment made by Major Edward 'Cannonball' Krause that night. He said, "We had history by the balls, but fate lifted his leg and farted on us."

Krause was sorry that the mission was cancelled, but none of the men were. There is no doubt that the Division would have been fighting for their lives. General Maxwell Taylor's message of a trap came with three minutes to spare.

Some troopers recall they were already in the air when the order came to turn back.

On the night of the 13th September 1943, the Division made its second combat jump, this time into the Salerno beachhead, Italy, to help the beleaguered Fifth Army.

By the next morning the paratroopers were in the front line and the cry went up, "The 82nds here!" With that, the morale of the Fifth Army went up by leaps and bounds. The arrival of the 82nd stiffened the line and saved the beachhead, including the reputation of General Mark Clark. As they did in Sicily, the Division fought well and enhanced its already good name.

On 1st October 1943, Colonel James Gavin was awakened by a British Liaison Officer, he had been asleep on the floor of an Italian farmhouse.

The Britisher was elegant and impeccable in appearance, almost as if he was about to go on parade. He told Gavin in a languid sort of way that the 82nd. and his British 23rd Armoured Brigade had been ordered to fight their way into Naples.

Gavin said later, "From that moment on I found my association with the British Army a most pleasant and delightful one. In many ways they took the whole war far less seriously than we, but on the other hand, in matters of discipline and combat effectiveness they set very high standards."

It was a few days later, on the 10th October, that Gavin was taken from the 505 and promoted to Assistant Divisional Commander. As Ed Dugan said, "It was not the happiest moment for the men of the Regiment. We had been through a great deal together and he was sadly missed."

In the last week of November Gavin left Naples to journey to London to plan the airborne assault on Normandy.

****

The first hard fight that F Company, 505, had with the Germans was at Arnone, on the Volturno River, north of Naples. The best description of the battle was in a poem written by Lieutenant John H. Dodd. One year later he was dead, killed in action at the Nijmegen Bridge in Holland.

He called it:

'F' COMPANY, 505, AT ARNONE

The shelling was increasing, as we crawled up into town,
But it wasn't too annoying and we had time to hit the ground.
The Second Platoon had entered first and was set up to defend:
Company E was supposed to be on the left past the river's bend.

The First Platoon was next advanced and placed on the Second's right.
The Third Platoon was in reserve, but fully prepared to fight.
The Captain had his Command Post in the centre of Arnone,
From there he sent out and set up to the rear by telephone.

But don't forget, that through all this, the Jerries fire was growing:
Eighty-eight and mortar shells, artillery fire was snowing.
Not to mention the generous spray of their rapid fire pistol,
A thing of amazing Rat-a-Tat and a too late warning whistle.

They seemed to know the co-ordinates of every spot we held,
And every place to which we moved was forthwith heavily shelled.
By the time the Third Platoon came up, the shrapnel was so thick,
Advancing through the stuff was really quite a trick.

Casualties were mounting and our Aid men worked like mad,
And men who were near the wounded used all the packs we had.
Jerry was fording the river, about half way between the bridges,
We threw a couple of mortar rounds that appeared to hit the spot.
If they stop that goddamn shelling we'd give them all we've got.

Jerry's plan was obvious and a well devised one too,
He's cutting around our left and sealing our Waterloo.
But Jerry hadn't noticed, and we praised the Lord for that,
Company E was on our left, so Jerry's plan fell flat.

By now the fire was so intense, withdrawal had to be,
And so we did, but no one felt it was disgracefully.
We gathered up the wounded and moved through the rough,
One stretcher case was improvised and portaging was tough.
Then came the Battalion Medics with litter bearers for the rest,
And the sight of them relieved us — for we knew we'd done our best.

Arnone is just in shambles now and the booby traps are sprung,
And the church is not the place it was when sacred hymns were sung.
Our own artillery is striking now where Jerry had his day.
Our Allied friends, the British, are taking up the play.

I'd like to pay just tribute to the men of Company F:
To those who read this history and to those whose ears are deaf.
You didn't hold the town Arnone, but though you were detained,
You showed a gallant spirit and that spirit never waned.

****

On 7th October 1943, Chaplain George Wood went into Arnone to recover the bodies of the 505 men who had been killed the day before. They included the body of Lieutenant David L. Packard of E Company.

It was necessary to make several trips to bring them all out as a large percentage of the sixty casualties were fatal. The town was 'no man's land', but the Germans respected the Red Cross flag and the party was not fired on.

Commanding F Company during this period was Captain Neal Lane McRoberts who won his first Silver Star for his actions at Arnone, his First Sergeant being John 'Jack' Field.

Captain Robert 'Doc' Franco remembers McRoberts well. He explains, "We were all friends in the 505, but a few people were somehow special. McRoberts was a clean-cut, handsome young man who led F Company, our 'tough company'. I clearly remember him when we were attacking on the Volturno River and not moving very well. I was told that I was wanted at the Company Command Post. When I arrived, through heavy fire, I met with McRoberts who looked like a kid. I marvelled in all the bedlam that youngsters like this had the lives and fates of one hundred and twenty men in their hands, and looking calm and composed through it all. He was a fine man and a good officer."

When the paratroopers arrived back in Naples from the front line their uniforms and equipment were in tatters. They were in need of new jump suits and their distinctive jump boots. The Division's supplymen were told that no jump boots were available.

The paratroopers soon realised why there were no jump boots, every other American serviceman in Naples was seen walking the streets wearing them. Tempers ran high and raiding parties from the Division were out taking jump boots off the feet of personnel who were not entitled to wear them. Many an officer had to walk home in his stocking feet.

Complaints were made direct to General Matthew Ridgway for him to stop this highway robbery. His answer was "My men are entitled to new jump boots, and I want to know why they are not available at the stores." New supplies of jump boots were quickly found.

Several sources have told stories about a Polish American paratrooper by the name of Stisic. He never seemed to have any colour in his face which was always dead white. When the 505 got to Naples, Stisic bought a wooden coffin for himself and carried it to the billet. Every night he used it as a bed and went to sleep with only his white face showing. To strangers he looked like a corpse. It was not long before he was transferred out.

Sergeant Charles Kaiser was in a Naples hospital when he heard on the grapevine that the 505 were on the move. He managed to sneak out, find a Jeep, and got himself back to the Third Battalion. Kaiser reported to Captain Robert Kirkwood on his arrival that he may be reported AWOL. "OK you're here," said Kirkwood. Kaiser was one of many who had discharged themselves from hospital.

The 504th Parachute Infantry Regiment was held back in Italy at the request of General Mark Clark and the British Prime Minister, Winston Churchill. They wanted a first rate regiment to stiffen the line.

General Gavin was later to write, "But when the 504 flew into Salerno, the Fifth Army was in desperate straits. The 505 was given the mission of crossing the Sorrento Peninsula and capturing Naples, which we did. We then went on to the Volturno River, which we reached at a point midway between Capua and the ocean. At that time we were pulled back. Ridgway was asked to provide a parachute regiment to operate on very high ground, the mountain tops actually, between the Fifth Army on the left of the boot and the Eighth Army on the right."

"I went up to visit the 504 about three times during the last couple of weeks before I left Italy. It was very cold, very rugged terrain and quite active. There was much carrying of rations on the back to get them up there, the same for ammunition. I believe there were mules too. It was a fine mission for a mountain division and Clark's confidence in the 504th's ability to do just about anything was unsurpassed. The regiment did a great job."

One of the signals sent by Churchill to General Wilson, C-in-C, Mediterranean, on the 6th February 1944, included a sentence which said:

"First, why was the 504th Regiment of paratroopers not used at Anzio as proposed, and why is the existing British Parachute Brigade used as ordinary infantry in the line?"

Even Churchill knew the value of paratroopers and he referred to the 504 in many of his signals extolling their virtues. In all of his *The Second World War* volumes the only Allied combat unit smaller than a Division he made referrence to was the 504.

On 18th November the 505th Parachute Infantry Regiment marched down to Naples harbour and boarded the *S.S. Frederick Funston*. They had no idea where their next destination would be.

Many years later John Rabig was reminiscing with Frank Bilich. Rabig claimed that he did not sail on that ship but on another one, a supply ship, the *S.S. James O'Hara*. Quite an argument started but Rabig was adamant he was correct. "I know what boat I sailed on. In fact on the voyage I had six meals a day. I ate with the crew and then with the men."

"How come?" questioned Bilich.

"I was hungry," answered Rabig.

"I'm sorry I asked that question," quipped Bilich.

SECOND LIEUTENANT JAMES J. COYLE
E COMPANY, 505

Escaping from hospital in Sicily I hitched a ride on a C-47 flying to Foggia, Italy, then on a truck going north and finally caught up with E Company in Naples. I reported to Lieutenant Talton Long.

The first thing he told me was that Lieutenant Dave Packard had been killed in a engagement the First Platoon had been in at the Volturno River. This had been E Company's first real fight with German troops, and quite different than anything that had happened in Sicily.

Lieutenant 'Pete' Peterson had moved over from the Third Platoon and was now Platoon Leader of the First Platoon. I was assigned as Pete's Assistant Platoon Leader. Shortly after I rejoined the Company, Lieutenant Long was promoted to Captain and transferred to Regimental Headquarters Company. Captain Clyde Russell was transferred from Battalion Headquarters to command E Company.

E Company remained in Naples for about a month on occupation duty with an occasional training hike just to keep the troops in shape. We were billeted in a partially bombed-out factory building and it was the easiest duty we had pulled since going overseas.

German bombers came over nightly to bomb the Allied ships in Naples harbour and the anti-aircraft artillery all around the city would put on quite a display. One night we saw search-lights catch a plane squarely. A dozen lights converged on it as it flew across the city for what seemed like at least five minutes with every gun firing at it. It did not appear to receive any hits and finally flew out of range. The men were expecting it to be shot down any minute and had a few disparaging remarks to make about the AA gunners.

On one of the night time training hikes we were in bivouacs on a hill about ten miles east of Naples. The men had dug slit trenches and covered them with shelter-halves and most were in the holes asleep. Those of us who were awake could see the ack-ack in the distance over Naples and could hear planes fly over us from time to time.

Suddenly, one of the planes went into a dive right above us. It was too dark to see it, but it sounded as if the plane was coming right at us. It didn't seem possible. The men had lit small fires to heat rations earlier but I doubt if they would attract the attention of a bomber.

The roar got louder and louder. The air around us seemed to vibrate. My thought was that the plane was going to crash in our midst. There was a tremendous explosion, but it wasn't the plane. It was a very large bomb about thirty feet from where I lay on the ground. The air was full of dirt and dust.

We could not see anything and for about ten seconds we were in a state of shock. The men started shouting in the Second Platoon area and Lieutenant Bill Meddaugh was pointing to the foxholes of men who had been buried alive. The bomb had blown a crater about 30 feet in diameter and 25 feet deep. At least six men had been buried under about two feet of earth.

By some miracle no one was killed, although several men were unconscious or in shock and were sent to hospital in Naples. I believe the German pilot had taken one look at the anti-aircraft fire over Naples and had jettisoned his bomb. E Company just happened to be in the way.

On 18th November 1943, the 82nd Airborne Division left Naples Harbour in a U.S. Assault ship *Frederic Funston* bound for the unknown. We left the 504th Parachute Infantry Regiment behind fighting the Germans up in the mountains, hoping they would be joining us soon.

We had no idea where we were going and after a voyage of about two weeks, in which we knew we had left the Mediterranean, we arrived in a large port. The Navy crew told us we were in Belfast, Northern Ireland.

From Belfast, we moved to a farm called 'Desertcreat' which was a few miles outside Cookstown. Years later I was to learn that my great-grandfather, Dennis Byrne, was born within a few miles of our camp.

Many new replacements joined us, but training them, together with the veterans in the Company was restricted to road marches and athletics because all the open areas were planted farmland. We did travel to a range at Strawberry Hill, near Lough Neagh, where the men had the oportunity to 'zero in' their rifles and fire the Company weapons, including machine-guns and mortars.

While we were there we ran obstacle courses and dug foxholes which we occupied while tanks were driven over us to prove it was safe. This made a change from our normal routine, but to the best of my knowledge no man in E Company was ever run over by a tank in combat.

The men were given three day passes and furloughs while in Ireland and there was a problem in connection with men staying 'absent without leave'. The AWOL rate took a sharp upward curve due to the fact that the Irish girls were the first English-speaking females the men had seen in almost a year. Clyde Russell, who had a very good sense of humour, called it 'Belfast Fever' and told the men at one formation that, "they weren't fighters, they were lovers."

For our brief stay in Ireland we were housed in quonset huts instead of tents, which was fortunate as the nights were very cold and damp. Another disadvantage was that it stayed pitch dark until 10am on the winter mornings.

Despite the climate the E Company men loved Ireland. It was too good to last however, and in the middle of February 1944 we boarded a ship in Belfast harbour and sailed to Scotland. From there we travelled by troop train to our tented camp in the village of Quorn, near Leicester, in the English Midlands.

Quorn and Leicester

In the first few months of 1944 the American Paratrooper became a familiar figure in Leicestershire. He was the elite of the U.S. Armed Forces, the pride of General Eisenhower, being easily recognised by his unique calf length jump boots and sporting the hard won silver parachute badge on his breast. He knew he was among the best.

The 82nd Airborne Division arrived in Leicestershire from Italy on the 14th February. One of its Regiments was the famous 505th Parachute Infantry Regiment who were camped in Wood Lane, Quorn, known to them as Tent City.

Since leaving the States the 505'ers had excelled themselves in Sicily and Italy fighting and defeating some of Hitler's best troops, such as the Hermann Goering Panzer Division. After two successful combat jumps their confidence showed that they were ready for anything.

Their arrival in the green rolling countryside of Leicestershire was a welcome break from the rigours of the Mediterranean. Where they had come from there were no liquor stores around, and when available a bottle of scotch could cost $40. Gone were the North African sand storms that always seemed to arrive at chow time. There was no way to separate the sand and flies from the food. Another unpleasant experience left behind were the problems of dysentery and the overloaded latrines.

Jim Coyle remembers his first impressions of Quorn. "Our new base consisted of pyramidal tents pitched in a park at the edge of Sherwood Forest of Robin Hood fame, between Leicester and Nottingham." (Editor's note: Those are Jim's words. In fact Sherwood Forest is about twenty-five miles away to the north).

"A liberal pass policy was initiated and except when night training problems were scheduled, groups of men on a rotation basis were allowed to go to nearby towns almost every night."

The men of the Division made friends very easily and the Leicestershire people took them to their hearts. Lifelong friendships were formed and Quorn is always remembered at their reunions. Still talked about, and relished, 50 years on, are the fish and chip suppers wrapped in newspaper that could be bought from Atkins, the village 'chippie'. Their favourite pubs were the White Horse Inn in the centre of the village and the Bull's Head where they drank their 'mild and bitter' beer; and still do today whenever they make their frequent visits to England.

Sergeant Charles Kaiser and his friend, Ray Cridland, used to favour the Bulls Head pub. "It wasn't so rowdy as the others. We learnt to play darts and drink their warm beer. Two old maids ran the pub, and one night Ray

Camp Quorn, Leicestershire. A parade of the First Battalion just before D-Day, being addressed by Colonel William E. Ekman, the 505's Commanding Officer.

told them that the Americans liked their beer cold. From that night there were supplies of iced beer for us, and the locals started asking for it too.''

John Levitsky of I Company made sure he always walked slowly out of an English pub because the fresh air, after drinking 'mild and bitters', could knock you out even if you were built like a weight-lifter.

At the weekends they made sorties into Leicester to have a drink in the city pubs and to dance at the Palais de Dance in Humberstone Gate. The Grand Hotel was exclusively for officers, or so they thought. One Paratrooper found a way to gatecrash that select club. Private Ken Geis of I Company used to meet his art student girlfriend, Margaret, at her house. She had a brother away at the war so Ken used to change into one of the civilian suits hanging in the wardrobe. Aided by some GI gasolene, thoughtfully brought in a jerry can, the car in Margaret's garage was sprung into life and provided transport to the Grand. Much to Ken's surprise and delight the car was a luxury Rolls Royce.

The officers never suspected that a GI Joe was in their midst. Forty two years later Ken told the story with some glee.

Just before D-Day Ken and Margaret got engaged and she was given his coveted jump wings. As he recalled the happiness didn't last long, Margaret sent him a 'Dear John' letter which he received in Normandy. ''Oh how I loved that girl,'' he told me wistfully. I was able to tell him that Margaret still treasures those jump wings to this day.

On their nightly tours of the Leicester pubs, drinking as much as they could, there was usually trouble. If a guy fell down drunk then his friends would take him outside and prop him up by the side of the road. The trucks going back and forth to the camp would then stop and throw him in the back.

If the MP's had to step in they would do the honours for transport. Next day you would be in front of Colonel Vandervoort who would chew your ears off, but that would be the end of it.

Robert Veria of Headquarters Company remembers the White Swan Hotel in Leicester's Market Place. The bar was on the second floor above some shops. One night several 505 men were drinking there when one shouted out, "Stand up and hook up!" Then standing on the seat by the open window gave the order, "Lets go!" With that he jumped to the pavement, about fifteen feet below, followed by the rest of the party.

The Barmaid took sometime to get over the shock of seeing her customers disappear out of the window so high up. From then on it became a regular feature of the evening's entertainment. On Sunday nights the Salvation Army Band use to play in the Market Square nearby. The drummer was always ready to give a special roll on the drums as the Paratroopers did their graceful exit and fell to the ground.

The 82nd Airborne Division were not the first Americans to be based in Leicester, already here were an all-black U.S. Transport Battalion. The Paratroopers were mainly from the Southern States, so right from the start there was trouble. On the night of the 28th February war broke out on the streets of the city. The warriors had found the Blacks in command of the city and the girls. There were dozens of fights and well over twelve servicemen suffered knife wounds. The interior of the American Red Cross Club, opposite the Y.M.C.A. on Granby Street, was wrecked.

It was a rule that only a limited number of men received passes every night to leave the camp. On that night in question a number of 505 men were injured in the fighting. The Regimental Commanding Officer at that time was Lt. Colonel Herbert Batcheller whose home town was in the Southern State of North Carolina. As the men were forming up for lunch the next day he personally announced that, "Everyone is on a pass tonight!" His intentions were obvious.

That night every available paratrooper came to Leicester looking for revenge.

General Matthew Ridgway toured the city for several nights in his Jeep to calm his boys down, and he was the only man who could do it. He doubled the MP's on the streets and the Black unit was quickly transferred to Kettering, some 28 miles away.

There it was reported that they broke into an armoury to obtain weapons to get their revenge on the Airborne. Roadblocks on the A6 were set up and the situation quietened down.

Not one word of this got into the local newspapers as it was a military secret that the United States 82nd Airborne Division was here in England. Searching through the official records of the day there is only one mention of the troubles. In the Minutes of the Police Committee No. 12, held in the County Rooms on 24th June 1944, it is recorded that, "Nineteen members of the U.S.A. Forces were dealt with by their own Courts Inquiry."

Ridgway ordered an inquiry and on the 21st March, Lt. Colonel Batcheller was relieved of his command and transferred to the 508th Parachute Infantry

Regiment who had just arrived in Nottingham. This was not the first time that Batcheller had committed an indiscretion but was given a chance to redeem himself with the command of the 508's First Battalion.

The new C.O. of the 505th Parachute Infantry Regiment was Colonel William E. Ekman who commanded until the end of the war.

Herbert Batcheller was killed in action on D-Day.

It was later claimed by General Ridgway that no one had been murdered in the troubles, contrary to many rumours. Recent information from Jack Sneiderman, together with the knowledge that a body of a Military Policeman, Corporal Arthur A. Abrams, is buried at American Military Cemetery at Madingley, Cambridge, gave serious doubt to that statement. On research it has been found that the violent deaths of two American servicemen occurred nine weeks later outside a public house, the Dixie Arms, in Humberstone Gate only a few yards from the Clock Tower.

The answer was found in the Last News Edition of the *Leicester Mercury*, dated 3rd May 1944. There is a front page news report which states:-

U.S. ARMY POLICEMAN KILLED IN LEICESTER

A Military Policeman was one of the two American soldiers who received fatal injuries in Leicester on Monday (1st May). One of the victims died from a knife wound in the neck, the other is stated to have died from self-inflicted wounds.

The affair occurred round about closing time outside a public house in a main street near the centre of the city.

The American military policeman received fatal injuries when trying to create order.

The two men were dead when they were taken to the Leicester Royal Infirmary. Others received minor injuries.

All the investigations are being made by the American military authorities, who state that the matter was purely a military one, and had nothing to do with the civilian population.

In the circumstances no inquiry will be held by the Leicester City Coroner.

The date of the death of Corporal Abrams is listed in the records as 1st May, 1944. No other 82nd Airborne trooper is listed as having died that day, so it is possible his assailant, the other American, belonged to a different unit.

****

In the last few days of February, as usual for the time of year, snow fell and the camp sites were carpeted in white. The main problem for the boys was to keep warm and dry. Later the English spring blossomed forth and life took on a brighter hue.

There were several Divisional dances held in the city, at the Palais de Dance for the men, and at the Grand Hotel for the officers. The 82nd Airborne Orchestra supplied the music. It appears they had a private running joke with General James Gavin because when he entered the Hall the orchestra would stop and break into a jazzed up version of 'Maresy Dotes and Dosey Dotes'.

The 82nd Divisional Band gave a concert in the Town Hall Square and the locally based ATS girls joined with the paratroopers to produce the musical comedy, 'Together We Sing'.

Surrounding Tent City was a high stone wall. As Tom McClean of D Company said later, "If you had a pass you went out the front gate. If you didn't have a pass you went over the wall, and if you came back late you came over the wall." Part of that wall is still there today.

Climbing over that six foot stone wall was the only way of missing the guard on the front gate. Scaling the section of the wall nearest to D Company's tents meant crossing a piece of private land belonging to Quorn House. This was, unfortunately, the home of a very large bull mastif dog. He had a head as large as a lion and didn't take kindly to trespassers. The dog's name was Wallace, named after one of the Kings of Scotland. The wary latecomer's technique was to make a quick sprint across the open ground with this huge dog snapping at their ankles. In the end it became a game of which trooper could beat the dog to the wall.

One trooper remarked that when you heard that dog bark you quickly realised that it came from "no little dog."

Once over the wall into the camp it was a race to get into bed before the Orderly Officer came round to check that everybody was in. Lieutenant Tom McClean would come down the lines with his flashlight which meant there was little time to spare.

Frank Bilich would quickly take off his jacket and jump into his bed, pulling up the blankets and turning his face to the tent wall. Tom McClean said many years later, "You guys thought you were clever. Do you know I could see the outline of your jumpboots under the blankets. I knew who was in late."

D Company's mascot was a little sausage dog by the name of Herbert. Nobody seemed to own him, but everybody fed him on scraps. He met his fate in the jaws of the bull mastif, Wallace, and he was killed.

Not only did Wallace terrorise the GI's, he also terrorised the villagers of Quorn. The local village policeman, Police Constable Bobby Norman, threatened to shoot the 'bugger' on more than one occasion.

There is one lady, Dorothy Waddingham who worked at Quorn House, who claims that Wallace was not as fierce as he looked. She said, "He was always my friend as I prepared his food. I can see him now, the way he used to chase any wary visitors."

Dorothy's parents had a house which backed on to the camp and she well remembers the quick trips the lads used to make over the wall and down their garden path to the Mill House pub across the road.

One of the attractions of Quorn House was a Land Army girl by the name of Edith. She helped in the vegetable garden. It is reported that she had many 505 suitors.

The stable block had a cobbled yard which had been concreted over and used as an outdoor dance floor for weekly socials. The staff of Quorn House made a number of lasting friendships with the GI's, and many of them wrote letters to their families back in the States.

Carl Clawson of B Company has many fond memories of Quorn. "The generous manner in which the populace accepted an overwhelmingly large contingent of young, sometimes very raucous soldiers, has always put Quorn in a unique place in the minds of all of us fortunate enough to have had the experience."

"I recall the Bulls Head Inn and the 'regulars' who were kind enough to permit our joining in their dart and cribbage games. The wartime allocation of ale was in effect — but the supply was shared without hesitation. Quorn enjoyed magnificent weather during your Spring and the area was so beautiful. I recall almost enjoying the arduous forced march programme inherent in our training."

Carl and his wife Betty visited Quorn in 1962 and as he was looking over the old camp site was observed by the people living close by, and they promptly invited them in for tea. "We had a great time and corresponded with the family for sometime after."

Another local pub was the Pig and Whistle in Station Road. The paratroopers had a problem in understanding the Licensing Laws in England. If they had a supply of beer then they would open at 6pm and close at 10. Frank Bilich remembers the publican at the Pig and Whistle would shout at 10pm, "Time Ladies and Gentlemen please, and that goes for you bloody Yanks too!" Nobody would argue with him, they would do as they were told. One thing the 505 boys never got used to was the warm beer. Frank called it then as he does now — Horse Piss.

"We enjoyed the social life of the pub," said Frank. "The sing-songs with everybody joining in. There were no English men around, they were all in the services. The pubs were full of girls, ATS girls (Auxillary Territorial Service, later to become the Women's Royal Army Corp) from the camp at Woodhouse Eves, Land Army girls and WAAFS from the airfields. It was just like being in heaven."

"One thing I remember about the English is that nobody 'bitched' about anything, and they had it tough with their rationing. The same with the British Army, they used to say 'What's the hurry Yank, the war will still be there tomorrow.'"

Tony DeFoggi came as a replacement to join the 505 after their return from Italy. He relates his adventures on arriving in Europe and joining his new regiment in Leicestershire.

"You probably did not know this, for it was the best kept secret of the war. Why? Because I was so sea-sick coming across the Atlantic Ocean I did not care if ever I fought the war or not."

"We landed in Northern Ireland and our first camp was just outside Newtonards which we immediately named Camp Starvation. I was told by the guys that if you get put on KP's then steal some food. Of course, being a new arrival I was soon put on that duty. When I left the mess hall that night they were missing a whole ham. The men in our Q-Hut thought I was a hero."

"Next day I received a pass and went into town. There I was minding my own business and admiring the view when an old Irish lady called out, 'Yank,

B Company, 505, take a break during a training hike by the stone wall which surrounded Camp Quorn, 1944.

Six officers from B Company. (Left to right) Captain Harold Miller, Lieutenants — Charles Christian (who was later transferred to I Company and features in the Tucker Diary), Max Domina, Stanley Weinburg, Harold Carroll and Carl Clawson.

you are in trouble. The MP's are coming. Get into the house.' I did as she told me.''

''A record player was playing 'I'm dreaming of a White Christmas' by Bing Crosby. There was a knock on the door. 'Go hide under the bed,' she said. I did. I could not hear what was being said, but here I was hiding under a strange women's bed listening to Crosby. My Mother would never believe this; she knows I am not even a fan of this Crosby guy, I dislike him. Like me she's a Sinatra fan.''

''It was after dark when I arrived back at camp and there I was told to pack up as we were being transferred.''

''The ferry landed us at Stranraer in Scotland and we stayed in a camp for a week. Here there was plenty of food and we ate well. I also met a nice young lady in a blue uniform. I think she was a W.A.A.F. (The British Womens Auxiliary Air Force).''

''From Scotland we travelled to Leicester and then on to Camp Quorn. I was assigned to F Company and reported to Sergeant Leo 'Hoss' Pizarro (he called everybody Hoss). He picked up my bag and told me to follow him. I thought this was great, a Sergeant carrying my bag. We stopped at a tent and he said, 'This will be your home while we are here'. Boy, was I disappointed — a tent with full blown air conditioning from everywhere. But we got to love it after we came back from Normandy.''

''They put us through some hard training and we made a few jumps. Every night after dinner we went into town. If you had a pass you would go through the gate, if you did not, you jumped over the wall.''

Troopers of F Company, 505, with Tony DeFoggi standing in the door of the C-47.

"Meanwhile I met this young lass and we would walk around the Square, looked into the Pubs and watched the older Yanks make fools of themselves (now I do it). One evening I noticed this Cop was following us. 'Sheila, I think that policeman is following us!' 'Pay no attention, he is my father,' was the reply."

"At curfew time we caught the truck back to camp. It made two stops, one by the wall and the other at the gate. That night I got off by the wall for I had no pass. When I arrived at my tent the Platoon Sergeant Bonnie Wright (he died of wounds in the Ardennes) told me to report to the Command Post."

"At the C.P. there were men lined up waiting to see what was going on....and we shortly found out. When I got in there I was asked where I was when there was a call for Formation. Everybody else made an excuse that they were in the showers or something but I told the truth and said I was in town. The First Sergeant, John Field, nearly fell off his chair and he ordered 'Report to your quarters and don't leave.'"

"Dark and early the next morning I was told to dress in full battle gear with a complete full-field pack and go to the Supply Room and draw a day's rations. The day was Easter Sunday. Because I told the truth the Company Commander, Captain Hubert Bass; the First Sergeant, Jack Field; the Platoon Leader, Lieutenant Joseph 'Little Joe' Holcomb; the Platoon Sergeant, Bonnie Wright; my Squad Leader, Leo 'Hoss' Pizarro and the Assistant Squad Leader, George Ziemski all had to make the day's march. It became known as the Easter Parade."

"At the noon-break I was sitting under a tree all by myself when Hoss came by with a bunch of K-Ration boxes. He wasn't very happy, 'Here eat, for this is your Easter Dinner,' he said sarcastically. I felt very small. Right there, sitting under that tree, I promised I would never tell the truth again. When we got back to camp nothing was said about the march, and I made sure that I never went on one again."

"We kept on training hard. Then on that fateful Monday we were herded to the airfields. A week later the 5th June jump was cancelled. Ike gave the green 'Go' for the 6th and then he wisely went to bed with his driver, Kay Summersby."

"It was my Platoon Leader, First Lieutenant Joseph 'Little Joe' Holcomb, who, on 19th September 1944, dragged me off a Nijmegen street to safety when I got hit. He must have forgiven me for the Easter Parade. I have not seen him since and I have tried for years to locate him......I owe him something, he saved my life."

The Easter Parade was the result of Colonel William Ekman's arrival to take over the command of the 505. He decided that the discipline was getting a little slack and the men were leaving the camp without passes at night.

On the evening of Easter Saturday, 25th March, he ordered a 'Charge Call' to be blown at 8pm. Every able-bodied Trooper in the camp had to stand in formation for a role to be taken. Anyone missing and not on an official pass was declared AWOL. The next day the absentees, together with their officers and NCO's, went on an all day hike as a punishment.

Charles Kaiser reports that Princess Elizabeth, then in the ATS, came on a visit to Quorn and was invited to sit in the reviewing stand as the 505 paraded. The men could not believe that 'a real live Princess' was in their midst. This researcher has been unable to find any facts about this visit, but somehow this event is firmly fixed in several veteran's memories. Somehow and somewhere that pretty twenty year old Princess captured many a paratrooper's heart and it is known that some jumped into Normandy with her picture in their pockets.

The Regiment did receive other official visits, there were several from the local Police Constables in search of 'missing' bicycles from the village. Some official representatives also came to note that several trees had disappeared from the camp site and used for firewood.

The village baker, Eric 'Dud' Tomlyn, was kept busy in his bakehouse which backed on to the Churchyard. The 505 cooks found the ingredients and 'Dud' worked overtime baking the fruit cakes, which were made in large three by four foot tins, and the two foot long milk loaves.

All this was watched by his young daughter, Dorothy, who marvelled as thousands of doughnuts were produced. These were transported to the camp in a back of a jeep threaded on long canes. One trooper's name has stayed in her memory all these years as it rhymed with a famous bandleader of the day — Harry James. He was Sergeant Larry James, the 'Mister Fix-it' from the Headquarters Company who organised all the ingredients.

Once 'Dud' said he was short of cooking oil and Larry arrived soon after with a fifty gallon drum of it. Dorothy's father puzzled for days over the correct amounts to use. She remembers the family ate bright yellow cake for a week until he got it right.

Dorothy, or 'Billie' as she is known in the family, had a constant supply of chewing gum which caused so many sticky problems in the village school. Eventually it was banned and the children were punished with the cane on being caught with it. Dorothy remembers suffering that fate.

Those few months for the Tomlyn family, when the paratroopers were their neighbours, were the brightest of the war years.

A newspaper boy, thirteen years old Tony Gale of Quorn used to deliver for Joyce's newsagents around the village. Forty seven years later the happy memories came flooding back. Tony recalls the evening when he first met the 505'ers settling into their camp. The Americans seemed to be very organised.

He used to sell many copies of the *Daily Mirror* at the camp gates. During the day, he and his friends used to prop their bicycles against the wall and stand on the cross bars to look over into the camp. They used to watch the men boxing with big red gloves in a boxing ring.

The paratroopers used Tony as their messenger boy and sent him for fish and chips from Atkins Fish Shop on the main road. The young boy used to climb over the wall to deliver them to his favoured tent. "The tent used to be full of smoke, no filter tips in those days, and there was usually a game of cards going on or some dice rolling," reminisced Tony. "The village was always full of friendly GI's wearing their famous jump boots and I can remember them sitting on the low wall outside the Pig and Whistle drinking the warm beer, just as if it was yesterday.''

It was an open house where Mrs Elizabeth 'Bess' Sutton lived in the nearby village of Barrow-on-Soar. She had an old farm house at 12 Church Street. The boys used to gather in her parlour to warm themselves on the cold evenings. She remembers Henry Voges from Texas, and she did correspond with his mother until after the war. Another was Fred Schrefler who was saving to get married to an English girl, Lilly Hills, who worked at Quorn House. He gave his money to Bess for safe keeping and she hid it under the linoleum floor covering in her bedroom.

The wedding never took place as the romance failed. Fred had his money back before the 505 left to fight again. Bess Sutton always knew when combat was in the air. ''The boys used to have very close haircuts and get very quiet, I knew when they were getting ready for something. They used to bring me all sorts of food. I did worry where they got it from but they assured me they hadn't done anything wrong to get it.''

One of the mysteries of the camp at Quorn was the identity of the 'Green Hornet of Quorn'. It appears that on dark nights several of the HQ Company troopers returning from the pubs felt a tap on the shoulder, and on turning around received a heavy punch in the face, usually resulting in a black eye. The assailant was always described as a little guy who immediately ran away towards the Second Battalion area, through D Company lines heading for E or F Companies. To catch the Green Hornet they assigned Joe 'Tiny' Horvath of the HQ Company, described as 6 foot 4 inch giant, with arms hanging down like a gorilla, to act as a decoy. He patrolled the area on several nights, acting as though he was drunk. He never was attacked.

The prime suspect was a tough little New Yorker of F Company who was a member of the Regimental Boxing Team, 'Teddy' Tedeschi, weighing in at 118 lbs.

Pfc. Richard 'Teddy' Tedeschi, aged 22 and 5 foot 4 inches in his socks stretched himself as much as he could on his medical to reach the required 5 foot 5 inch minimum. He is still accused of being the culprit forty-seven years later, and still denies it. Although he did say recently ''I used to drink with Tiny in a pub — that's why I never hit him.''

The 'Green Hornet' was the talk of the camp and everything that happened was blamed on him. One night they heard some shots being fired, ''Now he is shooting us,'' somebody cried.

'Teddy' Tedeschi enlisted in the army on 1st March 1942, in New York City and standing next in line was Andy Kilcullen. Their serial numbers were consecutive. There a 'father and son' relationship was formed which lasted forty-five years. Both did basic training together, joined the 505, with Andy in B Company.

Tedeschi is still parachuting and organises the Old Tymers Parachute Club which jump at the annual reunions. In 1987, at the age of 67, he parachuted into the grounds of the Dutch Liberation Museum at Groesbeek as a prelude to its opening by Prince Bernhard of the Netherlands. The strong wind carried the light-weight Tedeschi away from his intended target and he finished up in a tree in the Old Mill Hotel next door. He was rescued by the

Richard 'Teddy' Tedeschi is rescued from a tree in the car park of the Old Mill Hotel, Groesbeek.
Richard, aged 67, made this special parachute jump to open the Liberation Museum in 1987.

Dutch military and pictures of the episode appeared in all the Dutch newspapers. His excuse was that he felt like a beer and landed as close as he could to the bar.

Another of the Regiment's boxers was Carl Beck, a huge genial man and a College footballer. He was a good soldier both in combat and in garrison, but he wasn't perfect. He milked his position on the Regimental Boxing Team for all it was worth by claiming he needed time for boxing training instead of going out with the troops in the field. To be fair, any good soldier would take advantage of any angle to beat the system, and Carl did win the Division's light-heavyweight Championship.

Carl had a friend who, though a good man in combat, was considered a 'heartache' because of his tendency to get in trouble. Beck's friend failed to show up after a three-day pass, and Carl with the best intentions — or so he claimed — got a pass and went looking for his friend. Carl too went missing and when he returned was charged with going AWOL.

Beck was up for a Summary Courts Martial, but the Company Commander agreed to waive this if he would accept Company punishment under the 104th Article of War. When his Lieutenant, Jim Coyle, informed him of this, Carl asked him his advice. Coyle told him to accept the punishment, which he did.

Coyle knew that Carl's Private First Class rating was at stake, and so it was, and the memory of that lost stripe has stayed with Carl all these years.

(Left to right) Larry Wiefling, Jim Coyle, David Wills (son of the author) and Carl Beck. In England in 1984.

Jim Coyle has never been allowed to forget it. As Jim says, "For forty-seven years at reunions, Carl has reminded me that my advice cost him his Private First Class stripe. He claims that I failed him as his Defence Council (a position I might have held only if I were assigned at a Courts Martial). My explanations are of no avail. At the last E Company Reunion, Tony DeMayo went to the local army supply store and bought a set of Pfc. stripes."

"When Carl was called upon to say a few words, he included an account of the loss of his Pfc. stripes. Tony went up to the podium and made a formal presentation of the Pfc. stripes to Carl, who laughed along with the rest of us. However, I am not sure that I have heard the last of Carl Beck's lost Pfc. stripes."

As you can imagine these young paratroopers were a pretty wild bunch. Don McKeage recalls that it seemed that everytime someone got into trouble, somebody recognised him as a 'Mac', or someone would hear a shout of "Hey Mac!" It was a regular thing for every 'Mac', or 'Mc' in the Regiment to be ordered to report to the Regimental Headquarters in Class A uniform for an identity parade.

"A couple of times I recall this happening, once when some trooper beat the living hell out of a local girl, his buddy finally hollered "Hey Mac, lets get the hell out of here!" Another time when Major Edward C 'Cannonball' Krause was leaving the Officers Club, someone knocked him down with a big club. 'Cannonball' regained his feet, jumped over the stone wall that surrounded Camp Quorn and chased his assailant into the woods. He lost him but he thought he recognised him as a 'Mac'."

It was Captain Robert Kirkwood of the Third Battalion who gave Krause the nickname of 'Cannonball' when writing up the Field Orders for Normandy. He was looking for a suitable code name to be used in battle. From then on the Third Battalion adopted the insigna of a cannonball and it was painted on their helmets.

The 505 trained in the areas of Charnwood Forest and the Sherwood Forest of Robin Hood fame. The local country lanes saw them on their training hikes. In the old county of Rutland a parachute school was established on the airfield at Ashwell. Everyone was getting ready for the big day, but when that would be they could only guess.

The first hour of the training schedule each day was thirty minutes of callisthenics followed by a thirty minute run. While no one took pleasure in this activity at 7am in the morning, they were all in good physical condition and the only ones who had a slight problem with the exercise were the men who had been on pass the night before and had a little too much to drink.

E Company was typical, but Lieutenant Jim Coyle noticed that one of his men, Private Joe Yoni, would occasionally fall out of the column during the run. Jim questioned him about the problem but Joe denied that he was suffering a hangover, he would just say he could not go on.

One night Jim Coyle went to the Palais de Dance in Leicester and there to his amazement found Private Joe Yoni was the main attraction for the English girls. He was an excellent dancer, particularly adept at the 'Lindy' or as the

English called it, the 'Jitterbug'. He never lacked a partner and danced non-stop for hours.

The officer began to get the picture, and the next morning when Joe Yoni fell out of the column during the run he shouted back at him that he had been seen in action the night before at the Palais de Dance. Now if he didn't finish the run he had danced his last Jitterbug as there would be no more passes to Leicester.

The threat struck home, the English girls and the Jitterbug won. Yoni sprinted to catch up with the rest of the men who were laughing so hard that they nearly fell out. Private Joe Yoni never fell out of a run after that, even after a hard night at the Palais.

Several mass training jumps took place. On Saturday, 6th May, there are reports of hundreds of parachutes coming down over the east side of Leicester in the Scraptoft and Tilton area. Eager troopers quickly rolled up their chutes and ran towards their allotted rendezvous.

Jim Coyle's main concern was training his Platoon for the next combat jump. "Around Quorn there were plenty of open fields in which to manoeuvre, so training problems were conducted on a daily, or a nightly, basis. On the third manoeuvre which was to include a jump, the planes became disoriented due to bad weather and E Company flew around for several hours before finally landing at, what I believe was, an RAF fighter base. I don't know where it was located but it was a long ride back to camp in trucks."

"Due to this incident and my experience in North Africa and the Sicily jump, I was becoming quite concerned with the Troop Carrier navigation. However, a Pathfinder group was formed with the best pilots and navigators to drop paratroopers with small radar sets ahead of the main body of jumpers. They would send signals from the Drop Zone that could be picked up by the approaching planes."

"When they heard the lead planes approaching they would be able to turn on lights which would identify the Drop Zone to the pilot and the jump-master in the plane. This gave us a little more confidence in the success of our next mission."

Allen Langdon had memories of one practice jump. "We were doing a practice night jump somewhere near Bradgate Park and I was the next-to-last man in the stick. We were jumping near high tension cables but we were told that the electricity was turned off."

"Sergeant Wartick was the last man — he hit the cables but the electricity had not been turned off. They shorted, the sky lit up, and we all thought he was dead, but all he had done was burn his boots."

Corporal Thomas Burke, a very brave soldier who was later killed in action in Holland, was one of E Company's authentic characters.

He was very proud of a full-page picture from *Life Magazine* portraying him kissing his girlfriend goodbye at Pennsylvania Station in New York City. In the picture, an approving Military Policeman stood smiling nearby. Burke carried the picture with him always and would show it to every new replacement who joined E Company. The picture was something of a joke amongst the veterans of the Company, because one of them remembered that Burke was AWOL at the time the picture was taken.

One of Burke's favourite stunts, after a few pints in the English pubs, was to break into a loud song. Unfortunately, Burke's entire repertoire consisted of IRA revolutionary songs, but his act was much appreciated by the English people.

One of Lieutenant Jim Coyle's favourite stories about Burke did not concern combat, but it gave Coyle a pretty harrowing time. It occurred at the famous — or infamous — E Company party in Barrow-on-Soar, which is a village adjacent to Quorn.

Coyle relates. "After the party had been underway for about two hours, I had my hands full trying to maintain a semblance of non-violence. In the midst of the action I was called to the door of the rustic pavilion in which the party was being held, to be greeted by a very big and very irate Military Police Lieutenant. He had been on patrol in the village. He informed me that his Jeep had been stolen and since the E Company party was the only game in town, he was certain that one of my men was guilty."

"He was giving me a hard time and it crossed my mind to ask him where he was and what he was doing when his Jeep was stolen. However, in view of his justifiable anger, I realised that this would not contribute anything helpful to our conversation. I assured him that none of my red-blooded American boys would steal his Jeep, and after some discussion he and his Sergeant left."

"With 'Double British Summer Time' it was still daylight, and I watched the MP's go out of sight around a corner up the road. At almost the same time I saw a Jeep come weaving up the road from the opposite direction with Burke at the wheel and a large barrel of beer in the back!"

"With the thought of saving the party and E Company's fairly unblemished reputation, I reacted quickly: I got Burke out of the Jeep, had a couple of men take the beer into the pavilion, told a young soldier, who appeared to be one of the fairly sober men present, to drive the Jeep several blocks away, park it on a side street somewhere where the MP Lieutenant would find it, and return immediately to me."

"The young soldier was barely out of sight when I realized that in my haste to get rid of the Jeep in the event of the MP Lieutenant should return, I had not had sufficient time to consider all the angles to this problem. It suddenly struck me that if the MP Lieutenant spotted the Jeep with my man still in it, Burke would have a fellow defendant at his Courts Martial — Me! The young man who drove it away was acting on my order."

"The next ten minutes seemed like hours as I waited in the road for the return of the young soldier, praying he would not be accompanied by MP's. When he returned alone, I breathed a sigh of relief and returned to my duties inside. The party was wild as ever, but I was at peace."

Raymond Rodriguez and Joseph Przybyla both went through Jump School together in the States, but somehow they finished up in England in the 30th Infantry. They tried to get back to the Airborne without success until one day their Captain spoke to General Eisenhower. "That's the kind of men we want!'' exclained Ike, and the very next day a truck from the 82nd picked them up. They both served in I Company, 505. Private Joseph Przybyla was killed in action in Normandy.

D Company, Frank Bilich claims, were 'goofy' in garrison, but excellent soldiers in the line. ''They were the best guys in the world to be in a tough spot with. We had some crazy guys, I remember two of them. One, Pfc. William 'Swamp Rat' Skinner was over six foot tall, and he was matched up with Pfc. Dominick 'Dippy' Deppolito, who was only five foot five, as a machine-gun team. Skinner always let Dippy carry the machine-gun because he said Dippy liked it that way. Skinner, the large guy carried the tripod.''

Later, Deppolito was to win the Silver Star for bravery in Holland.

''There was Pfc. Frank 'Trigger' Schneider who was blind as a bat without his glasses, and he was the Company runner. I suppose if anyone could find his way in the dark it was him. He once fell down a hole. He did get shot in the arse but he always claimed it was 'high in the thigh'. He started the war with four pairs of glasses and broke his last pair in the Holland jump. The Dutch found him another suitable pair so he could carry on with his war.''

''The worst words Sergeant Stanley 'Saddlebags' Kotlarz heard after he fired his machine-gun at a suspect image was, 'Guess what Sergeant, you've shot one of your own officers in the 'ass'. The officer concerned was Lieutenant Isaac Michelman.''

''Sergeant Milton Schlesener had a built in radar system. He never got lost. He was a good soldier and an excellent shot. In Holland he had his picture taken by a Dutchman which was subsequently used in several Dutch publications and later in the museum at Groesbeek.''

''One guy who never swore was Bryant Jones, even when he was hit. A piece of shrapnel took his thumb and a finger off as clean as a whistle. 'Well I'll be, look at that', was all he said.''

''There was an American Indian by the name of Herbert Buffalo Boy Canoe from the Oglala Sioux tribe who finished up with the Silver Star, a Bronze Star, plus two Purple Hearts. I believe he was the most decorated Indian during the war. If you saw him sober he would scare the hell out of you. We had a little skinny guy, Roy Stark, he was the only one who could handle him.''

''One guy who was always terribly sick in an aircraft was Paul 'Little Nellie' Nelson. He used to lay on the floor in pain, but he made the jump everytime — never missed. He came from Playingfield, New Jersey, and after the war he was found dead in the street. He was a vagrant, a street bum, and he finished up in a pauper's grave.''

The wild men of D Company Frank Bilich remembers were M.P. Brown, John Haggard, a guy called Robert Niland, Kenneth 'Red Dog' Auther, Frank 'Barney' Silanskis, Charles 'Smiley' Manovich, Joseph 'Big Joe' Skolek and Tommy Thompson.

''John Haggard was a wild one. One time a piece of shrapnel went right through his helmet and that never slowed him down. He was killed in action in Normandy.''

"Niland, 'The Beast' we used to call him, had an awful mouth full of teeth that showed when he smiled, which was not often."

"Tommy Thompson got into many fights in Leicester. One night he fought with the MP's and knocked a Provo Marshal on his back."

"I don't remember why he was called M.P. Brown, maybe he only had initials to his name, (Editor: from the records it was Melvin P.) but he was a tough fist fighter who could take on four or five men at one time. He had huge hands and built like a tank."

"Brown was always in trouble. When he came out of a combat zone you knew he would be off AWOL, and you could not do much about it. He was the best combat soldier you ever saw, a sort of guy you would want next to you in a tough spot."

John Rabig, his Staff Sergeant, takes up the story. "M.P. Brown? That guy was a play-boy in garrison, he wanted wine, women and song. He was going to get that, what the hell the circumstances were. Brown was once again in the camp stockade. A barbed wire enclosure with pup tents to sleep in."

"Brown was due out of the stockade after serving five weeks for something or other. One day I was sitting in the Orderly Room when the phone rang. It was the MP's to tell me that Brown's time was up and he was due out now. So I go down to the stockade and get the son-of-a-bitch."

"As we are walking back to the Company, he says, 'Will I get a pass tonight?' Now this is the guy I've just got out of the stockade and he is asking me for a pass."

My answer was "No!"

"Why not?" Brown asks.

"Because you are on Guard Duty tonight. You happen to be on the roster."

"Brown was not very happy."

"I told him, 'You go on Guard Duty tonight and I'll see you get a pass for tomorrow'. He agreed. It was a combined Company guard, with about six men from each Company forming the guard to police the camp."

"So Brown stood guard that night. I'm sitting in the Orderly Room later and the phone rings."

"I answered, 'Company D, Sergeant Rabig.'"

"Is M.P. Brown in your Company?"

"Yes, he is on Guard Duty tonight."

"The voice on the other end of the phone says, 'No he ain't, he's in the Guard House.'"

"Oh shit! I just got him out of there and now he is back in. So down I go to the Duty Officer and found out they put him in charge of the prisoners at the stockade, his friends who he had spent the last five weeks with. It appears that the prisoners were supposed to be clearing up the garbage around the perimeter of the camp. The Duty Officer had found Brown's rifle leaning up against the wall, Brown was holding a baby while his two charges were with two dames in the bushes."

"The Duty Officer throws all three in the Guard House. I go and see Brown the next day. He says, 'Well, they were my friends.' What the hell can you do with a guy like that?"

Kelly the Medic, alias Corporal James Kelly used to go into Leicester regularly to get drunk. He sometimes managed to mess up his uniform during this activity. One night he borrowed Staff Sergeant John Rabig's jacket for a sortie into town. There he got into trouble with the MP's for being drunk and was sent back to Quorn under escort.

Colonel Vandervoort saw him and ordered Captain Taylor Smith to find out whose jacket he was wearing.

Captain Smith came into the Company office, found Rabig there and said, "Find out whose jacket Kelly was wearing tonight?"

"It's mine," admitted Rabig.

"God damn it, you had better report to Vandervoort," was the order.

Rabig went to the Battalion Office and found Vandervoort sitting at his desk. "I've come to see you about the jacket Kelly was wearing tonight."

"Whose was it? Vandervoort questioned.

"It was mine," admitted Rabig.

"God damn it. Get out of here." was the reply.

John Rabig also tells how he became the First Sergeant of D Company, "You got to remember that this was a civilian army, not like the British with rigid discipline. Anyway the Company was short of a First Sergeant and I, as a Staff Sergeant, had been acting as the First."

"Colonel Vandervoort gets the whole Company lined up and presents to them a First Sergeant Turner who has just come over from the States. The Colonel being very diplomatic says, 'Anybody who wants Sergeant Turner to

John Rabig (left) and Frank Bilich at one of the C-47 Club reunions in Williamsburg, Virginia, in 1987.

be your First Sergeant raise your hands.' The whole Company in one voice shouted, 'Get that son-of-a-bitch out of here.' They all knew him.''

''Vandervoort then told Turner to return to F Company and gave the order, 'Sergeant Rabig, fall the Company out.' ''

From then on Rabig was a First Sergeant.

Sergeant Turner jumped into Normandy but broke his leg on landing. For him the war was over and he returned to the States soon afterwards.

Rabig was never worried when his men went AWOL. ''They always came back when they were broke. They maybe AWOL from camp, but when the rumours started that the 505 were moving out, they would come streaming back. Even the hospitals used to empty. I remember one guy, Pfc. Frank Thierry, coming back with his broken leg in a cast saying, 'You bastards are not jumping without me.' ''

Thierry had broken his leg on a practice jump and was in hospital when the rumours were circulating that the 505 was pulling out. He went AWOL and returned to D Company, had his plaster cut off and his ankle and foot tightly taped. A bigger jump boot was obtained to enable him to make the combat jump into Normandy.

The best story about being AWOL that John Rabig remembers is when the Commanding Officer, Lawrence Price, asked him to take a look at a telegram he had just received. It was from two troopers who were adrift. It read, ''Safe and sane, on a train, will be late, but can explain.''

''What the hell am I supposed to do with this?'' Price asked.

One man Frank Bilich remembers with sorrow was Pfc. George J. Rajner who was married with five children. He refused to buy his ten thousand dollar GI Insurance because he thought that his mother-in-law would benefit if he was killed, and this fate he was expecting because of a premonition. He tried to go seaborne for Normandy but was refused. His premonition was correct, he was killed in action attacking Hill 131 in Normandy. His last words, as he lay dying, were, ''Make sure my scarf gets back to Pennsylvania.''

Frank often wonders how his young family fared.

Many young hearts were broken. A sixteen year old Loughborough girl, Dorothy Cumberland, met nineteen year old Private David Berardi of A Company and they fell in love. The meetings had to be in secret as Dorothy's parents did not approve. Promises were made that David would return after the war to claim her as his bride.

Private David Berardi was killed in action in the Ardennes battle on 6th January 1945. Dorothy still visits his family in the States to this day.

The Mystery of Papillon Hall

The Billet of the 319th Glider Artillery Regiment

The men of the 319th Glider Artillery Regiment were billeted at Papillon Hall at Lubenham, near Market Harborough, Leicestershire.

Little did they know that Lubenham and Papillon Hall has for centuries had its stories of ghosts, murder and mystery. There is an account of how the 17th century mistress of the Hall, Anna Marie Castell, on her death bed at the age of 84, asked that her silken slippers should always be kept there in case she wanted to go for a walk when she came back. If the slippers were removed from the house she added, a terrible curse would descend on the building.

This Spanish lady had married Frenchman David Papillon in 1615. His ancestors had come to England from Normandy with William the Conqueror in 1066.

For many years her request was strictly adhered to, until someone decided to remove the slippers for a joke. It is reported that straight away two people in the house became ill and only recovered when the slippers were returned.

In 1920 when the Hall was owned by Mr Frank Belville, the shoes were lent to an exhibition in London. Immediately three people in the Hall died and four of Mr Belville's polo ponies were struck by lightning. The slippers were hastily recovered and to ensure they would never be moved again, the key to the alcove door, where they were kept, was thrown away with the shoes locked safely inside. When the 350 year old Hall was rebuilt in 1922 the slippers were again moved, this time in a glass case high up over a fireplace.

Associated with her ghost-like memory there are reports of the 'four-in-hand coach' being galloped along the main road from the Hall to Lubenham village. White ghost-like apparitions in the area have been seen, the last time in 1965.

The village folklore recalls that the 319th Glider Artillery Regiment of the 82nd Airborne Division took over Papillon Hall in February 1944, and again the curse struck. The story goes that a souvenir-hunting GI forced open the bottom of the case and took one of the slippers away with him. Later the trooper met his fate by being killed in action and the slipper was hastily returned. That is the story of the local legend and it has been difficult to unravel the truth.

Joe Clowry of the Headquarters Company of the 319th Glider Field Artillery, now living in Lockport, New York, has recently told his story to put the record straight. He writes: ''We were billeted in the main house of Papillon Hall, in one the many rooms containing as many double bunks as could be squeezed into each room.''

''Before settling in, we were lined up and given a briefing on how to behave in England and especially warned not to become involved with a pair of slippers that were encased and hung over the fireplace in one of the main rooms.''

''Naturally enough, as soon as we were dismissed, we all headed for the house to search out the slippers. If I recall rightly, there was a large high-ceilinged room to the right of the main entrance with a fireplace to the left. Secured high up over the fireplace, near the ceiling was a glass case containing two slippers. They were hanging together with the toes pointing down.''

''As best as I can recall the story that was circulated explained that the slippers were worn by a young bride, in the distant past, at a Ball held in the room in which the slippers were housed. Apparently she died shortly thereafter and the slippers were enshrined in her memory.''

''The story gave us the impression that the house was haunted, but events never revealed any ghost-like aberrations appearing during our stay.''

''It was either after the first or second night we were there that on the following morning we were all lined up again and advised that one of the slippers was missing from the case. This disappearance was a serious breach of etiquette that must be rectified by the return of the slipper...or else.''

''To the best of my recollection, the slipper was back in the case within a day or two and remained there for the rest of our stay.'' ''I am not aware of how the slipper vanished or how it reappeared, nor who was responsible for its disappearance, other than I believe an irreverent, unthoughtful GI who stole down to the room by flashlight in the middle of the night. His intention was to procure a souvenir. I also felt that, because of the high location of the case, there was more than one individual involved.''

''We were at the Hall until late May when we left for Membury Airfield for participation in Operation Overlord. We returned to Papillon Hall in July and left again in September for Market Garden. We never returned to Papillon Hall, and as far as I can remember, the slippers were still in their proper place when we left.''

A final piece of evidence has been supplied by another 319 veteran, Edward R. Ryan of Hyde Park, New York. He says, ''We knew that the slippers were to bring bad luck to whoever touched them. One of our fellows stole them and was in the process of sending them home when he had a terrible accident with a Jeep. He returned the slippers quickly as the curse seemed to be still working.''

''There were stories of the 'Duke' who owned the place, he was an officer who was stationed in the British Isles. He visited the Hall once during my stay there. I understood he was heir to the Colman Mustard fortune.''

The 'Duke' was in fact a Mr Rupert Belville who fought with General Franco's forces in the Spanish Civil War. He was a major share-holder in the Colman company and he died in 1952.

Another legend was that the French Crown jewels had been hidden in the Hall after the French Revolution. When the Hall was demolished in 1950, it was carefully taken apart stone by stone without anything being found.

Today, the only visible remains of Papillon Hall are the holes in the ground where the cellars had been, but the legends go on. Folk tales are impossible to kill. Both slippers now safely reside in a Leicester museum.

Cottesmore & Spanhoe Airfields

Early on the morning of Monday, 29th May, the 505 paratroopers climbed aboard trucks for the journey to two airfields to prepare for the greatest invasion in the history of the world.

As Harold Carroll recalls, "That morning as we marched out of the camp to meet the trucks, the street was lined with our friends. The people of Quorn had a much better 'grape-vine' than we did." That was Harold's last sight of Quorn, he never made it back. He was captured on D-Day, spent the next eight months in a prisoner-of-war camp, Oflag 64, to be finally released by the Russians in January 1945.

James Coyle writes, "At the end of May we loaded our equipment on trucks and moved to the airfield of Cottesmore. Here we were told that we were restricted to our assigned area, a row of pyramidal tents. The field was patrolled by Military Police and we knew that this would not be a practice jump this time."

The two airfields were Cottesmore and Spanhoe. The Second and Third Battalions of the 505 went to Cottesmore, situated in the old county of

The lines of C-47s waiting at Cottesmore Airfield to load up with paratroopers for D-Day.

Rutland and is still an active military airfield today. Spanhoe was a temporary airfield three miles to the north of Corby, Northamptonshire, and received the First Battalion and the Regimental Headquarters. The two airfields were about ten miles apart.

Also included were units from the 307th Engineers and the 456th Parachute Battalion of Field Artillery.

The 505 were hardened veterans, the premier assault troops of the United States forces. They realised a long time ago that they were counted as expendable. They knew that to survive they had to hit first and hit hard.

Generals Ridgway and Gavin were hard taskmasters and this was the way they trained the men. In their briefings they pulled no punches. Ridgway told the men, "Some of you will die, this particpation in world history may be just a thought that you can take with you. You are assured by me that you will be on the winning side." Gavin put it a little kinder when he said, "Some of us will lose our way."

They had been waiting for Y-Day, or Ready Day, as it had been known for months. That was the first day of June. Thereafter each day was numbered plus 1, plus 2 etc. until the date was set for D-Day.

At Cottesmore seventy two C-47 aircraft were waiting, while at Spanhoe forty eight C-47's were ready. At Spanhoe, 864 Paratroopers crowded into a hangar for their sleeping accommodation. In all 2095 men of the 505 were standing by.

Both airfields were sealed off from the outside world by the Military Police. The only movement between them were the two Chaplains and their escorts to hold the religious services. George 'Chappie' Wood and the Catholic priest, Father Matt Connelly, both remember that the attendance was better than usual. Both Chaplains promised to see them in Normandy, as they would be jumping too.

"We didn't have long to wait for our Normandy briefing for D-Day," said James Coyle, continuing his story. "E Company was to set up roadblocks at Neuville-au-Plain, a small town a few miles north of Ste-Mere-Eglise. Ste-Mere-Eglise was a main road junction which the German reserves would have to use in order to attack the Fourth Division which was landing on the beaches, east of our objectives. The Third Battalion of the 505 was to take Ste-Mere-Eglise. The Second Battalion, which included our Company, was to protect the town from attack from the north by holding Neuville-au-Plain."

"We were briefed on our mission on large scale maps of the area and low level aerial photographs of the town of Neuville-au-Plain. We were advised on 3rd June to get a good night's sleep because we would be taking off the next night to jump into France. The next day, however, we woke up to heavy rain and strong winds."

Craps and poker games were in full swing to help pass the time. The stakes were dollars and the recently issued French invasion money. Fortunes were won and lost in the seven days they were cooped up waiting for the word 'Go'. Private First Class 'Dutch' Schultz won and lost $2,500, more money than he had ever seen at one time in all of his twenty-one years.

With a change in the weather it was late in the day when the word was passed down that the invasion had been postponed for 24 hours. The pre-planned dinner on the Sunday night had to go ahead. The grim-humored comments were to the effect that 'the condemned men ate a hearty last meal'. The dinner was one of the best they could remember since going overseas.

The 5th June 1944, dawned bright and clear. It was announced at reveille that the invasion was definitely on for that night. By early afternoon all was ready. Last minute briefings had been held, weapons checked and cleaned once more, knives and bayonets sharpened. Many men, because of the tension, could not sleep and they just stretched out in their cots in the large aircraft hangar. Others took the chance to write their last letters home.

Some of the 505'ers chose to blacken their faces. Orders were to have their hair cut to a half an inch in case of head wounds. Everyone was checked to make sure that the two metal identity tags held by a thin chain were around their necks. This was a long running joke amongst the 505 as they were always losing them. Many a local girl around Quorn and Loughborough, and the ATS (British Army) girls from Woodhouse sported jump wings or a set of identity tags.

First Sergeant Rabig lined D Company up for a last inspection. "Who hasn't got their identity tags?" One hand went up, it was William 'Rebel' Haynes, "I ain't got no God damned dog tags!"

"God damn it", raged Rabig, "Where are your dog tags?"

"I've lost them," said Rebel.

"Its too late now, write your name and number on two pieces of paper and tie them with string round your neck. Serves you right if you get killed and finish up as the Unknown Soldier. I don't give a shit no more." Rabig had had enough.

Major Krause packed carefully the old worn Stars and Stripes which had flown over Gela in Sicily and the Post Office in Naples. In a dramatic speech to his Battalion he stated. "Tomorrow morning I will be sitting in the Mayor's office in Ste-Mere-Eglise and this flag will be flying over the Town Hall."

One piece of equipment that wasn't packed was Frank Bilich's gas mask. He threw it away and filled his case with coffee powder, candy bars and rations. His Mother had sent him tins of Nescafe which kept Frank in fresh coffee during all the campaigns in Europe.

At ten o'clock as the daylight began to fade (British Double Daylight Time) the order 'Chute up' was given. Equipment bundles had been fixed on racks under the planes to be dropped at the same time as the men. The parachutes were laid out by the Supplymen, everybody picked his main and reserve out of the pile and proceeded to adjust the harnesses.

Each man was now carrying at least 150 pounds in weight. On the command 'Load up' the Troopers made for the tailplane of the C-47 to relieve themselves — a paratroopers ritual: not the easiest thing to do with all that equipment and the parachute harness on. Willing hands helped the bulky bodies up the short ladder and through the door of the aircraft. After ten minutes in the plane there was always somebody who wanted to head for the tailplane again.

Many of them looked out for their friends to shake hands and say "So

Checking the equipment at Cottesmore airfield during the loading of the C-47s for D-Day. On the left is Lt Harold Carroll with Lt Stanley Weinburg, both of B Company, 505.

long" or "Take it easy buddy." A lot of them would never see their friends alive again. Most realised that they would be lucky to see this operation through in one piece.

Their thoughts were also on the fact that in the invasion of Sicily, out of one serial of the Division's one hundred and forty four C-47 aircraft, twenty-three were shot down by friendly naval gunfire. Six were shot down before the parachutists had a chance to get out.

One aircraft carried a stowaway. He was the American Sioux Indian, Herbert Buffalo Boy Canoe, veteran of the Sicily and Salerno jumps. He had been ordered to stay in England but there was no way the 505 were going to jump without him. He was not listed on the plane's roster so he was smuggled aboard by his D Company buddies. The only weapon he had was a grenade given to him by another trooper.

At the last moment, at Cottesmore, trucks loaded with carbines raced to the loading area and the men were given a choice of exchanging their M-1 rifles for the lighter weapon. Also the BAR men were given a sling harness which, when attached to the Browning Automatic Rifle, made it possible to lower it to ground just before landing.

A group of Pathfinders before they boarded their C-47s to be the first to land in Normandy during the first few minutes of D-Day. On the left, back row, is Tony DeMayo; standing on the far right is Robert Bales; fourth from the right, back row is Larry James; far right in the middle row is James J. Smith.

As the troopers were boarding their planes the two Chaplains walked among them reciting the Lord's Prayer and the Paratrooper's Prayer. They were prepared for battle and the feeling amongst the men was as tense as it had been during the previous combat jumps. These were men who had already tasted battle and won, so there was some assurance as to what to expect when they met the enemy on reaching the ground.

At Spanhoe just before take-off a Gammon grenade carried by one of the men of the First Battalion Headquarters Company exploded. Four were killed in the C-47 of Flight Officer Harper of 43 Squadron, USAAF, fifteen were wounded, one being the aircraft's radio operator. The only man unharmed was Corporal Melvin Fryer, who, not wanting to be left behind elbowed his way on to another plane. He was killed twelve days later in Normandy.

Two of the dead are buried at the American Military Cemetery at Cambridge. They are Corporal Kenneth A. Vaught and Pfc. Robert L. Leakey.

The codename for the 82nd Airborne drop was 'Boston'. At 11 o'clock the C-47's took off. In the darkness of the Normandy countryside identification was going to be made by the password 'Flash', to be answered by 'Thunder', and by little toy crickets which clicked. With the passing of time many paratroopers now mistakenly recall the passwords as 'Thunder and Lightning'. In daylight, recognition of positions would be made by orange flags.

Private First Class William 'Bill' Tucker recalls his memories of that night. "It was just twilight, and the sound of all those men marching in single file to their planes was like a drumbeat. Nobody was talking. The roar of engines was everywhere. I looked out of the door of the plane and saw all those English people, cooks and bakers watching us. It was like a silent prayer, or salute. As young as we were, we all knew it was the biggest thing in our lives."

The Commander of the Pathfinders was Major Neal Lane McRoberts. The leaders of the Battalion teams were Lieutenant Michael Chester (First), Lieutenant James J. Smith (Second) and Lieutenant Robert B. Bales (Third).

The Pathfinders and their volunteer security teams, who included Elmo Jones, Robert Murphy, Larry James and Tony De Mayo left from the airfield of North Witham in twenty C-47's. They took off at 21.30 hours with two hundred pathfinder paratroopers on board. Not all were from the 82nd, about half were from the 101st Airborne, the 'Screaming Eagles'. At 00.15, fifteen minutes into D Day, these parachutists landed on French soil to mark the Drop Zones with lights and radar beacons. The 505 team were the only ones to mark their Drop Zone accurately.

Tony DeMayo, a member of E Company, successfully made all four combat jumps and was awarded the Bronze Star for bravery, and being wounded twice he had two Purple Hearts. It is always said that any man who made the four combat jumps was extremely lucky to survive the war.

He told a story about one incident when the two men either side of him were killed by an exploding artillery shell. Tony felt a blow on his chest and when he looked at the bible he carried in his breast pocket he found a piece of shrapnel embedded in it. If it hadn't been for that bible Tony would have been killed too.

On the occasion of the presentation of the first Silver Star to Captain Neal Lane McRoberts. (Left to right) Lieutenant-General Matthew Ridgway, Brigadier-General James Gavin, Captain Neal Lane McRoberts and Major-General Maxwell Taylor. March 1944.

The McRoberts wedding in New York in 1945. (Left to right) Neal Lane McRoberts, his wife Augusta, and the Best Man, Captain James J. Smith.

Tony returned to Loughborough Parish Church in 1945 to marry his girl, Ethel, and take her to New York. He had met her through playing darts in a pub, the Loughborough Hotel in Baxter Gate, with her father. Tony always joked that after the game of darts and the pub had closed, he used to take Ethel dancing.

Their happy marriage lasted 45 years until Tony died in 1990, aged 72. They had five children, and at the last count, eleven grandchildren.

Both Jones and Murphy became prominent business men in the States. Jones in the manufacture of plastics and Murphy as an Attorney. Both these men were still making parachute jumps in the 1980s.

Neal Lane McRoberts was awarded two Silver Stars for his bravery in Italy and Normandy. A recurrence of malaria caught in North Africa as the Division was getting ready for the Market Garden Operation stopped him getting his fourth combat star. He returned to the States and took command of the Jump School at Fort Benning. In 1945 Major McRoberts married an English girl, Miss Augusta Haywood, and fellow pathfinder James J. Smith was the best man. Later the couple came to England to reside when he opened a branch of the Bank of America in the City of London.

Miss Haywood was the sister of the Lord Lieutenant of the County of Rutland and they met when the Major was based at the North Witham airfield. He took the part of the English country squire and regularly rode with the famous Cottesmore Hunt, living in the Old Hall at Ashwell. He attended an 82nd Veterans Convention in Atlantic City in 1966. Shortly after his return to England, in the December, he was killed during a fox hunt when his horse fell at a fence.

Just before dark, about 21.30 hours on 5th June 1944, the English countryside heard the sound of aircraft engines warming up. Large numbers of C-47's from numerous airfields across the country took off, circled until they got into formation, and headed across the English Channel to Normandy. The invasion of Hitler's Europe had begun.

Normandy

Because of the flak and nervous tension the pilots did not always throttle back and reduce their air speed as they approached the Drop Zones. This meant that the troopers had to jump out at speeds in excess of 150mph. The opening shock tore off musette bags, binoculars, watches and anything else which was not securely fastened.

General James Gavin lost his wrist-watch in this way. He replaced it later by taking a dead German Lieutenant's watch, as well as a map showing the German positions around La Fiere. On turning the map over, Gavin was surprised to see a map of the English Midlands, exactly where he had come from.

Gavin, the youngest General in the U.S. Army since the Civil War, at 37 years old, looked much younger. His men, noting his slim boyish looks, nicknamed him 'Slim Jim'. Such was his charismatic leadership that they would follow him anywhere.

Jim Gavin was a soldiers' General and the men loved him, even after forty-five years the affection was still there. He went on in his Army career to be President Kennedy's Marshal at the Inaugural Parade and later to become the United States Ambassador to France. Not bad for an orphan who joined the Army as a Private in 1924.

Don McKeage of F Company, 505, left from Cottesmore airfield. As he said, ''All went well until arriving near the DZ 'O', the C-47's did not slow up for the drop. Everyone in the Second Battalion agreed that it was the highest, fastest jump ever made. Eyeballs had to be screwed back into their sockets. The Second Battalion landed on or near the DZ. Except for one stick from F Company and they headed for the centre of Ste-Mere-Eglise.''

The main problem in those first few minutes of the 6th June was the low cloud which obscured the target areas. It was the Second Platoon mortar squad of F Company, 505, that mis-timed their exit and landed in the Square of Ste-Mere-Eglise. Thirty minutes before, two sticks of the 101st Airborne's 506th Parachute Infantry Regiment had jumped across the east side of the town. Four were killed by the German guards and this alerted them to the 505 error.

It was Private First Class A.J. Van Holsbeck of F Company, 505, who died falling into the house which was on fire on the south side of the town square. The house had been accidently set alight and the Germans allowed the villagers, under guard, to break the curfew to fight it.

An eye witness account has been given by Frenchman Raymond Paris who lived in Ste-Mere-Eglise. He was 20 years old at the time. He said that a fire broke out in a house at about 10pm (midnight British time). A German sergeant gave Mayor Alexandre Renaud permission to rouse the populace and for the priest to ring the church bell. The people set up a bucket brigade in the light of the flames. As they were fighting the fire, American planes appeared low overhead, so low that Paris could see their open doors. Paratroopers began jumping out by the hundreds.

"I saw one paratrooper drop on the road, but he was killed by a German before he could get untangled from his parachute," Paris said. "Another was killed near me. I will never forget the sight."

In May 1991, Raymond Paris contacted the C-47 Club Flyer with another story from that night in Ste-Mere-Eglise. He wrote:

"During the night of 5/6 June after the parachute jump, as I was coming back in the darkness from the house which had burned in the square, we found in the middle of the street, twenty metres from our home, a parachutist of the 82nd Airborne who appeared dead."

"We carried him a few metres away to the edge of the square and covered him with his parachute."

"The next morning as I went back and I was amazed to discover that there was no body under the parachute. Nearby a parachutist was sitting on the steps of a truck left behind by the Germans the night before. He spoke French and told me he was from Louisiana. I told him that the night before we had carried one of his friends who had been killed. He burst out laughing and told me that it was him. He had been wounded in the shoulder by a bullet and that he had shammed death in order not to be killed by the Germans."

"When he heard us coming, without knowing if we were French or German, he kept playing dead. We spoke a long time together, but I did not see him again. If that individual is still alive, I would be pleased to hear from him or to see him again."

PRIVATE KEN RUSSELL, F COMPANY, 505

He recalls his memories and this is what he wrote in a letter in 1982, more than thirty eight years later:

"I have heard and read so much on this I wonder where all these people were in Ste-Mere-Eglise in the early morning of 6th June, 44."

"I jumped with the Second Platoon, it was commanded by Second Lieutenant Harold Cadish. I don't remember all the stick in our plane but I know Pvt. H.T. Bryant, Pvt. Ladislaw 'Laddie' Tlapa and Lieutenant Cadish were most unfortunate. They were the fellows who were shot on the power poles. My close friend Pfc. Charles Blankenship was shot still in his chute, hanging in a tree, a little distance down the street."

"When we jumped there was a huge fire in a building in town. I didn't know that the heat would suck a parachute towards the fire. I fought the chute all the way down to avoid the fire. One trooper who had joined our Company shortly before D-Day landed in the fire. I think his name was Van Haheck, or similar to that." (It was Pfc. Alfred J. Van Holsbeck).

"Facing the church from the front, I landed on the right side of the roof, luckily in the shadow side from the fire. Some of my suspension lines went over the steeple and I slid down over to the edge of the roof. This other trooper came down and really got entangled on the steeple, I didn't know it was Steele at the time.''

''Almost immediately a Nazi soldier came running from the back side of the church shooting at everything. Sergeant John Ray had landed in the church yard almost directly below Steele. This Nazi shot him in the stomach while he was still in his chute.''

''As you know sergeants jumped with a 45 calibre pistol. While Ray was dying he somehow got his 45 out and shot the Nazi in the back of the head killing him. Sergeant Ray saved my life as well as Steele's. It was one of the bravest things I have ever witnessed.''

''I finally got to my trench knife and cut my suspension lines and fell to the ground. I looked up at the steeple but there was not a movement or a sound and I thought the trooper was dead.''

''I got my M-1 assembled and ducked around several places in that part of town hoping to find some troopers, but all of them were dead. I got off several rounds at different Germans before they drove me to a different position with intense gunfire.''

''Working my way back past the church, I was the most scared and loneliest person in the world. I thought I was the only trooper alive in the midst of all those enemy soldiers. I was finally spotted again and I believe every German in the area opened up in my direction. Dashing across the street I ran down to a park or wooded area not far away. How the enemy with so much fire power didn't get me I will never know. After I short distance I came to a field. I heard a noise ahead so I started crawling towards it. I got very close and snapped my cricket. A cricket snapped back in return. What a relief!''

''It was a trooper from the 508, a 'live' trooper. We started back towards the trees and came across three more, one from the Third Battalion 505, one from the 506 and one other from the 508.''

PRIVATE JOHN STEELE, F COMPANY, 505

Two men landed on the church, John Steele was caught up high on the tower, and Private Kenneth Russell hit the church with his chute on the lower part of the roof. Private Steele was wounded in the foot by flak as he floated down. He was later rescued by the Germans and taken prisoner.

The Platoon Sergeant was John 'Jack' Field. Unaware of what was happening to his men, he had landed in a walled courtyard of a motor repair business and it took him some time to find his way out in the dark. Forty years later this researcher walked with Jack Field around Ste-Mere-Eglise trying to locate the yard without success.

Jack Field was awarded a battlefield commission during the Normandy fighting.

One man was so close to John Steele that night but never met him face to face. He was a German soldier, Chief-corporal Rudolph May, who commanded a patrol of ten men.

These are his own words as he related them forty years later:

''That evening on the 5th June, my friends and I were enjoying ourselves trying to break a cycle speed record around the church at Ste-Mere-Eglise,

The church at Ste-Mere-Eglise, Normandy, in 1984, with the parachute draped over the corner of the tower where John Steele was hanging during the early hours of D-Day.

just to kill time. At 10pm I resumed my post in the steeple — a telephone at my side. Around midnight (2am British time) I heard planes passing overhead and saw 'objects' falling from the sky. During this period a house began to burn. It was the light from this fire that made it possible for me to see hundreds of parachutes falling from the sky as the airplane motors droned on. They fell on the roofs, in the streets and even in the trees of the church square. The sky was studded with parachutes.''

''Suddenly everything in the steeple became dark. Through an opening I saw that a parachutist had fallen on the steeple, hanging by the ropes. He appeared to be dead, but after a moment I heard his voice. There were two of us on duty at the post, and my companion wanted to shoot him. 'Are you crazy,' I said, 'if you shoot we'll be discovered.' ''

Rudolph May cut the parachute lines with his pocket knife to release Steele so he could be taken captive. John Steele and Rudolph May were never as close to each other as during the course of that famous night.

''John Steele came back to Ste-Mere-Eglise on several occasions, and so did I, but we were never able to meet one another. Personally I regret it, we would have had many things to talk about.''

The reason that May kept returning to Normandy was to visit the grave of his brother, a pilot, killed in 1944.

Rudolph May died in 1986 in the small village of Niederzier, between Cologne and Aix-la-Chapelle, where he had lived since the war.

John Steele became the local hero in Ste-Mere-Eglise. After the war they named the hotel and restaurant after him. To this day, on every anniversary

John 'Jack' Field of F Company with his wife, Bede, in the square of Ste-Mere-Eglise in June 1984.

of 6th June the French townsfolk hang a parachute on the church tower in his memory. Steele was a natural comedian with a great sense of humour, he kept the world laughing around him.

While at Quorn he used to act as the Company barber and charged the men 50 cents or one shilling a time. The boys nicknamed him 'The Sheep Shearer'. The officers were charged one pound for the service. Lieutenant Joe Holcomb, the Executive Officer, got John to cut his hair and was charged one pound. A short time later 'Little Joe' Holcomb returned and told Steele, "You cannot do that to the officers." Steele looked at 'Little Joe' and said, "Sir, I have just gone out of business."

After the war every one knew when Steele was around because he carried a duck call which he use to blow at the most inopportune moments. At one reunion when General James Gavin was addressing the veterans a duck call honked out. The General paused for a moment, looked up and said, "I know you're out there Johnny Steele." Joking to his last breath, he died of cancer in 1969.

Because of the film *The Longest Day*, the adventures of Steele became internationally known. His part in the epic story was played by the comedian Red Buttons.

LT. COLONEL BENJAMIN VANDERVOORT, 505

Lt. Colonel Ben 'Vandy' Vandervoort broke his ankle on the jump and being on the heavy side there was no way he could travel. He felt his ankle 'go' as he landed in an orchard, realising help was near to hand he quietly called to Lyle Putman, the Regimental Doctor. Putman confirmed the fracture. In fact his left tibia had broken about one inch above the ankle. So Vandy asked him to lace up the jump boot as tightly as he could so as to act as a support. "What ever you do, don't take it off," ordered the Doctor. Then as Putman watched, Vandervoort picked up a rifle to use as a crutch and said to the men around him, "Well, lets go!"

Just then he saw two 101st Airborne sergeants pulling a collapsible ammunition cart. Asking for a lift he got the short answer of "We havn't come to Normandy to pull a damn Colonel around." The two sergeants got an equally short answer when, as Vandervoort noted later, "I persuaded them otherwise." Soon after he 'won' one of the Gliderborne Jeeps, which greatly increased his mobility, and much to the relief of the two 101st Airborne sergeants. In Ste-Mere-Eglise he was able to borrow crutches from a crippled French housewife.

Although the 82nd and 101st were sister units there was no love lost between them. The 82nd were battle hardened whereas the 101st had never been tested in combat. The 101st won their first battle honours within hours.

Vandervoort's Second Battalion was lucky, twenty-seven out of the thirty-six sticks hit the Drop Zone five minutes ahead of schedule. Vandy had been watching carefully the position from the aircraft and when he received a 'green go' signal from the pilot he knew that it was far too early. He simply told his crew chief to go back and tell the pilot to turn it off until he got to where he was supposed to go.

Lieutenant Colonel Benjamin H. Vandervoort (left) and Major William J. Hagan, at Cottesmore Airfield waiting for D-Day.

Back in Quorn, waiting for Normandy, Vandervoort was, to say the least, unpopular. The men of his Battalion found it hard to have any confidence in him. He never allowed himself to get close to his men, a relationship that most other officers enjoyed. Vandervoort had been the Regimental Plans and Training Officer, never the most popular of jobs, and during the fighting in Italy was given the command of the Second Battalion.

Most of his men were hardened veterans of North Africa, Sicily and Italy and were thoroughly combat wise. Vandervoort was subjected to having some cruel nicknames. One, because when he stood to attention his right leg used to tremble, was 'Shakey Jake'. After Normandy, where he proved his leadership beyond all doubt, there was never any mention of nicknames.

Frank Bilich, a Pfc. in D Company, added his praise of Vandervoort by saying, ''A lot of guys didn't understand Vandervoort in Ireland. They probably didn't understand him in England when he was preaching training, training, training. I tell you one thing, when we came out of Normandy it would not make any difference if you understood him or not; he won the respect of everybody — he had a lot of guts. In airborne language, he had 'balls'. After that if he had told us to follow him to hell, we would have gone with him, no doubt about it.''

Bilich's favourite story of Vandervoort in Normandy tells us a lot about the man. There were three American tanks attacking down a narrow road with

E Company in the field one side and D Company on the other. Vandervoort was hobbling alongside the leading tank which was firing its machine-gun. All of a sudden the tank stopped firing. Vandervoort started beating on the turret. The turret opened and the Tank Commander's head appeared. "Why have you stopped firing?" Vandervoort demanded.

The Tanker was taken aback by this crazy Airborne officer and explained that he was out of ammunition. "Get that God damned tank out of here and get another one," came the order.

"I've seen him," recalls Bilich, "when a burp-gun opened up nearby and he would just stand there, he would never duck. It was if he was covered in armour, or something."

Vandervoort was awarded the Distinguished Service Cross for his actions in Normandy and his name is still a legend today. His ambition was to stay in the Army after the war but was, unfortunately, later wounded, losing the sight of one eye. He retired from the Army in 1946.

Towards the end of his life he lived quietly in retirement in North Carolina after twenty years service with the Central Intelligence Agency, serving in Washington and overseas. He died in November, 1990, at the age of 75.

In the film, *The Longest Day*, the role of Ben Vandervoort was portrayed by the actor John Wayne.

After the battle for Ste-Mere-Eglise, Jim Gavin, surveying the scene a day or two later with Ben Vandervoort said in jest, "Van, don't kill them all, save a few for interrogation."

LIEUTENANT TURNER 'CHIEF' TURNBULL, D COMPANY, 505

A strange happening took place on D-Day at about 1300 hours as Vandervoort was taking up the defensive positions for Ste-Mere-Eglise. He was talking to Lieutenant Turner Turnbull (known as 'Chief' because of his American Indian heritage as he was half Chereokee) of D Company's Third Platoon who had set up a road block. A Frenchman rode up on a bicycle and announced in English that some American paratroopers were bringing a column of German prisoners down the road from the north.

When they looked, sure enough there was a column of marching men coming down highway N-13. There appeared to be paratroopers on each side of the column waving orange flags. All seemed to be in order when Vandervoort noticed that two tracked vehicles were following in the rear.

He ordered Turnbull to have his machine-gunner fire a short burst just to the right of the approaching column, which was now about 800 yards away. When the machine-gun fired, the flag wavers and the marchers dived into the ditches and opened fire. Turnbull's men returned the fire and pinned down the infantry. The two Self-Propelled Guns continued to move forward and at 500 yards they opened up. Their first shots knocked out the bazooka team at the road block but a 57mm gun with some fast and accurate shooting knocked out both vehicles. Meanwhile the Frenchman had wisely disappeared.

The next day Turnbull was killed by an artillery round. He was recommended for a Distinguished Service Cross, but ultimately awarded the Silver Star Medal. It was Turnbull's defence of Ste-Mere-Eglise in the early stages that enabled the 82nd Division to stablise its position. John Keegan in his book, *Six Armies in Normandy*, commenting on Turnbull stated, ''He belongs with those who saved the invasion.''

PFC. ROY A. STARK, D COMPANY, 505

Stark was a member of Turnbull's Platoon manning the road block on Highway N-13. During the fierce fighting a mortar bomb exploded behind him knocking him to the ground and inflicting Stark with a serious head wound. As Stark said later, ''I thought I was dead, but I felt myself being moved. It turned out that a German soldier was going through my pockets for cigarettes.''

The Germans also thought he was dead. When he regained consciousness all his pockets were empty. The Germans gave him back his cigarettes and took him to a house, which was lucky for Stark because as the German counter-attack came through he was found very quickly. The Germans took him to Cherbourg and when that town was liberated, Stark was taken to England for medical treatment. After staying in five hospitals and under-goimg numerous X-rays his condition was described as inoperable. Finally a doctor took the risk and successfully operated.

Roy Stark returned to the 505 some seven months later when the Regiment was fighting in the Battle of the Bulge.

Years later in 1965 when he was making a celebration parachute jump with the Old Tymers Jump Team he was asked by a journalist, ''What do you think about all this?'' Stark looked him right in the eye and said, ''Well, I figured on D-Day plus one I was dead, so every day I got, I stay away from the Devil. I don't have one God damn complaint.''

(Left to right) Joe Gironda, Tony DeMayo, Roy Stark, Tom McClean and Paul Nunan, veterans of the 505, during a visit to Leicester in 1984.

He was anxious to return to Europe for the 40th Anniversary to visit England, Normandy, Belgium and Holland with the Division's veterans. Having already suffered a series of heart attacks the journey was in doubt. His buddies made sure that he went and pushed him around in a wheelchair and looked after him in the hotels. His wish had come true and he had the time of his life. On his return home his condition worsened and not long afterwards he died.

SECOND LIEUTENANT JAMES J. COYLE, E COMPANY, 505

James Coyle was a Platoon Leader in E Company and continues his story in his own words:

On the night of 5th June, we took off from Cottesmore airfield where we had been isolated under strict security for several days. I was the jumpmaster on our C-47 which carried 18 paratroopers. Our machine-guns and mortars were in bundles slung beneath the airplane, and could be released and dropped by parachute when we jumped.

I had a beautiful view of the English Channel as we crossed. The door of the plane had been removed, and as I sat by the open door I watched the moonlight shine on the waves. It was a peaceful prelude to the violent invasion. I can't recall all my thoughts as we flew in. I do recall one personal concern. We had removed six Fulminate of Mercury blasting caps from our demolition kit because of the danger of leaving them packed with the high explosives in the bundle under the plane. I had taped them in a wooden block to my left foot. They were very sensitive, and I was afraid they might blow up when I hit the ground.

Shortly after we crossed the western coast of the Cherbourg Peninsula the anti-aircraft fire filled the sky. This continued at intervals in the distance until we reached Ste-Mere-Eglise. My primary concern was that the pilot would locate our proper Drop Zone, and that we would be able to assemble all our men and equipment. The red warning light finally came on and I gave the order to 'Stand up and hook up'.

This order was relayed from man to man over the roar of the engines and each man checked the parachute of the man in front of him. Beginning with the last man '18 — OK', the count was relayed from man to man until the man behind me shouted 'Two — OK' then I knew we were ready.

The plane's engines slowed down and I knew we would receive the green light to go soon, but I still could not see the lights which were to be set up by the Pathfinders who had jumped earlier to mark the D-Z. Suddenly we made a sharp left turn and I picked out the blue lights in a 'T' formation directly in front of us. Just at that moment the green light beside the door flashed on and giving the order 'GO', I jumped.

I had no trouble on landing despite all the equipment we carried. As soon as I got out of my parachute harness and stood up I saw the green light which was our Battalion's assembly signal, a short distance away.

The first man I encountered was our Battalion Commander, Lt. Colonel Benjamin Vandervoort. He asked if I had found my medical aid man but I told him I was alone. At the time he did not mention that he was injured, but he had broken his leg on the jump and fought for weeks with his leg in a cast. He ordered me to continue to locate my men. This I did for the next hour and we were able to assemble the First Platoon and Company Headquarters of E Company. The Second and Third Platoons were dropped away from the drop zone. After we had located as many men and weapons as we could, we moved towards Neuville-au-Plain, which was our original objective.

However, before we reached our objective we were ordered to turn south to Ste-Mere-Eglise.

We entered the town just at dawn. One man came out of a house and spoke to me. He was the only person I had the opportunity to talk to during my brief stay in Normandy. He spoke little or no English and I spoke only a little French, but I understood him well enough to sense his concern. He wanted to know if this was a raid or if it was the invasion. Our orders were not to disclose any information on the invasion, so I could not tell him that this was the day he had waited for for four years. I did reassure him of one thing: ''Nous restons ici.'' As for us, we were not leaving Ste-Mere-Eglise.

Our Company was assigned an area in the town along the sea road, east of the church. We were not called on for action until about noon when my Platoon was ordered to go north to Neuville-au-Plain to provide the rear guard for a Platoon from D Company. This was commanded by Lieutenant Turnbull (he was part American Indian blood and we called him 'Chief' — he was killed in Normandy and is buried in the Cemetery at St. Laurent). They held the Germans north of the town but were outnumbered, and we were to give them orders to return to Ste-Mere-Eglise and cover their withdrawal.

We arrived at the southern edge of Neuville-au-Plain just as the German troops were cutting east along a road which would have cut Turnbull off completely. We engaged the enemy and prevented him from going any further in his plan of encirclement. We were able to hold them even though we were outnumbered. In the meantime Turnbull got his surviving men out of Neuville-au-Plain and on the way to Ste-Mere-Eglise. My Platoon then moved back to our position in the town. We did not lose a man in this action, but we inflicted many casualties on the enemy, principally by very accurate mortar fire provided by our mortar Sergeant, Otis Sampson.

Shortly after returning to Ste-Mere-Eglise, gliders began to land in the area. I was standing in a ditch along the sea road when a glider suddenly came crashing through some trees. I had not seen it coming, and of course it made no sound until it hit the trees. I just had time to drop face down in the shallow ditch when the glider hit the road, crashed across it and came to rest with the wing over me. I was not injured, but had to crawl on my stomach the length of the wing to get out from under the glider.

The trees had split open the fuselage and many men were injured inside. We helped carry them out, but the best we could do for them was to inject them with morphine from our first aid kits and put them in trenches wrapped in parachutes. The men who survived left to remove their artillery piece from a glider nearby.

Enemy artillery had begun to hit about us as we were removing the injured from the glider, and it continued to fall heavily on our position during the night. We were well dug in however, and only one of our men, Private Benoit, was wounded.

The next day I received an order from our Company Commander, Captain Clyde Russell, to go to the beach by Jeep with two men from D Company and try to make contact with the Fourth Division. We were in desperate need for one of their artillery observers to give us fire support. I was able to reach a unit of the Fourth Division as they were moving off the beach, but they had only one observer left alive and could not release him to aid us.

I noticed a tank unit along the road and explained our needs to the Lieutenant Colonel in command, but he could not release any tanks to me without orders from his command. It was frustrating to see all those tanks not engaged while we were fighting so hard a few miles away. But there was nothing a Lieutenant could do, so I returned to Ste-Mere-Eglise with one bit of helpful information: the tank commander was in radio contact with tanks which were assigned to us. He told me they were on their way to Ste-Mere-Eglise on a round-about route through Chef-du-Pont.

As soon as I reported back to Battalion Headquarters we were given an order to move into a position north of Ste-Mere-Eglise to prepare to attack the enemy who were closing in on the town. The Platoon took up positions along a road which runs west from the main highway. It is the road which has the last house on the north edge of the town. We were told that the 8th Infantry Regiment of the Fourth Division would arrive on our left flank, but by the time of our assigned attack no contact had been made.

While we were waiting for the preset time to attack, a tank unit came up from the sea road, but in the confusion of war they drove up the highway north to Neuville-au-Plain, apparently never knowing that they had passed both us and the enemy. I am not certain, but I think these tanks were the same ones that I had seen on the beach. If so, it was the second opportunity to help us that was missed. They went so far north that they did not contribute any aid in the battle that was about to begin. However, two tanks which had been assigned to us had arrived and they would cover our open flank as we attacked.

There was heavy machine-gun fire coming across the field from our front. My original order was to take my Platoon across this field, but in the interval before our jump off time, 17.15 hours, I got permission to take them north up a dirt road on the left of the field which provided better cover and conceal-ment. We advanced up this road with the tanks following, and when we reached the intersection of another dirt road running east to the highway we found the enemy behind the hedgerow.

Luckily we had come up on his flank and by pure chance he had left it unprotected. We poured fire up the ditch from our positions. One of the tanks joined in with its heavy machine-gun and after about fifteen minutes a white flag appeared in the ditch. I called for a cease fire and it was with some difficulty in all the noise of battle that I was able to get our firing stopped.

Lieutenant Frank Woosley, our Company Executive Officer, and I went up the road to accept the surrender, but before we got very far two hand grenades came over the hedgerow. He dived into the ditch on one side of the road and I went in the other. We thought at the time that we had walked into a trap.

I learned from M. Alexandre Renaud's book twenty five years later that these troops were Georgian. They were probably the ones who wanted to surrender, but the German officers and NCO's were fighting on.

We returned to our position and resumed fire. This time we did not cease firing until the enemy ran out of the ditch into a large field next to it with their hands raised.

When I saw that there were over a hundred of the enemy running into the field I went through the hedgerow with the intention of stopping them and rounding them up. But as soon as I got through the hedgerow into the ditch on the other side I was hit by machine pistol fire. The Germans had not yet quit. One of my men followed me through the hedgerow and fired an abandoned German machine-gun up the ditch ending any further resistance from the enemy.

In this battle E Company with two Platoons, (the other commanded by Lieutenant Theodore Peterson) captured 160 prisoners. We again received accurate supporting fire from Sergeant Sampson's mortar from a position which can be located today about 50 foot south of the 82nd Airborne Division sign at the intersection of the main highway at the north end of Ste-Mere-Eglise. I do not know the number of enemy dead left in that ditch.

Lieutenant Peterson's Platoon, which was on my right flank, captured the German Battalion Commander. Corporal Sam Appleby shot one German Captain as he tried to escape the trap. A Platoon of D Company commanded by Lieutenant Thomas McClean captured a great number who tried to escape across the main highway and ran into his position.

I was given first aid after the prisoners were collected and rode back on a tank to the Battalion Aid Station in the old school in Ste-Mere-Eglise. The next day I left the town in an ambulance to return to England and hospital.

The ambulance took me from the 505 Aid Station in Ste-Mere-Eglise, drove for about an hour and then unloaded its wounded on stretchers in a large field. The men who needed immediate attention and surgery were taken into nearby hospital tents.

I had been shot through both buttocks this time, the bullet being somewhere just below my left hip. Naturally, the Medics could not spend any time on me. They took one look at the holes in my rear-end, slapped the bandages back and gave me a shot of morphine.

I didn't know where I was in Normandy, but I did learn that I was in the 82nd Airborne's 307th Evacuation Hospital and that I would not be operated on until I got back to England.

Just before dark on D plus 2, I was loaded into an ambulance with five other wounded and headed for the beach. By coincidence, I recognised the glider pilot that I pulled out of the crashed glider in Ste-Mere-Eglise on D-Day. We didn't do much talking, however, because both of us were half out of it from the morphine and were not making much sense anyway.

The ambulance was bouncing over the rough roads and one of the wounded moaned constantly. I realised that his wounded leg had bounced off the stretcher and when I was able to replace it and secure it with a blanket, his moaning ceased. We finally arrived at another field hospital on the beach and spent the night there. It was impossible to sleep however, because of our artillery firing nearby.

The next day I was loaded into the hold of a Landing Ship Tank (LST) with hundreds of other wounded men and we sailed for England. I spotted another E Company man, Private Eads, on a stretcher near me and was able to determine that he was not seriously wounded and eventually would recover.

We landed at Plymouth and travelled by ambulance to the 55th General Hospital in quonset huts at Malvern Wells, Worcestershire. After the bullet was removed and I could get around, I went looking for E Company men in the hospital but I didn't find any. However there were several officers that I knew from the 505 in my ward.

After about three weeks I was discharged from the hospital and returned to Camp Quorn. The regiment was still in Normandy. They returned from France about a week later, but many of the men who were wounded after I was were still in hospital.

I learnt that Lieutenant Roper Peddicord had been killed and that Lieutenant 'Pete' Peterson was in hospital with a leg wound. I was also informed that Pete and I had received battlefield promotions to First Lieutenants.

MAJOR EDWARD KRAUSE, THIRD BATTALION, 505

The Third Battalion's Commanding Officer, Major Edward 'Cannonball' Krause landed in a garden to find fifteen of his own men had landed nearby. Within an hour one of his patrols returned with a drunken Frenchman. A patrol had knocked on his door to ask the way, the shock of seeing the invading forces soon sobered him up and he offered his services as a guide, the information he had was vital. He told Krause that there was only one German Company in Ste-Mere-Eglise, the rest were camped on high ground just to the south of the town. The Frenchman offered to show them the way, an offer which was taken up as he wouldn't be volunteering if it wasn't safe.

By 4am the Battalion had assembled one hundred and eighty men and they moved towards Ste-Mere-Eglise. After setting up road blocks, Krause moved into the town, the Frenchman pointing out the German billets where the troopers killed ten and took thirty prisoners. As dawn began to break, Krause walked to the Town Hall and raised the old, well worn, Stars and Stripes above it.

By the end of the first day Krause had been wounded three times. He reluctantly went to the Aid Station where the Surgeons cut a bullet out of his left thigh, but he was back in command next day.

Harry Anderson of E Company remembers Krause not only for his toughness but his sense of humour. ''One morning while we were all in our foxholes he took the rollcall in German. Scared us all to hell.''

Major Edward C. 'Cannonball' Krause of the Third Battalion, 505, in 1944.

PRIVATE CARL BECK, E COMPANY, 505

Carl's entry into Normandy was quite spectacular. His parachute did not open correctly. As he said, "My chute was a complete streamer, the only reason I didn't get killed was the trees slowed me down before I hit the ground."

"I wasn't hurt too bad. I finished up with torn muscles in my legs and burns from a tracer bullet on my hand. My mother got a telegram from 'Uncle Sam' saying I was slightly wounded in combat."

"I remember being evacuated from the beaches as they were clearing the dead GI's. The bodies were stacked like cordwood, a sight that I will never forget. After a spell in hospital I was sent to a replacement centre but I was determined to make it back to the 505. With the help of the Boxing Coach I went AWOL and arrived back at Quorn."

PRIVATE ARTHUR 'DUTCH' SCHULTZ, C COMPANY, 505

One of the loneliest men that night was Private Arthur 'Dutch' Schultz of C Company. Making his first combat jump he was separated from his friends. After searching through the hours of darkness he did not find a single soul. At first light he met Lieutenant Jack Tallerday and the group of men he had collected.

It was Tallerday who was in the situation of walking down one side of a small hedgerow in the dark when he was startled to see coal-skuttle helmets going in the opposite direction on the other side. The surprise was complete for both sides and they passed without contact.

MAJOR GENERAL MATTHEW B. RIDGWAY

General Matthew Ridgway, Divisional Commander of the 82nd had orginally intended to land by glider in Normandy. His staff were unhappy because the chances of a safe landing in the dark were very slim. But as D-Day approached he made a sudden decision to jump with his paratroopers. He had only made four training jumps in the past.

In the Sicily invasion he came ashore in a landing craft, and it is generally believed that he later regretted that he did not jump with his men.

His aid, Arthur Kroos recalls, "We got him a parachute and took it back to his house in Leicester (the house was Glebe Mount, in Glebe Road, Oadby). We fitted him out in the privacy of his quarters because he didn't want anybody else to see this. We made sure all the straps were exactly right and everything was properly taped down."

Ridgway chose to jump with the 505 flying from Spanhoe. He was put in the 'stick' of Captain Talton 'Woody' Long who had entered the army as a private in 1941 and now commanded the 505's Headquarters Company.

It was Long's job to brief Ridgway on the operation. "It was a rather demanding experience for a young Captain," he remembers. "However, I recall that General Ridgway sat there intently following every detail of my briefing. I don't think those piercing eyes left me once. Afterwards, he graciously thanked me and made some comment about seeing me on the ground."

Ridgway's fifth parachute jump landed him in a nice soft grassy Normandy field watched by a cow. To his relief, that cow meant that the field was not mined or booby-trapped. As he said later, ''I could have kissed her.'' He saw a movement in the shadow of the hedgerow and covering it with a pistol, gave the password. It was answered correctly. To Ridgway's surprise it turned out to be G Company's Commander, Willard 'Bill' Follmer, injured with a broken right hip. Surprisingly Follmer had been the first paratrooper he found in Sicily, then he was injured with a broken right ankle. Ridgway tried to cheer Follmer with the words, ''I guess you hope to God you never see me again.''

In Sicily, Follmer was able to lead I Company from the back of an ancient mule 'liberated' from an irate local farmer. There was no such luck in Normandy as the injury was far more serious.

Bill Follmer survived the war and lives in Florida with the U.S. Army Nurse, Kay, he met in England. They were married at Quorn Parish Church. To this day he is still troubled by the injuries he received during the war. In pride of place in their home in Orlando is a painting of 'their' church.

At the end of the day Ridgway watched his men bury their dead colleagues in temporary shallow graves. With the grim task completed, Ridgway walked back to contemplate the mounds of earth ''where so many of my boys lay,'' and saw that little children from the nearby villages had picked wild flowers and were placing them in bunches on the still moist earth. ''I was so overcome that I wept,'' confessed the General.

Hugo Olsen (left) and Willard 'Bill' Follmer, in England in 1984.

FIRST LIEUTENANT WAVERLY W. WRAY, D COMPANY, 505

Possibly the most courageous man of the 82nd Airborne. First Lieutenant Waverly W. Wray was a devoutly religious Mississippi woodsman of Baptist faith, with all the skills and courage of the First World War hero of the 82nd, Sergeant Alvin C. York. On several occasions Colonel Vandervoort offered him the command of his own Company, but he chose to stay with his own men of D Company, 505.

Pfc. Frank Bilich remembers with great pride that he was one of Wray's men. "He was a big man of 250 pounds or so. His strong legs were like tree trunks, you could see that by the wide lace-ups on his jump boots. Our parachutes were not designed for big guys like him, he dropped pretty fast on a chute. If you went out the door after him, you never saw him till you reached the ground. Sometimes we used to think that with his strong legs he didn't need a chute."

"There were two wars going on," said Bilich. "One was World War Two, and the other, the private war of Lieutenant Wray. Wray's attitude was if he killed all those 'John Brown' Tedeschis (Italian for Germans) today, there would be less to kill tomorrow."

In the defence of Ste-Mere-Eglise the Second Battalion stood firm. Wray armed with an M-1 rifle, a Colt .45 pistol and a pocket full of grenades carried the battle to the Germans. One of his one man patrols through the hedgerows outflanked the enemy until he found the headquarters of the German First Battalion, 1058th Regiment.

He ordered their Commanding Officer and seven staff to surrender. When one officer attempted to draw a pistol, Wray shot him. Two German soldiers nearby realised what was happening and opened fire with machine pistols, catching Wray's ear in the process. Wray shot the remaining Staff Officers and turned his attention to the two soldiers. They were dispatched with one shot apiece.

Later, Wray directed mortar fire on the rest of the German Battalion and broke them. Finding that they had no officers they fled north away from the town. Lt. Colonel Ben Vandervoort said later, "Wray shattered that German Battalion. He was nominated for the Congressional Medal of Honor, but the recommendation was downgraded to a Distinguished Service Cross."

Frank Bilich was in the D Company's Command Post during that action. He recalls, "In fact he came into the Company Command Post that time when he engaged all those Germans, his ear-lobe was shot off, he was bleeding, he had holes in his jump suit. He didn't come back because he was tired, he came back for some more grenades, he had run out. He was grabbing grenades, 'Who's got more grenades?' he was demanding."

"If there was some fighting going on in the Third Platoon he would be shouting, 'What's happening? I'll be right back.' If there was a firefight in the Second Platoon — he would be right up there in the thick of it."

"You could never say enough about Lieutenant Wray. He was more than a soldier or an officer — he was a real leader." Bilich became angry as he spoke. "And Boy! Why they took away that Congressional Medal from him I'll never know? If anyone deserved it, he did."

First Sergeant John Rabig takes up the story. ''Wray was a very religious person. He knew his Company needed his help. If any man did something wrong you answered to Lieutenant Wray, not Captain Taylor Smith.''

''He didn't use profanities, the strongest expletive he used when provoked was 'John Brown', an old Southern curse word amongst the Southern slave supporters.''

''If he said 'John Brown' then he was mad.''

''I called the Company out once and warned them, 'If Wray tells, calls or says to you 'John Brown' you had better fly straight because that is as mad as he will ever get.' If he came storming at you with pursed lips and the first thing he said was 'John Brown' and called you by name, then you were in trouble. But on the other hand he was an honest and fair man.''

''He wanted me with him on several occasions,'' continued Rabig. ''You know, I was scared to go with the man. I used to think this is going to get me killed.''

''This one time in Normandy he says, 'Follow me!' and we ducked down a hedgerow to where our artillery was coming into the next field. I could hear these Germans screaming as they were getting hit. Wray said, 'John, I wish that artillery would stop so we can go in after them.' Jesus! I thought, that artillery is doing good enough.''

''He was also a careful man, he took chances, but not reckless ones. He would disobey orders if he felt there was too great a risk for his men. He would not commit himself to ridiculous plans.''

First Sergeant John Rabig admired Wray. ''He insisted if you killed a German, you had to bury him. Wray would say, 'Well, we killed him, they deserve a decent burial.' That's the kind of guy he was.''

First Lieutenant Waverly W. Wray was killed in action in Holland on the afternoon of 19th September 1944, leading from the front, as he always did.

All these years later, Frank Bilich still feels that Wray didn't get the recognition he deserved. He recalls, ''I am proud to have served with him. What makes me mad is at a Fort Bragg reunion, when we came out of the Museum and saw all those stones along the walk there. On them they have all the names, ranks and Companies of our most decorated men who were killed in action. Guess what they got for Wray — Waverly W. Wray, Infantry, — no Distingushed Service Cross, no D Company, 505th Parachute Infantry Regiment, no 82nd Airborne Division.''

''We all protested to General Gavin and asked, 'Can't you get that changed, can't they at least put D Company 505?' I hope, one day, they correct that mistake to honour a great hero.''

CAPTAIN ROBERT 'DOC' FRANCO, 505

''In Normandy my own experience was unique in that it was a sort of a perfect jump. I landed on soft grass land, it was perfectly quiet. Within an hour quite a number of us had coalesced into a group and we took off. I still remember walking into Ste-Mere-Eglise in the dawn light; the hands on the church tower clock pointed to 4 o'clock. We established ourselves, set up perimeters, found a school building or civic building to use as an Aid Station and prepared for activity.''

''This was not long in coming, and the pressure from the north was pretty intense for a day or more. About noon on D-Day someone came into our Aid Station with word that a farmhouse, a mile or so away, was filled with American wounded. Our busy group was able to spare one man, me, and I followed the soldier. In the farmhouse there were dozens of wounded and I worked around the clock holding things together.''

''The next day it was possible to evacuate all these people via ambulances to the appropriate medical units. A few years ago I ran across a book by the well known author, Robert Ingersoll. It was about D-Day and he described the farmhouse and the lone medical officer working hard to stay up with his problems.''

''My three weeks in Normandy was an exciting experience and I recall a few details. One occurred while our unit was in reserve. Two of us were walking the two or so hundred yards to our slit trenches for a sleep when we saw some vague shadows or forms moving around. My companion, Pete Suer, a Dental Officer who was both smart and fearless, a quality that eventually got him killed (he died of wounds in the Ardennes), called out for identification. When none came, Pete, speaking clear German in his loud gruff voice, indicated that they were surrounded by Americans with automatic weapons. They were clearly seen, and if they did not surrender immediately they would be shot.''

''They did just that, throwing down their weapons and putting up their hands, saying, 'Nicht schiessen.' We now had a Dental Officer and a Medical Officer holding fifteen enemy prisoners. We made the prisoners lie down on their backs in a radial pattern with their feet almost touching and reminded then of the consequences of any movement. It was then Pete and I decided that one of us would have to walk back to the radio and the other — me — would watch the prisoners. I think these guys had had enough fighting and they gave no trouble. Afterwards I was thankful that it was too dark for my Red Cross armband to be seen.''

''A few days earlier a tragedy occurred when an ammunition truck exploded. We were in reserve and the men were lying in the hedgerow ditches when the truck stopped and immediately there was an explosion. No one ever explained why, maybe it was hit by a mortar or it was just static electricity. We all ducked into the safety of our ditches and waited for the whole truck to blow up.''

''Then came the horror: one of the men was trapped in the midst of the explosions, crying, blinded and barely able to move. It became clear that this lad was doomed, either by the continual small explosions or the eventual big one. I felt I had to do something so I ran to the truck as fast as I could and found that one of our Aid men had come in from the opposite side. We jumped on the truck, grabbed the boy and pulled him off and into a ditch. The explosions of grenades and bullets continued. The wounded boy was evacuated and we heard later that he had died.''

''The rest of the Normandy campaign was a long series of attacks. The Medics were always busy. When the penninsula was finally 'cut' on about

25th June, we went into a defensive stance for a while before preparing for the attack on La Haye-du-Puits. Here I managed, with sound stupidity, to get hit by artillery shell splinters and was evacuated to England.''

''My hospital was not far from the south coast seaside resort of Bournemouth, where I was able to visit two or three times in beautiful weather. It was a lovely place.''

Robert 'Doc' Franco was awarded the Soldiers Medal for rescuing the man from the ammunition truck. When he describes the time he was wounded by shell splinters he was, in fact, rescuing and attending wounded paratroopers under fire. For this action he was awarded the Silver Star.

PFC. TONY DeFOGGI, F COMPANY, 505

''Crossing the Channel was uneventful but when we hit the coast of France all hell broke loose. The Red Light came on to 'Stand up', and after a few minutes we got the Green to jump. When I made my exit from the plane it seemed like a giant hand grabbed me by the seat of my pants and pushed me to the end of the static line. The blast of air was so great that it was as though I had been hit by an anti-aircraft shell. The drop seemed an eternity until I landed in a field surrounded with tall hedgerows.''

''I looked around, I was all alone. My Squad's objective was to knock-out a particular bridge. In my musette bag I had the explosives along with my shaving gear, K-Rations and a photograph of a girl named Elizabeth, who is now the Queen of England. Finding a way out of the field, I found a dirt road, so I started to walk. I did not know where I was going. A bridge came into view. Was this the right bridge? I walked back and forth over it and then decided it was not.''

''As I was retracing my steps I heard a vehicle coming. It did not sound like one of ours, so I took cover in the hedgerow. When it passed I could see it was a motorcycle and sidecar with two Jerries. Moments later several shots rang out and then it was all quiet again. I learnt later that my Mother had a dream about this action.''

''Just as I was about to get on the road again I heard some men coming. They were American Paratroopers. I fumbled for my cricket and gave them the signal. If I had been a German I could have killed them all, and I told them so.''

''Because I was 505 they put me in command. These men were from the 507 and the 101st. I told them what my mission was so we set out to find the bridge. Further down the road we came across the Germans with the motorcycle. They were both dead. Our attitude changed, now we knew that this war was for real.''

''It was daylight by the time we found the bridge. I posted guards on the approaches and it was not long before we heard a vehicle coming and the paratroopers ordered it to stop. The Jeep contained an American Lieutenant, his driver and in the back seat was my best buddy, Larry Neipling.''

''Larry told me to get in. As we were driving down the road we were fired on. The officer jumped out on his side, and the driver out of the other. Me, I went over the back while Larry got in the front seat and put the 50 calibre

Tony DeFoggi in Leicester in 1984, with Anne Wills, wife of the author.

machine-gun into action. 'Tony, get me some more ammo,' and from that moment on I was his assistant.''

''Around midday most of our Battalion was organised into one area. Nearby there were a lot of German prisoners. We were ordered to go to Neuville-au-Plain, but because the Third Battalion was fending off a counter-attack at Ste-Mere-Eglise the orders were changed. The main body of the Battalion went to help, but forty-four of us went on to Neuville-au-Plain.''

''As soon as we arrived we immediately came under heavy fire. Artillery and 88 shells were coming in like rain. One man received a direct hit, George Ziemski thought it was me and I thought it was him in the confusion. When we got protective covering fire from our 50 calibre machine-gun we ran to the next hedgerow. There on the ground was a beautiful pearl handled German pistol in front of us. Word was passed along that it may be booby-trapped, so we sat there looking at it.''

''Climbing through the hedgerow I collided with a smiling German with his hands above his head. It scared the devil out of me. At the next hedgerow I was told to relieve John Zunder with the sniper's rifle, it was an 30 Springfield fitted with a telescopic sight. Zunder pointed out the area where the Germans were and it wasn't long before I saw a German carrying a bucket. I waited until he came back, I took aim and fired. Bulls eye...I hit the bucket and the Kraut quickly disappeared.''

''Although we inflicted a lot of damage there, we came back with only sixteen men. This was the action led by Lieutenant Turner Turnbull which was said later to be of great importance in the first few hours of D-Day. He was resigned to making a last stand, but because of the timely arrival of E Company we were able to pull out.''

"Our next major objective was the town of St Sauveur-le-Vicomte. Our last attack was made on Hill 131 which overlooked the town of La Haye-du-Puits. It was raining so hard that you could not see your hand in front of your face. The hill was a hard climb for me carrying a 30 calibre machine-gun up a very muddy and slippery slope. Luckily we did not meet much opposition.''

"Several days later we were on our way back to Quorn where I found my girl friend, Sheila, had got another boy friend.''

SECOND LIEUTENTANT LEON E. MENDEL, 325 GLIDER INFANTRY

Leon Mendel was a Second Lieutenant in the 325th Glider Infantry stationed at Scraptoft, Leicester. As he was proficient in seven languages he was soon transferred to Military Intelligence as an Interrogation Officer.

Assigned to be flown in by glider on Mission 'Galveston' on D-Day Plus One, he headed for Landing Zone 'W' to arrive at 07.10. As the glider came across the coast of Normandy it was hit by small arms fire which came through the floorboards. Several men were wounded. For most of the journey Mendel had sat there admiring the Garand rifle the man opposite was carrying. This unfortunate man was hit, so now by chance, Mendel became its proud owner.

"My glider made a beautiful landing at Ecoqueneauville and I made my way south to my assembly point at Les Forges crossroads. Here I got the bad news that I had lost half of my six man team in glider crashes. The good news was the others had already eight German prisoners for interrogation.''

"I started off with German but with little response, so I switched to Russian with the question, 'Vj Russkij chelovek?' (Are you a Russian?). Their reply was immediate, 'Da, ya khochu ekhat' na Ameriku' (Yes, I want to go to America). I slapped both my hands on top of my helmet and shouted at them, 'Durak, durak. Ya tozhe!' (Crazy, crazy. Me too!).''

PFC. JOSEPH G. CLOWRY, 319 GLIDER FIELD ARTILLERY

This was Joe's first combat glider landing although he had seen plenty of action in Italy, landing by sea at Maiori. This is how he recalls his D-Day.

"Outside the engines of the tow planes were warming up and the noise was such that any verbal communications had to be shouted. At last this was it, this was what we had been training for, and we were ready to go.''

"Sitting there, there was a feeling of anticipation. How would the flight go, the landing and after? There wasn't any external or internal signs of fear — this was a great adventure and, after all, what could happen to a twenty-two year old. It could happen to the guy across the way, or the one next to you — but never you.''

"Soon the roar of the lead C-47 was heard as it inched forward slowly on the runway at Membury Airfield. The tow line began to uncurl like a serpent from its preset configuration and the lead plane was off at 20.37 hours.''

"Then it was our turn, the tow-rope unravelled, tightened, and with a slight jerk our Horsa glider began to roll forward. We gathered speed and soon the rumble of the wheels on the runway was silenced and we were airborne.''

''The glider lifted off first and the taut tow-rope lifted the tail of the tow plane. We were veering off and climbing to the preset altitude for assembly.''

''Our serial was completely airborne with 418 airborne troops, thirty-one Jeeps, twelve 75mm pack howitzers, twenty-six tons of ammunition and twenty-five tons of other equipment.''

''The troop carriers were unaware the 82nd Division was diverting our flight to Landing Zone 'O' because of the supposedly better landing conditions and that Landing Zone 'W' was dominated by German weapons. The glider pilots had been briefed to turn 180 degrees to the right after releasing instead of the previously directed left turn because of the German strength in the area of 'W'. This turned out to be a mistake because at 'O' the German strength was to the right.''

''The two serials joined up and in a column of fours headed across Southern England in a ten-mile wide corridor, out over the English Channel heading for France. For the 200 mile flight we were accompanied to the French coast by groups of Allied fighter planes.''

''Whereas the parachute drops approached Normandy from the west of the Cherbourg Peninsula, the gliders came in directly over the Utah Beach area, roughly from the north.''

''I peered out of one of the port-holes lining the length of the Horsa and I could see the lines of towplanes and gliders droning on over the increasingly darkening water below. We passed over the armada of fighting ships; the larger ones, parallel to the shore, belching great balls of yellow and orange flames towards the shore.''

''As we approached Utah Beach the rushing noise of the wind passing over the wings and the side of the glider increased. The gliders were usually towed at about 100 miles an hour, but as we approached the shore the C-47 pilots increased their speed to what felt to be about 125 mph so that they could get in and out as fast as possible.''

''The sun had set a few minutes before we crossed the coast and as we headed inland the ground began to get darker and it was more difficult to make out objects below, even at 500 feet.''

''I could see what appeared to be a group of fireflies milling about on the ground in the darkness and then ascending in single file, increasing in velocity as they approached in streams until, with a swish, whizzed by the window. Realising they were tracer bullets, I felt that I had nothing to worry about because they could be seen. It was the other four or more bullets between each tracer that you had to look out for.''

''The intensity of the ground fire increased and more and more fireflies went streaming by.''

''The glider pilot finally cut loose, the noise of the rushing wind became silent, and starting a 180 degree right bank we began to descend into the darkness. I continued to peer out of the porthole, searching for any recognizable land feature. That was the last thing I remember....''

''The first glider release in our serial occurred at 22.55 hours, five minutes ahead of schedule. A large portion of the gliders were released over a mile short of Landing Zone 'O', while six gliders were released at least five miles to the east. The change in the Landing Zones took the towplanes and gliders over the German defences and into heavy ground fire.''

''Small fields, some only a hundred yards long, hedgerows, tall trees, darkness, enemy fire and some glider pilots disregarding orders to land at a slow speed, all played havoc with the landings. Including some damage done by enemy fire after landing, of the eighty-four Horsas, only thirteen were undamaged. Fifty-six were totally destroyed.''

''Eight of the fourteen CG-4A's gliders were destroyed. The eight surviving were damaged. Ten of the 196 glider pilots were killed, at least twenty-nine wounded or injured, and seven reported missing. Of the troopers, twenty-eight were killed and 106 wounded or injured.''

''The next thing I recall was total darkness and the continual sound, of what seemed to me, of crunching and splintering caused by someone jumping off a roof of a house into a large pile of wooden match boxes. I realised it was someone tearing away the plywood from on top of me. Then some dim shadows with arms extended to assist in extricating me from the wreckage.''

''There were two other men, one sitting each side of me, so that I was sandwiched between them and they must have absorbed some of the impact. I recall seeing a Fourth Division insignia on one of the rescuers. While laying on my side, I spotted, about ten to fifteen feet away, the Jeep tipped over on its side with a complete oval-shaped section of the glider floor still attached to it by the tie-down ropes. I felt relief that it had not landed on me.''

''Blood was running down my face and my entire body was sore and aching. I had a swelling and a gash about an inch above the outside corner of my left eye and a number of slashes across the top of my head in a ear-to-ear direction. Someone bandaged me up with two compression bandages; one across the top of my head and tied under my chin, the other over my left forehead and tied at the back.''

''Amid the usual din of war I made my way, in the darkness, to a nearby stone wall. I pulled up about me an abandoned parachute and leaned back, hardly moving to prevent antagonising the soreness I felt all over. There I sat to see what the six hours of summertime darkness might hold in store.''

''When daylight came, I made my way to an Aid Station that had been set up at a nearby crossroads. The tent, marked with a Red Cross, had wounded laying on stretchers around it, tagged and waiting to be evacuated.''

''I was cleaned up a bit and tagged. Orders were that anyone with a head wound was to be evacuated immediately. Waiting outside the tent I noticed a P-47 fighter plane that had seemed to have been hit by enemy fire and was obviously in trouble. I recall subconsciously asking myself why the pilot didn't bale out. I was relieved when I saw a human form falling from the plane. I waited for the chute to open, but the figure continued to plummet earthwards and disappeared into the trees down the road.''

''When we reached the beach, a DUKW took us out to an LST waiting off-shore. Back in England I remember being in a cot in a large circus-like tent and being checked over by a nurse. They shaved my head around my wounds. I was then sent to the 62nd General Hospital further inland from where I was later released to return to Market Harborough to await the return of my unit from Normandy."

"Both the men on either side of me in the crash suffered broken vertebrae in their necks. The gilder pilot had a bullet in his leg. The Lieutenant who had acted as co-pilot sustained a broken back and was unlucky enough, while waiting on the beach to be evacuated, to be strafed and killed."

PRIVATE ALBERT NELSON, 325 GLIDER INFANTRY

Albert Nelson was another gliderman who had a disastrous D-Day. He was in a glider that crashed into a tree on landing. In a brief moment of consciousness he saw that the two GI's sitting on either side of him had been killed.

"I don't even remember the cast-off when we were unhooked to land. I just recall looking at the two friends who had died, and looking out to see what was happening outside."

"I remember nothing after that until waking up on a ship taking me back to England. They thought I had a broken back. Luckily I didn't, but I spent a month in hospital near Chester."

Albert returned to his Regiment at Scraptoft, Leicester, and met his future wife, Barbara. They married in March 1945 in Leicester. They had forty-five years together, staying in England and living not far from his old camp site. They had five children and six grandchildren. Sadly, Barbara died in 1988.

STAFF SERGEANT PAUL NUNAN, D COMPANY, 505

Staff Sergeant Paul Nunan looked up and checked his canopy as he drifted down towards an orchard. Two Germans standing on a roof had opened up with machine pistols and he felt the twitches as the bullets went through the parachute.

"It wasn't the best of landings," recalled Paul, "In that part of the world big trees grow out of the hedgerows and the biggest was waiting for me. I thought that this was going to hurt as I swung into the trunk and collapsed into the ditch below."

Paul pulled out his knife which was strapped to his boot to cut himself free. The tough harness would not part so he had to resort to undoing all the buckles. Two minutes work seemed like two hours. Then came the assembly of the three sections of his rifle. Somehow they would not go together and in a frantic effort to get it to work, accidently fired off seven rounds. "It sounded like a bag-pipe band coming down the road," he said later.

As he got up to walk he realised that he had sprained his knee. The air was full of the sound of metal crickets as men gathered together and he joined a Company which was setting off to set up a roadblock.

By now the knee had swollen up and it was judged by a Lieutenant that he was a hindrance and was ordered to take cover until daylight. Much to his own astonishment after settling down under a hedgerow, he fell asleep.

He awoke to find a whole column of the 505 heading for Ste- Mere-Eglise and tagged along with them. In the evening, for the defence of the town, his platoon was guarding a cross-roads. Paul was digging himself a foxhole when his platoon leader, Lieutenant Oliver B. Carr of D Company, ordered him to go across the road to supervise the machine-gun team. He was annoyed as he wanted that foxhole dug for cover for the night, but he obeyed orders, leaving his knapsack behind.

Five minutes later the position was hit by an 88mm artillery shell with a direct hit on the knapsack. Three men were killed. By the end of D-Day, Paul Nunan was one of the only two of the platoon's seven NCO's still on their feet. The others were either killed or wounded.

By the end of the war Nunan had made four combat jumps, awarded the Silver Star, the Bronze Star, earned himself a battlefield commission and collected three Purple Hearts. Not bad for a man who was blind in one eye and managed to fool the doctor at the Syracuse Recruiting Office by a well-practised sleight of hand during the test.

PFC. ANDREW 'ANDY' KILCULLEN, B COMPANY, 505

Pfc. Andrew F.'Andy' Kilcullen of B Company was in the platoon led by Lieutenant Jim Irvin, which were misdropped near Cherbourg. Several were wounded. "We dropped a long way off our target and spent all day running around trying to get the guys together. We were trying to keep the Germans off and wait until it got dark, but nobody told us it never really got dark at that time of the year."

They quickly assembled with the strays from the First Battalion H.Q. Company which brought their numbers up to about fifty. Andy carried a comrade named Gramall to an Aid Station after he had been hit with a wooden dum-dum bullet and there met two more members of B Company, Willy Hall and Mike Vuletich. On his return he found that only about fifteen of his group were left out of the original fifty.

"We dropped about 1am and there was a lot of confusion. Planes were coming down all around, and finally the Germans caught me." Andy was a man of few words when it came to recounting his experiences.

He was captured at 9pm. Andy, remembering his training manuals on what to do if captured, upgraded everyone to non-commissioned officer rank, which kept them altogether as a group. Their home for the next six months was Stalag 3-C at Krustin, near the Polish border. Andy spent his time digging an escape tunnel and when the Russians arrived and the camp was in turmoil, Andy and Joe Foley hid in it. When all was quiet they emerged to find the compound empty. It was learned later that most of the American prisoners had been strafed and killed by the Russians.

After dark the intrepid pair went through the barbed wire fence and started a long trek to freedom. They were still wearing the same clothes they had been captured in.

The Russians treated them no better than the Germans, but some friendly Polish people put them in hospital and cared for them for two weeks. It was the British Red Cross who came to their rescue and supplied them with clean clothes, which happened to be British uniforms, and decent food. From Odessa on the Black Sea he sailed on a British ship to Naples. Andy arrived back in New York in April 1945 only to find that his family had been notified that he had been killed in action some months before.

Lieutenant Jim Irvin made it back to Quorn to rejoin his Battalion after posing as a French civilian for two months. He had been captured, but escaped while being transported back to Germany and helped by the French Underground to safety. 'Chappie' Wood, the Regimental Chaplain, was in the act of mailing a 'sympathy letter' to Jim's parents when he was surprised to see him at the Regimental Headquarters.

Also captured on D-Day from B Company were Carl Clawson and Harold Carroll who both finished up in a Prisoner-of-War camp, Oflag 64, in Poland. They were released by the Russians in January 1945 and made their way to Odessa. After a somewhat cool reception from the crew of an American freighter they found a British troopship in the harbour returning Russian prisoners from Germany. They were provided with immediate hospitality and a passage to Port Said.

Harold Carroll, who had an arm wound, went back to the States where he learnt that his brother, Lt. Colonel Robert C. Carroll serving with the 501st Parachute Infantry Regiment, 101st Airborne, had been killed in action on D-Day and had been posthumously awarded the Silver Star for his bravery.

Carl Clawson rejoined B Company in Germany and crossed the Elbe only to be wounded the day before the war ended.

After the war Andy Kilcullen was one of the organisers of the 505 and 82nd Reunions, both in the States and in Europe. He became a First Grade Detective in the Homicide Squad of the New York City Police and retired after 30 years service. He was everyone's visual idea of a New York cop. His death in 1987 was a great loss to the veterans.

Retired New York Police Detective Andy Kilcullen is arrested by the French Gendarmes on the Utah Beach in June 1984. The arrest was 'fixed' by the author but the Gendarmes seemed to take it too seriously.

PFC. ANTHONY ANTONIOU, B COMPANY, 505

"Quorn and Loughborough were second homes for me. I had the best time in my life there at the age of eighteen. After being in Africa, Sicily and Italy, jolly old England was like paradise. It was a buddy in my Company, Andy Kilcullen, who taught me how to drink and play with the ladies. I fell in love with a girl named Rita and went steady with her until we left England. I was going to marry her, but after I was on the battlefront I found out that she was going with other guys. I was heartbroken...but I got over it."

"On Monday morning, 29th May, the Regiment climbed aboard trucks, and by early afternoon we were sealed in the departure airfield, cut off from the outside world. Briefings took place to where we were going. That was no surprise, but I was sweating it out like everyone else. By the time the eighteen of us from the Third Platoon of B Company climbed aboard our plane I was at peace with myself, I had said my prayers and I was sure I was going to make it. As I sat there my thoughts were back in England with my girlfriend Rita and all the good times we had together. I also thought of some bad times too, in combat in Sicily and Italy."

"As we were reaching the coast of Normandy our C-47 was hit three times, wounding two or three men. In the confusion one of them fell against the equipment bundle switches, releasing them. The wounded were unhooked and told to stay in the plane."

"Continuing on, we were hit again, this time without injuring anyone. Then, just as we were reducing airspeed for the jump we were hit with a flak burst that put everyone down in the aisle. Seven or eight were wounded. They included Pfc. Bert Eason and Corporal James Cook. By the time I got to the door to jump, the co-pilot came over and told me to stay and take care of the wounded. I said I was going out. He pulled a gun on me and ordered me to stay."

"By the time the able-bodied had got the wounded comfortable and treated as best we could, we were back over the Channel. The pilot headed for the nearest airfield, which I believe was near London. People there came over and asked what was going on. I told them the invasion of France had begun and everybody started to cheer."

"The next morning, several of us who were uninjured went out on the resupply planes and jumped. But my luck was still very little better, we were misdropped. I was first at the door and kicked out two bundles before I jumped. As I was going down I could see tracer bullets hitting my chute. The pilot, thank God, was flying very low, no more than three hundred feet. I felt the opening shock and seconds later hit the ground very hard."

"I landed near a hedgerow and before I had time to get out of my harness I saw three Germans coming my way. I pulled my 45 pistol out before they spotted me and I shot two before the other ran away. After about ten minutes, seven of the guys that jumped with me came by with my buddy, Pfc. John Skirko, leading the way."

"After walking very carefully, as there were Germans all over the place, we came across about twenty troopers from the 507 Regiment who were also lost. In our travels we found a suitable farm house near a highway and we formed a defence perimeter around it. Here we were constantly attacked by a big force of SS troops. They shelled us all day and all night, some of the guys got hit so we used the farm house as a First Aid Station.''

"Finally on the third day a German officer came over carrying a white flag and wanted us to surrender. We told him to go to hell. After that they started to shell us again, more than ever this time.''

"We had with us an American Indian who used to go on patrol at night by himself. He would come back with the ears cut off the Germans he had killed. The fourth time he went out he did not return, maybe he was killed or captured, we never did find out.''

"It took about a week before our troops reached us. After I rejoined my Company we were in constant combat. We kept attacking, and we gave them hell. Two days later I was hit in my testicles with a piece of shrapnel. The Medic pulled the shrapnel out and patched me up. Captain Harold Miller told me to stay with them as they were short handed. Everybody was laughing at me, making all kinds of jokes, because of the way I was walking, with my legs spread apart.''

"Three days later we were dug in, holding a position, when a shell exploded in a tree and I was hit again, this time in my rear-end with three pieces of shrapnel. Thank God, it was just serious enough to be evacuated to a hospital. Everybody was saying, 'You lucky guy, you are going back to England.'''

"John Skirko survived the war and was awarded the Silver Star for his bravery. He was a real good buddy but I've never seen or heard of him since.''

Private First Class Anthony Antoniou came through the rest of the war after fighting in Holland, Belgium and Germany, altogether being wounded five times. With his war medals he has five Purple Hearts, and those Parachute Wings, which he still proudly wears, are adorned with those rare four Combat Jump Stars.

PFC. HOWARD MANOIAN, FIRST BATTALION, 505
Howard Manoian was typical of the men who jumped that night. He arrived in England in September 1943 and was assigned to the First Battalion of the 505 Regiment as a replacement in April 1944, after the Division returned from Italy.

"Like many of my companions I waited impatiently for the moment to fight the Germans.''

During his long stay in England he participated in six exercise jumps, the last one taking place in April and then he waited. During May he was still waiting until his unit was transported to the airfield at Spanhoe.

"On the 3rd June in the evening, during a briefing, a Corporal showed me a map of our jump zone. Everything was marked down — the river, the bridge, the railroad tracks, the manor, some houses — all except the name of the place. Nevertheless, we guessed that the objective was in Normandy. We waited to leave and then came the counter-order.''

"On 5th June, during the course of the afternoon, we were together in the hangars. It was there that our Sergeant, the chief of my 'stick' of 18 paratroopers, revealed to us that our objective was the manor of La Fiere, near Ste-Mere-Eglise.''

Later, armed with two parachutes, the Garand rifle, two belts of cartridges, eight regulation grenades (he had taken four extra), an anti-personnel mine and K rations he boarded the C-47.

It was a time of great anxiety for Manoian, this would be his first combat jump. ''I remember, I don't know why, perhaps for fear of being hit by the German fleet, that I sat down, like a few of the others, on my heavy helmet. Not until we were flying over the Normandy countryside did Sergeant Owin give the order to 'Hook up' a few minutes before the jump.''

''All of our 'stick' were released and before touching the ground I thought I saw a fire and a great dark mass: Ste-Mere-Eglise. I did not know where I was or if anyone was around me. I took off my parachute harness, removed my haversack in order to put a packet of rations in my pocket, a bar of chocolate and...a pair of socks.''

While advancing carefully in the dark, the gun in my hands, I slammed into a wall. I jumped over it to see what was on the other side and found myself, with some fear, looking at crosses in a cemetery.''

''In the midst of mooing cows I made my way towards a house — I believe that it was somehow connected with Marcel Mauduit — and with a small dictionary in my hand I asked where I was and the directions for the road to La Fiere. I must have asked the question several times before learning that it was four or five kilometres away. I swore to myself and went off into the night.''

''Along the road I met some other paratroopers of the Third Battalion of the 505 and I remained with them in the southern part of Ste-Mere-Eglise in a defensive position.''

''At about 8 o'clock (morning) on 6th June a Lieutenant assembled about twenty of us to counter-attack the Germans who were arriving from Reuville and we lost no time in closing in. We pursued them and for a quarter of an hour we had a scuffle.''

''With the incident over we caught up with the others at Ste-Mere-Eglise where, for more than twenty-four hours, there was a combat with the Germans. The tanks and reinforcements having arrived I was able to rejoin my company at La Fiere bridge on 8th June.''

After the war Howard Manoian served in the State of Massachusetts Police Force. Today he is enjoying his retirement in the village of Chef-du-Pont, Normandy, only a few miles from his wartime exploits.

CHAPLAIN GEORGE 'CHAPPIE' WOOD, 505

This was Chaplain George 'Chappie' Wood's third combat jump and as he landed he was caught up in a tree. ''I remember thinking at the time, Here it is, the great invasion of Europe, I just made the best jump of my life and I'm bouncing two feet off the ground.'' He looked around, he was completely alone, so he remembered the cricket.

''I got mine out while I was hanging from the tree and started clicking. Next

Chaplin George 'Chappie' Wood in Normandy in 1944.

The town square of Ste-Mere-Eglise on the morning of the 6th June, 1984, the 40th Anniversary of D-Day. 'Chappie' Wood is giving an address during the wreath laying ceremonies. Also in the picture are Don McKeage, Tony DeFoggi, George Ziemski and Andy Kilcullen.

thing I knew, a voice from behind me said 'For God's sake Padre, stop that noise, or we'll all get killed.''' Meekly 'Chappie' Wood followed the paratrooper out of the field.

By the afternoon 'Chappie', together with doctors, Captain Lyle Putman, Captain Robert Franco and Lieutenant Alexander Suer were busy tending the wounded, from both sides, in Madame Angele Levrault's schoolhouse. It was 'Chappie' who led the group sent out to cut down the dead paratroopers from the trees around the town's square.

The son of the Ste-Mere-Eglise fire chief, Andre Feville, assisted in the gathering of some two to three hundred American dead near the school. Later he was on a burial detail.

'Chappie' Wood went on to become the only United States Army Chaplain in the Second World War to make four combat jumps. The Catholic Chaplain, Father Matt Connelly suffered a broken vertebra on the Normandy jump which ended his parachuting career.

CAPTAIN ROBERT KIRKWOOD, THIRD BATTALION, 505

Bob Kirkwood had a photograph taken as he smoked a cigar before he boarded the C-47 at Cottesmore airfield. With him was Lieutenant Pat Ward, the Battalion's Intelligence Officer, and twenty men in the 'stick'.

Waiting to board their C-47 on the evening of the 5th June, 1944, for D-Day at Cottesmore. Captain Robert Kirkwood (left) and Lieutenant Pat Ward with a platoon of 505 troopers.

At least three 'sticks' from the Third Battalion were dropped off target at Montebourg, about six miles north of Ste-Mere-Eglise. Kirkwood, Ward and Lieutenant Jack Issacs of G Company managed to get together and assemble thirty-three men. In the subsequent fighting the group were dispersed and many casualties sustained.

Captain Bob Kirkwood said later, "It took me three days to get back to our lines, and in those three days I saw more Germans than I ever wanted to see again."

Lieutentant Pat Ward and most of those thirty-three men were captured. Bob Kirkwood and Jack Issacs were able to rejoin their Battalion on D+3.

Kirkwood never saw that photograph of himself until it was published in a Leicester newspaper in 1989, forty-five years later.

FRED MORGAN, MEDIC, 505

Fred Morgan a 505 Medic of Edgartown remembers, "I was scared stiff. I had landed in a tree and couldn't see the ground. As I reached to cut my risers, my hands were shaking so hard that I dropped the knife. I could not get down. Then after a while I heard voices in the darkness under me. After what seemed like hours, I finally whispered the password: 'Thunder'. Somebody below me said 'Lightning', and I knew they were Americans."

PRIVATE M.P. BROWN, D COMPANY, 505

Never far from trouble, M.P. Brown was dug in alongside a road on the second day. The weather was warm so he stripped off his shirt, vest, shoes and socks. He was just wearing his jump suit trousers.

Along the road came an unsuspecting German motorcycle and sidecar. Brown fired his M-1, killing the officer in the sidecar and wounding the driver. The officer was carrying a briefcase full of maps which looked extremely important, so Brown, realising their value immediately took his find to the Company Headquarters.

His Company's First Sergeant, John Rabig, later said that Brown should have received a citation, but all he got was 'his ears chewed off'. The Company Commander exclaimed, "Brown, God damn you, you're out of uniform!"

STAFF SERGEANT HARRY ANDERSON, E COMPANY, 505

Everything has it humorous side. Harry Anderson of E Company remembers Sergeant Victor Schmidt in his company. "He was a very tall German Jew with a very large nose. On two occasions when he was prone on the ground he was wounded in the 'ass. We all used to tell him, roll over on your back Victor and let them knock four inches off your nose."

PFC. ROBERT WILLIAMS, I COMPANY, 505

William's nickname was 'Little Willy' and he was in I Company. This was his third combat jump and he had been wounded in Sicily. When the green light came on the paratroopers started leaving the C-47 until one man, on his first combat jump, froze in the door. Williams, with another man named Elba

R. Walker, prised him loose from his hold and took him to the back of the plane. By the time they had jumped they were 20 miles behind the German lines. This was the only jumpstick from I Company that went astray.

On landing Walker broke both his insteps and lay helpless. For three days Williams and Walker hid in ditches until they were surrounded and so became prisoners of war.

'Little Willy' became POW No 81716 in Stalag 4-B. He tried one escape but was soon recaptured. Later, in September, he and many others were transported in a boxcar to Stalag 13-B and condemned to a Czechslovakian coal mine to work with Russians, Belgians and Americans. They had to hand mine 12 tons of coal a day or stay in the mine without food. Breakfast was at 5am when the rations were four boiled potatoes and one cup of burnt rye coffee. After twelve hours the next meal was a bowl of 'Rutabaga' soup and one loaf of bread divided between eight men. The bread was made with one third sawdust.

Robert Williams was released from captivity on the 23rd April 1945.

What happened to other troopers on that plane is still a mystery. Private James A Rund was later found bayoneted to death near Monteburg.

'JACK OF DIAMONDS' AND 'BLACK JACK', FIRST BATTALION, 505

The 505 left two of its greatest characters in Normandy, they had been both killed in action. They were Major Frederick Kellam, known as the 'Jack of Diamonds', and Major James McGinity who had the nickname of 'Black Jack'. This was the reason that the First Battalion had the 'Diamond' insignia painted on their helmets.

Kellem was the First Battalion Commander and was killed by a mortar shell. McGinity, the Battalion's Executive Officer, met his death by a sniper's bullet.

Stories abound about these two officers who are still referred to as 'a couple of pretty wild characters'. One of the favourite stories told is how they commandeered a C-47 while in Casablanca and flew it to another base were they loaded it with booze. These two regularly acted as 'altar boys' for Father Matthew Connelly, the Catholic Chaplain, at his Midnight Mass.

****

The time came when the 82nd's job was done. The foothold in Northern France was secure and new Divisions were taking on the fight. The paratrooper's casualties had been heavy and it was time to withdraw, regroup and to wait for another task.

From 8th July to the 12th the 505th Parachute Infantry Regiment was held in reserve. New uniforms were issued and transport arrived to take them to Utah Beach for the boats to return them to England. Their days of combat in Normandy were over. Many could not believe they had survived more than thirty days in continuous combat.

It was true what General Matthew Ridgway had told them. To all of them, D-Day, 6th June 1944, would be remembered for the rest of their days.

Major Frederick C.A. Kellam (left) who had the nickname of the 'Jack of Diamonds'. He was killed in action in Normandy. On the right is Colonel William E. Ekman, the Commanding Officer of the 505. Pictured at Cottesmore airfield waiting for D-Day.

Delbert Bradley Humpston (left) of the 325 Glider Infantry Regiment photographed with his brother, Jesse Herbert Humpston of the 95th Infantry Division. The photograph was taken in Evansville, Indiana, October 1945.

DELBERT HUMPSTON, G COMPANY
325th GLIDER INFANTRY REGIMENT

These are the memories and experiences of Delbert B. Humpston, a veteran of the First Squad, First Platoon of G Company, Second Battalion in the Normandy invasion. He writes:

This story was written not only in honour of the brave men, living and dead, who I fought alongside in combat, but perhaps to help future generations in their research for what actually happened in Normandy, the greatest invasion the world has ever seen. By many librarians and researchers my account would be called a primary source.

I have purposely tried to omit all the gore and horrible things which I experienced in combat that took the lives of some of the closest friends I ever had.

There are many details I have failed to mention, for they have become too vague in my memory.

Naturally, there are always conflicting experiences or different opinions about any story that is written, but regardless, this is my version.

OPERATION OVERLORD

With the long awaited invasion of German occupied Europe becoming more of a definite reality with each day, the men were getting very impatient, most wanting to go so that they could help end the war and return to their normal lives.

We didn't know the day or the hour but we did know that we were waiting for the very minute, the very second, for the invasion to begin.

Intense training continued until the middle of May, but from then on inspections took up most of our time. Officers checked our personal equipment and we received new issues for anything that was not in good condition.

Passes to town were stopped, so this appeared to be the real thing coming up. Before we were sealed to camp, a G Company party was held in nearby Leicester with plenty of beer and eats laid on. The three men from G Company who had been in the guardhouse were released for the party. As it later turned out, this was their last taste of freedom as all three were killed in action during the invasion.

At last the entire 82nd Airborne Division, with the exception of the 504th Parachute Infantry Regiment, received orders to move to their respective airfields. The 325 left Scraptoft at 10am on the morning of Monday, 29th May, by a convoy of trucks to Leicester where we boarded a troop train at 11am. We arrived at Hungerford, in southern England at 7pm and were taken by trucks to Camp Williams, a marshalling area and airfield fifteen miles northeast of Exeter. The airfield was called Upottery, taking its name from the nearby Devonshire village.

After being assigned to tents, we had chow at 9.30pm, dug foxholes in case of air raids and went to bed.

For the next few days the weather changed to rain and fog, and our time was spent with lectures about the French Resistance, how to use rubber life rafts in case our gliders were forced down in the Channel and many other details vital to our forthcoming mission.

Our clothing and equipment included O.D. (Olive Drab — used to describe the U.S. Army wool uniform) pants and shirt inpregnated against gas, field jacket with an American flag sewn on the right sleeve, steel helmet with camouflage net, impregnated leggings, boots, gas mask, a light pack — which contained a shelter half, raincoat, pair of cotton underwear, two pairs of socks, shaving equipment and towel. Also a cartridge belt loaded with armour piercing ammunition, a bandolier of ammunition, two hand grenades, one smoke grenade, two anti-tank grenades, M-1 rifle, bayonet, trench knife, three 'K' rations, six 'D' rations and a 'Mae West' life jacket.

At the camp the meals were very good and the PX supplies were plentiful. We all appreciated those things but we also realised how much they would be missed after we landed in France.

We were permitted to take a shower in the Air Corps shower room, but an officer had to accompany the men every time they left the limits of our tented area.

One day was spent laying a runway for glider takeoffs and we noticed the enormous gathering of gliders and C-47's parked everywhere.

With the weather clearing we could feel the tension rising with every hour. Finally we were briefed on our mission, studied maps of the terrain where we would be landing and fighting and issued with four dollars or two hundred francs of invasion money.

We were ordered to turn in all pictures and tape our dog-tags to keep them from rattling together and making the slighest noise. In the operation we were about to take part in, complete silence was of great importance.

For a little diversion to take our minds off the crucial days that lay ahead, the 82nd Airborne Division Band entertained us by playing some of the most popular songs from home. A movie show at the airbase helped us to relax while we patiently waited.

D-Day finally came on the 6th June, which has gone down in history as 'The Longest Day', the greatest military invasion the world has ever experienced.

With the parachute regiments already dropped in Normandy, where they were meeting stiff resistance, orders were received to commit the 325th Glider Infantry Regiment into the fray.

The Second Battalion was awakened at 2.30am, D-Day plus One, and given a quick breakfast a half hour later. From there we returned to our tents and hastily secured all our equipment.

Each Company was formed into platoons and marched to the airfield where gliders and the C-47 tow planes were lined up on the runways, ready for loading. Both the American CG-4A gliders, which carried thirteen troops and two pilots, and the much larger and less manoeuvrable British Horsa gliders were being used on this mission. Thirty-one or thirty-two troops, including the pilot, was the normal load for the Horsa.

It was not known to me why or how the men were assigned to the various gliders, but my squad drew the short straw for the Horsa. Our group was made up by the First Platoon, some from the Second Platoon and some from Company Headquarters. The First Sergeant of G Company, Daniel L. Abner of Hazard, Kentucky was with us and in command was Second Lieutenant Guy Gowen of Concord, New Hampshire, being the First Platoon Leader.

Like most everything else in the army it was hurry up and wait, for it would be almost an hour before we climbed aboard.

This was the first combat mission for most of the pilots who joked and kidded around with us until take-off time. They tried very hard to give us the impression that they were sure of themselves and capable of accomplishing the task that lay ahead.

As we sat around waiting, the conversation drifted from one subject to another. One man remarked how lucky he really was to be in an outfit that rode in 'flying coffins', 'tow targets' or 'flak-hacks', as the gliders were so often called, receiving no jump pay, but never a dull moment as he was pulled into combat on the end of a rope.

Perhaps many others felt the same way, but the secret of the whole thing was not to let the other fellow know how scared you really were.

We had been well trained, and we were a part of the best combat Division in the world, being taught how to survive and how to kill the other fellow first. Most of us felt ready and believed that we would accomplish our mission and live to tell our grandchildren about it. There were always those who had premonitions that they would not survive the war and return home. Two men in particular that I heard make such a statement were both killed in combat.

One man in our group had a pen or marker and wrote his name on the side of the glider, so I and several others followed suit. As the C-47's began warming up their motors we received orders to board the gliders. It was about 6.30am when our long wait was over.

After taking off we circled the field a few times until all the planes were in formation, then headed in the direction the paratroopers had taken before us. Our fighter protection of pursuit planes, mostly American P-38's and British Spitfires, were flying above us in every direction.

By the time we reached the Channel the sun was shining and we could look down on a vast armada of ships and boats of every description heading for the coast of Normandy; hundreds of ships that would eventually land men and much needed supplies for the beach-head forces.

As we were buffeted about I vividly remember looking around the glider at the different expressions on the men's faces. Some appeared to be napping, they could have even been offering up a silent prayer. Others were just staring off into space as if in deep meditation. The man next to me was reading from a New Testament that the Chaplain had given him at Fort Bragg. Of course, there is always a joker in any bunch, as someone hollered out, "Is this trip really necessary?" This brought chuckles from a lot of us, for most still had a sense of humour.

We had seen the 506th Parachute Infantry Regiment of the 101st Airborne take off before us and had heard the planes return from that first flight. We also knew that some had not come back and that others were riddled with flak. In spite of all this knowledge there wasn't the tenseness that one would expect, instead just calmness and determination.

The German Luftwaffe never made an appearance during our flight and only a few gliders came under anti-aircraft fire as we approached the north eastern tip of the Cherbourg peninsula. One glider was seen going down in flames and the fate of those men was never known.

When the French coast was first sighted the pilot shouted out, "Get ready Boys, there's Normandy!" After being in the air for a little more than two hours we came over Utah Beach at a very low altitude. Smoke and the signs of battle were everywhere as we flew five or six miles inland from the beach to just east of the village of Chef-du-Pont. Our original designated landing zones were found by the Pathfinders to be heavily obstructed with large poles, trees and other obstacles. These had been hastily set up by the Germans in the few open fields previously selected for our landings. Now the pilots had no opportunity and little precious time to select a decent landing site. Gliders can land safely in small fields if the pilot has sufficient altitude to make a proper and slow approach.

All the fields were very small and each completely surrounded by hedgerows and trees. Flying at an altitude of only two hundred feet, we circled the landing area picked out and watched the pilot cut loose from our tow-plane. As we clutched our rifles tightly, we hoped there was a spot below where the clumsy Horsa could find enough room for a decent landing. It was only going to be a matter of seconds and we braced ourselves for the worst to happen.

All the gliders were circling the small fields and coming in from every direction, smashing into one another, ripping through the hedgerows, spreading men and equipment everywhere.

Sitting in the second seat directly behind the pilot, I watched the distance between us and the hedgerows diminish rapidly. As we got closer and closer to the ground the large posts were clearly visible in the field. Looking down, the actual seriousness of the situation became a reality.

I was hoping that our pilot would attempt to select another field, but is was too late. The big Horsa glider banked sharply with a loud swishing sound, travelling at ninety miles an hour we barely cleared the hedges. In a matter of seconds after the skids touched the ground we clipped one of the large posts which tore off part of our right wing. This caused the glider to change direction suddenly and we ran over the wing of an American CG-4A glider that had landed directly in our path. Still travelling at a great rate of speed the pilot shouted, "Look out boys!", as we crashed head-on into two large trees at the end of the field, just short of the hedgerow.

The glider broke in half, the nose was completely demolished and the floor was torn up by the stumps of the trees we had knocked down. Everything was in a state of total confusion. I could hear the groans of the men, many seriously injured. There were the familiar cries of "Medic!", "Medic!", everywhere.

I had been thrown up front through the hole in the floor, landing on top of several bodies, including the pilot who had been killed on impact. The men had been thrown in every direction, but luckily, except for some severe bruises and some-what dazed, I was unhurt.

Captain Louis P. Murphy, the Regimental Medical Officer, who had been under the other wing of the glider we had run over on landing, said later that he had not expected to find any survivors from our group.

To complicate the situation we were being shot at by snipers. Immediately Pfc. Howard Gilmer, an expert rifleman in the Company, took off with Pfc. Shelby Fraley and another man in search of the snipers. Evidently they must have accomplished their mission as the firing soon stopped, but not before one man, handicapped by a broken leg, was killed while attempting to crawl away from the wrecked glider to the safety of a hedgerow.

Hurriedly, those of us who were not injured were trying to help the others. With the assistance of Sergeant Frank Pozar we managed to get First Sergeant Daniel Abner and Pfc. Fred Kampfer out of the glider and lay them on the ground. Later, we learned that Sergeant Abner had suffered a broken shoulder, several cracked ribs and severe lacerations. Kampfer had several cracked vertebrae amongst his injuries.

Pfc. Thomas Roberts was killed instantly, and Pfc. Glenn Lego, who was unconscious and bleeding from the mouth, was still alive when we left the scene but he died later the same day. Lieutenant Guy Gowen, who was the Glider Group Commander, and Pfc. Francis Higdon were thrown out of the glider and their bodies were found lying close together on the ground. Lieutenant Gowen's field glasses were still around his neck.

Leaving the casualties behind for the Medics to look after we headed for our predesignated assembly area. Looking back as we left there was a scene of complete destruction, the field was full of wrecked gliders. There was even a dead cow, killed while grazing by one of the big Horsa gliders.

When we reached our assembly area I was thankful that I had survived such a terrible ordeal. I remember kneeling down and kissing the ground. The Company quickly re-organised and waited until the Battalion was intact and ready to move out.

The Regiment had suffered 11 per cent casualties in the landings, but as a Company, G Company's percentage was much greater. On a head count we had thirty five casualties, more than double of any other. We had joked that men and gliders were considered expendable, now we knew it was true. Only one out of every four gliders landed without damage.

With orders to move out we made our way through the hedgerows in the direction of Chef-du-Pont, never knowing what was waiting for us on the other side. Again we came under heavy harassment from the inevitable snipers who were taking their toll along the way.

As the Platoon were walking along a hedgerow, approaching an apple orchard, I heard a rustle in the vines and bushes at my feet. Startled, I quickly turned and almost fired when a French women crawled out from the over-hanging underbrush with two small children. Very scared they had been burrowed in like rabbits for a long period of time.

Extremely excited, she pointed through the orchard towards a farmhouse in the distance, shouting "Boche! Boche!" Although my knowledge of the

French language was very limited I understood that she was warning us that Germans occupied the house. I handed her a bar of chocolate for the children and took off. This was my first experience of this kind but we later learned this was a common situation.

French civilians often left their homes in the midst of the fighting and fled to fields, ditches, under bridges and many other places, trying to find safety.

As we advanced through the orchard and came near the farm we began receiving increased small arms fire. Spreading out we surrounded the house. Several men took cover behind the stone wall in front and down one side of the building. Sergeant Clinton White, Pfc. Paul Block our B.A.R. man, and myself followed a hedgerow down the other side to get around to the rear. As we started towards the outbuildings which adjoined the house, a German darted out of a stable towards some woods at the back. I opened fire and shot him in the arm, which caused him to stagger a little. Block then killed him with a burst from his Browning Automatic Rifle. After a thorough search of the house and stable we found no other Germans, so he could have been a sniper left behind to harass or was somehow separated from his unit.

We moved into a bivouac area near Chef-du-Pont which had been captured by the paratroopers. No sooner had we dug our foxholes than we were ordered to move to an area east of the railroad, near La Fiere and north of the Ste-Mere-Eglise/Amfreville Road. While on the march my Battalion was hurriedly diverted and ordered to join up with another unit west of Ste-Mere-Eglise. We arrived in time to receive orders for an attack timed for midnight.

Fortunately, except for a few isolated pockets of resistance and clearing a few snipers, the main body of the enemy had withdrawn and the Battalion took up a defensive position just south of Fresville at dawn. Here we stayed for a much needed rest which was interrupted by two German planes hedge-hopping our area. On 8th June at 2300 hours we received orders to pull out at midnight and move north, closer to Fresville.

While in that area we experienced the eerie sound of the Nebelwerfers or 'screaming meemies' for the first time. Their power was less than an artillery shell but the fragmentation effect was greater. It was a six barrelled weapon that scattered its shells, and very much feared for that reason. It was classified as a type of mortar, they made a frightful noise and threw out powerful jets of flame as it was fired.

On 9th June we had orders to attack at 04.00 hours. The Battalion's objective was the village of Le Ham, about three miles to the north west, and was heavily defended by the Germans. We were told that this would be a big attack, which later proved to be true.

With very little sleep we moved out at first light and crossed the line of departure near Grainville at 06.30. The sky was overcast and light rain was falling. After advancing about a half mile, mortar shells and occasional sniper fire began to rip through the ranks. One of the forward scouts called our attention to a movement a short distance ahead. In front of us, through an opening in the hedgerow we could see a narrow road leading to a farmhouse. Through field glasses several Germans were spotted as they ran across the opening on the other side of the hedge. The next time one darted across the scouts opened fire, and then all hell broke loose.

The German machine-guns halted the Company abruptly: mortars, artillery and the deadly 88's laid down a murderous barrage. This area must have been zeroed in previously, we had run into the main line of the German defence. The whole Battalion was pinned down, unable to move, and unable to get supporting artillery fire.

As in all Airborne units, during actual combat, our officers led the men from the front instead of directing the action from a safe rear area. Our Company Commander, Captain Irvin Bloom, well respected by every man in G Company, was killed by artillery while leading us.

With the Captain at the time was Pfc. John Nero and he was severely wounded by the same shell. Seconds later T/Sergeant Carl Smith and Pfc. Carl Gessner were killed and Sergeant Frank Pozar seriously wounded. The shelling was so intense that we could scarcely raise our heads even for a second. The cry of "Medic!" rang out repeatedly, and although I was only about fifty feet away lying in a shallow creek bed, it was impossible to get to them.

Finally, we did get a heavy barrage going from our artillery, but as soon as it lifted we once again received the same heavy concentration of fire from the Germans. We tried several times to advance but were unable to do so. Word finally reached us that Captain Robert Dickerson, the C.O. of E Company had been wounded, the calf of his leg was almost blown off. Captain Dickerson was from my hometown of Henderson, Kentucky.

Casualties increased and the Germans were now threatening to envelop the open left flank. The Battalion was forced on the defensive to protect itself. With our machine-guns knocked out, the very heavy casualties and our C.O. dead, we were in a serious situation. During a lull in the fighting we finally reached Nero who was unconscious and had a large hole in his lower back, so large I could stick my fist in. He had lost a considerable amount of blood. After the Medic did what he could, I was one of the men who helped carry him back to where he could be picked up and taken to an aid station.

Just before midnight we were relieved by the First Battalion of the 505 Paratroopers and went back to a bivouac area to rest and re-organise. The main attack was resumed the following morning, with our Second Battalion remaining on the defensive to protect the flank of the entire operation. All the time we were under heavy and constant shelling by mortars and 88's. We all had learnt many things in a very short time, through bitter experience, things that could never be learnt from field training or any army handbook. The loss of Captain Bloom was felt by everyone in G Company, he was admired and respected.

The Company's strength was now down to eighty six men and only two officers. It fell to Lieutenant George Cockle to be in command. he was formally the Executive Officer of G Company. The other remaining officer was Lieutenant Gerald Kirk, who was later killed in action.

Two Stuka dive bombers strafed our positions causing us to stay close to our foxholes, but no casualties were reported. I remember being near a foxhole as the plane came over. Two of us raced for the same hole, I lost my helmet but managed to dive into the hole headfirst and the other guy came in on top of me.

On 11th June the drive against Le Ham reached its climax, the Battalion was ordered to attack. Leaving all unnecessary equipment behind, including gas masks, we were to attack German positions to our west. Carrying extra bandoliers of ammunition and fixed bayonets we jumped off supported by artillery and heavy mortars. Urging the men forward, General Jim Gavin stood on the line of departure which was a road raked with enemy fire from mortars and 88's.

Several pockets of stiff resistance were soon wiped out, for the men were very determined to even up the score for those already lost. All the approach routes were covered by German strongpoints in the hedgerows.

Under heavy fire we moved up to a road and a railroad track which the Germans had zeroed in. The terrain in front of us was very open, swampy and cut by canals. Beyond the railroad track was an open field that had to be crossed to get to the German positions in a wooded area on top of a hill, about a thousand feet in front of us.

After a heavy barrage when our artillery peppered the German positions, we prepared to cross the railroad track in clear view of the enemy. I distinctly remember Lt. Colonel John 'Swede' Swenson standing on the track watching the operation. We were receiving intense fire at this point.

This was the day that Lieutenant Cockle, now our C.O., distinguished himself as a true leader. He shouted only two words, ''Lets Go!'' and without hesitation he was across the railroad track, ahead of our scouts, into the open field. For the first time those words which are inscribed on our regimental crest really meant something.

With those two words ringing in our ears we swarmed across the track taking the open field on the run and firing from the hip. The fighting was severe and very costly as we were getting heavy machine-gun fire from the right flank. When the empty clip from my M-1 sprang out I stopped running momentarily to secure another clip and reload. With that completed I had only taken about another three steps when I felt a hot, burning sensation that knocked my leg out from under me. Looking down I discovered that I had been shot through the left knee.

Looking around I found I was approximately two hundred yards from the railroad track that we had just crossed, and remembering a drainage ditch that ran along the track, I decided to crawl for it. Mortar shells were dropping all around us and that would offer me a little cover.

Making it back to the ditch I found three other men from my Squad lying wounded in there, and learned later that everyone in the Squad had been hit except one.

As the attack progressed Lt. Colonel Swenson was severely wounded by shrapnel. Many were killed in the attack, including one of my closest friends, Pfc. Fred Fuhrman of Chicago. Several of us were shot at by a German 88 at almost point blank range, and that was a terrifying experience, one that I shall not forget.

After the German positions were captured and the shelling subsided, I was picked up by the Medics, placed in a Jeep and taken to a Field Hospital. I had attempted to bandage my knee the best I could, but my wound was looked at, re-bandaged and I waited to be transferred to the 128th Evacuation Hospital near the beach. The Jeep that picked me up passed a house with an American CG-4A glider lodged on the roof.

Littering many of the fields were the bloated carcasses of cattle killed, possibly by artillery, during the fighting just a few days previously. The signs of battle were visible everywhere.

Riding in the same ambulance with me was Pfc. Herbert Sanderson who was mortally wounded in that last attack. It was quite evident that although he had been given morphine he was in great pain, yet he talked to me on the way. After we reached the hospital we were separated and I never saw him again. Perhaps I was the last man from G Company to see Sanderson alive, because I was informed that he died a few minutes after the end of our journey.

I remained at the 128th Evacuation Hospital until 15th June when I was taken to the 261st Clearing Hospital on the beachhead. From there I was loaded onto an amphibious DUKW and taken out to sea to an LST boat. The LST took us out further out to sea where I was transferred to an English Hospital Ship. Here we sat at anchor all night during a number of German air attacks on ships in the area.

At 16.00 hours on 16th June we left the French coast for Southampton, England. In the early hours of the morning I left the ship and was taken by ambulance to the 110th Station Hospital, less than ten miles from the docks. My Mother's birthday was on 17th June and I remember it well, the Germans mounted a big air raid on Southampton during the night. England was still suffering, V-1 rockets and 'buzz bombs' were now hitting the southern cities and ports regularly.

There were quite a few of us from the 325 who were transferred by train on 20th June to the 53rd General Hospital, near Malvern Wells, arriving at 0330 hours. Later, when I was fully fit I was sent to the 10th Replacement Centre at Lichfield to eventually rejoin my Regiment at Scraptoft, near Leicester.

After thirty one consecutive days of combat, without replacements at any time, the Regiment was finally relieved. By that time G Company had suffered more casualties than any other company, not only in our Regiment, but in the entire 82nd Airborne Division.

When we left for Normandy our Company's strength was one hundred and fifty men and five officers. Only one officer and five men from G Company stepped off the train at London Road Station in Leicester when the Regiment returned from France on the Sunday night of July 9th. These figures were verified by the Company Clerk of G Company, Corporal Carl A. Helgren who was there to meet the men.

Because of the success of the operations the 325th Glider Infantry Regiment was awarded the Presidential Unit Citation.

Since Normandy I have tried, unsuccessfully, not to think about the Germans I shot, killed or helped to kill. Nor will I ever forget those brave men of the 325th Glider Infantry who I fought alongside. Especially always in my memory are the thirteen men from G Company, including our C.O. Captain Bloom, who are still buried in a Normandy Cemetery over looking Omaha Beach.

I have always been thankful that I survived to live my life to the full. I can certainly vouch for that wise statement, ''There are no atheists in foxholes!''

Footnotes on Del Humpston's story:

Humpston fought his way across Europe, through Holland, the Ardennes and into Germany itself. He returned home to Henderson, Kentucky, met a girl called Betty and married her. They have two daughters and four grandchildren. Del and Betty have made several trips to Europe to visit his old haunts.

The Regimental Records show that the First and Second Battalions lost one hundred and sixty six men killed in action in Normandy, 1944.

****

There appeared in the *Glider Tow Line,* Winter 1987/88 a letter from Edwin 'Tad' Lainhart, a Second Battalion Medic of Holton, Indiana. He described the battle on 9th June:

In the early morning hours of 9th June in Normandy, we started an all out attack toward the village of Le Ham. Casualties were heavy and I found myself exposed continually to German small arms fire and directed mortar and artillery fire.

Captain Bloom of Company G was killed by an artillery burst. Captain Dickerson (E Company) was wounded in the leg and could not walk. I gave him first aid and while doing so a barrage of shells came in at which point Dickerson called out, ''Boys, it's too hot here, let's get moving!''

I really don't see how any of us got out alive. The calf of Dickerson's leg was almost blown off but he made it through the hospitals and is alive today.

Lt. Colonel John (Swede) Swenson, a West Point Officer was wounded the second day of this attack. Prior to being disabled he had ordered the men of Company G to fix bayonets and go through the hedgerows after the Germans. The action was fierce. I found my best friend, Herbert Sanderson, mortally wounded. On my way to get a litter squad for Sanderson I came across Colonel Swenson propped up against the trunk of a tree. Someone had already bandaged his wounds but I could see that he was suffering intense pain. I asked him if he would let me give him a shot of morphine. He replied...''No, it would knock me out and I want to be alert and know what is going on.''

I sent a litter squad after Swenson and went to find my buddy Sanderson. Although I had done all I could for Sanderson before leaving him, it was not enough. His family was among the many who received a notice 'killed in action.'

I did not think that Swenson could make it and heard that he had died, but 42 years after the war I learned he was among the living, Praise God!

In her book *My World War II Diary* Edith Steiger Phillips, the 325 Red Cross girl wrote:

We stood so alone under the only light at the Leicester railway station the night the 325 men returned after thirty-three days of battle without relief. It was Sunday, 9th July, and the night was pitch black. The light we stood under must have been a twenty-five watt. It gave so little light I could not recognise any of the men as they marched by us. When I asked Colonel Lewis how many men were returning he got all choked up. He wasn't too sure but he thought about a third! I was prepared for a few hundred but a third, never!

The soldiers got off the train slowly and walked up the stairs like tired old men. I strained my eyes to recognise a face but didn't see anybody I knew. The men were unshaven, mud-caked and they slumped.

Back at the camp that night Colonel Lewis insisted on going to the mess hall where the men were to be fed but a coughing spell racked him and he had to sit down on the ground. He leaned on the driver and me and went to his HQ shack where he put his head on his arms as he tried to get comfortable at his small desk.

I left the Colonel and ran to the mess hall to help pour coffee but the men just sat there staring into space. They didn't eat. They fell asleep at the table. I didn't say a word to anybody. I noticed, however, that the GIs sat here, there and everywhere in the hall as though returning to a place where they had sat before. I dare not ask where this or that boy was. I knew.

****

In the *Glider Tow Line* of Summer 1987, Herb Heubschen (HQ-325), now living in Beloit, Wisconsin, remembered:

Iris and I were at the London Road Railroad Station at Leicester in July 1944 when the troops of the 325th, what was left of them, returned from Normandy. I had already returned to Scraptoft from a hospital, having been wounded on June 14th in Normandy. Colonel Lewis was there on the platform too, looking for familiar faces, saluting the returning soldiers and openly shedding tears for those poor bedraggled guys.

The girl, Iris, he mentions was a Leicester girl he later married and took back to the States as his GI Bride.

Colonel Harry Leigh Lewis was the Commanding Officer of the 325th Glider Infantry Regiment but was relieved from duties after the first few days in Normandy. Officially it was termed as 'Combat fatigue', but he was suffering from cancer. Within eight months he was dead.

****

Daniel L. Abner, First Sergeant of G Company returned after Normandy only to be killed in action in Holland on 28th September, 1944.

On research it is found that the following, who are mentioned in Del Humpston's story, survived the war to return home:

John 'Swede' Swenson became a cattle rancher in Wyoming.

Robert Dickerson lives in Palmetto, Florida.

Captain Louis P.Murphy lives in Scranton, Pennsylvania.

Lieutenant George Cockle lives in Omaha, Nebraska.

Howard Gilmer died in Bremen, Indiana on 24th January, 1981.

Shelby Fraley, whose home state was West Virginia, whereabouts unknown.

Frank Pozar lives in Struthers, Ohio.

Fred Kampfer lives in Pacific Grove, California.

Clinton White, whose home state was West Virginia, whereabouts unknown.

Paul Block, informed that he is now deceased.

John Nero lives in Akron, Ohio.

Carl A. Helgren died in 1988 in his hometown of Newport, Michigan.

Two other original members of the Company who have died are:

John Thompson of Chicago died in a mental institution.

Steve Serva of Akron, Ohio, committed suicide by hanging in February 1971.

Of the killed in action of G Company, thirteen are buried in Normandy, five in Margraten and one in the Ardennes, both in Belgium. Delbert Humpston has made a pilgrimage to each one of these graves on his European tours.

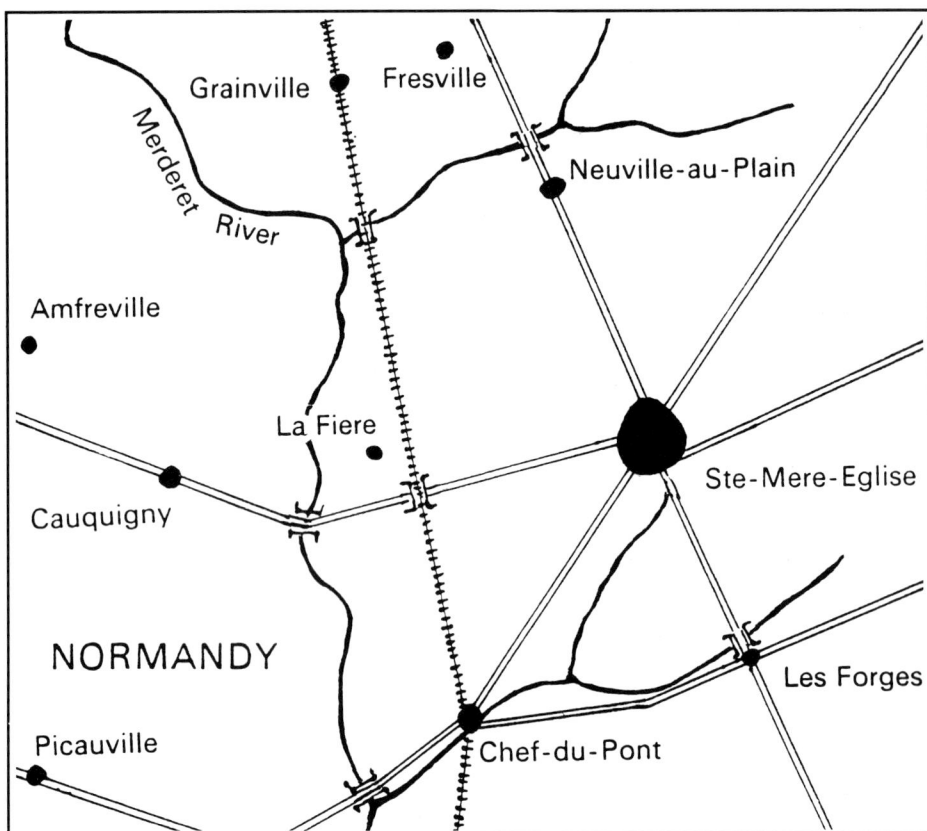

The Return to Quorn

On 13th July the 505 said goodbye to Normandy as they left Utah Beach in a flotilla of Tank Landing Craft after 38 days in combat. They left behind 186 comrades who had been killed in action or died of wounds. Many others were wounded, missing or prisoners-of-war.

The actual figures were:

A total of 2095 men of the Regiment parachuted into Normandy. Out of those 186 were killed, 60 missing in action, 492 wounded in action, 164 injured in action and 51 were captured. Those losses totalled 953, so only about half the paratroopers who left Quorn just over a month before returned for their glass of 'mild and bitter' in the village on that first night back — a casualty rate of 46.18 per cent for the whole Division of 11,770 men.

As 'Chappie' Wood said later, "When the men got off the boats in England they knelt down and kissed the ground. This to them was hallowed ground."

Many of the villagers came looking for their friends and were distressed to learn that they were either dead, missing or wounded. Even so the losses were less than General Eisenhower had feared. He knew that without the 82nd's determination the invasion may have had a different outcome.

Bill Tucker of I Company recalls, "Side by side, as a machine-gun team, we marched out of Quorn, some thirty five days before, heading for the Normandy jump. The Company of 144 men were in columns of threes and our Platoon of about forty eight men. Now we were returning with 45 men in columns of twos with about sixteen men left in the Platoon."

Ridgway had given orders to the Military Police that if any of his boys went 'over the wall' from the hospitals they were to be helped to return to their Regiments. As the wounded were released from the hospitals there was a danger that these paratroopers would be sent to a holding unit for reassignment. Many went AWOL from replacement depots to get back to the 82nd Division. The General wanted his boys back, even if they were unfit for combat. The 505, like the other Parachute Regiments, always found places in their service companies for the 'old men'. Nobody was transferred out, except at his own request.

One of the most remarkable escapes from hospital to return to the 505 was recorded by Pfc. Charles Kunesh. When the Division was moved from Italy, Kunesh was in a Naples hospital. Eight months later he turned up unannounced in Quorn in time for the Normandy invasion. Charles Kunesh was killed in action in Normandy when his foxhole had a direct hit with an 88mm shell.

Generous leave passes were handed out and the GI's headed for various cities, but mainly for the sights of London and Edinburgh. Richard Tedeschi and his friends got on a train for Edinburgh to taste the delights of Bonnie Scotland. By the time they reached Leeds they were in need of a beer, so they got off the train and found the nearest bar in a public house. Seven days later, still in Leeds, they headed back to the railway station to return to Quorn. ''We never did see Edinburgh, and come to think about it, we never saw much of Leeds either,'' said Richard.

Tony DeFoggi returned to find his girl in Loughborough had deserted him, so he was soon off to find fresh fields to conquer.

''Larry Neipling and I went to Scotland for our furlough. One evening he came back, very excited, 'Tony, we are going to Berlin tomorrow as Tail-gunners.' He had met up with some Eighth Airforce guys. 'Oh no Nip,' I said, 'I've got a date.'''

''He came back from his mission without firing his gun. Me? I got a complete surrender from this young lady and arrived back in Quorn a 'MAN'.''

''On 18th August 1944, I won the 505 Lightweight Boxing Championship. On the same night I had to go on a fifteen mile hike with the Company....remembering the Easter Parade. But I did refuse to go on to the Division's Boxing Finals. Other Companies allowed their fighters time off to train, but not ours, so I quit.''

''It was many years later, on 18th August 1982, to be precise, that I finally received my award. Don McKeage retold my story to Lt. Colonel Keith M. Nightingale, the Commanding Officer at Fort Bragg, and he made sure I got a citation....thirty eight years late.''

There was another citation that Tony DeFoggi forgot all about too. He was wounded as he was advancing on the Waal Bridge in Nijmegen in September 1944 and he never received his Purple Heart. At the 505 Reunion at Las Vegas in 1991 a special presentation of the medal was made to him....this time it was forty seven years late.

Harry Anderson, E Company, 505, had heard about the Lancashire seaside resort of Blackpool as being the fun place of England so he headed there. On the first day he realised that good booze was in short supply here too. In those days he liked a bottle a day. On the first day he decided he needed a haircut and a shave so he found a barbers shop. Luck was on his side, not only did the the barber make him look smart but he was able to supply a bottle of the 'good stuff' a day, at a price, because his son-in-law was in the Merchant Navy.

After his leave Harry Anderson was fed up being a Sergeant with all the pressure of duties and elected to return to being a Pfc. His aim was to miss all the parades and find himself quiet jobs on KP.

One day when there was a big parade due he managed to get in the cookhouse on KP's to peel potatoes. Later Captain Clyde Russell came looking for him in a rage, he was not happy as he had just had his ears chewed off. ''Here, this is for you, why weren't you on parade?'' He threw something at Harry who caught it amongst his potatoes. It was a Silver Star medal that would have been presented at the parade. Harry had won it in Normandy. Harry didn't stay a Pfc. for long. Vandervoort made him the

Supply Sergeant for E Company before the next mission.

Charles Kaiser, 505, also heard of the delights of Blackpool but he found it was too noisy for his liking. "There were fights in the streets with the Air Force guys. I just wanted peace and quiet. I returned to Leicester, rented a room for three or four days before I returned to camp."

Peter Clarke was a young boy living in Quorn. His father, Reginald, owned the Off Licence in Freehold Street. An Off Licence is the same as a liquor store. Peter remembers the 505 men arriving regularly at the shop with a jerry can to be filled with beer to take with them on their night problems. The five gallon can always came back to the camp empty.

The Clarke's house was also a haven of rest for the ATS girls stationed at the nearby Garats Hay camp. One the girls, Helen Brown, met an American Paratrooper named Private William 'Bill' F. Mulligan and they got married at St Peter's Catholic Church in Loughborough. Reginald Clarke was the best man.

Mulligan was suffering with malaria, caught in North Africa, and spent a long time in a hospital in London. One of his friends planned to travel to Loughborough to be the best man, but somehow failed to turn up. Reginald was pressed into service at the last minute. The date of the wedding was 20th September, three days after the Regiment jumped into Holland. Mulligan returned to the States soon after.

Bill and Helen Mulligan settled in Boston after the war and raised a family. They kept in touch with the Clarke family in Quorn until Bill died some years ago.

On his return to Quorn from hospital, Lieutenant James Coyle took over as the First Platoon Leader in E Company. Lieutenant Pete Peterson returned to the Company but his damaged leg eliminated him from parachute duty and he was classified as 'limited service'.

Jim Coyle continues: "We received replacements and gradually some of the wounded were able to return from the hospitals to active duty. Captain Clyde Russell was suffering from recurring malaria attacks and returned to the States. Captain James J. Smith, who was one of the Pathfinders in Normandy, took over as the E Company Commander."

"One of the first things that J.J. did was to set up an E Company party. He explained that he would turn over the Company fund to the enlisted men and they would run their own party. He also told me that I would be responsible for the party and after a brief 'Courtesy Call' by the Officers, they would all leave, except for me. I was to stay for the evening to keep an eye on things. I didn't know what to expect."

"E Company had never had a party before (and never had one again!). The party was held in a pavilion in the backyard of a pub in the little village of Barrow-on-Soar."

"It was a wild night. The beer flowed freely and there were a few fights. I had my hands full, separating the pugilists and breaking up the party at the appointed time. The pavilion was a wreck but I brought a detail of hung-over men back the next day to clean up. The landlord was satisfied and a good time was had by all — except me."

"The Company was now up to organised strength and after the men returned from furloughs training began again. Since our previous combat jumps were all part of invasions, there did not seem to be any logical places left to invade. We had no idea what our next mission would entail. We continued to hold day and night manoeuvres, one of which included a training jump."

Dennis Force was a replacement for the men lost in Normandy, arriving in Quorn in early July. He was put in I Company along with other replacements which included, John Siam, Calvin Gilbert, William Martin, Frank Federico and John Lebednick. All were assigned to Sergeant Charles Matash's squad in the Second Platoon. Charlie treated them like sons.

Dennis said later, "When I started hearing the war stories and the combat record of the 505, I was in awe. I wasn't sure if a rookie like me was in the right outfit."

One of the first to greet them was Pfc. John 'Scotty' Hough, the platoon runner. Now Scotty was the best food scrounger in the 505 and he was always showing up with something to cook after 'lights out'. On their first night, the new men sat down to pork chops, eggs, coffee and lots of bread and butter. He kept a small gas stove in his tent, just for the after hours cooking. It was his way of welcoming the new guys to the Company. Scotty was one of the original men of I Company, and he survived the war.

The one real character in the group was Cal Gilbert and most of his activities revolved around his many visits to the local pubs in Quorn and Loughborough.

He would walk into a pub and after a few beers would pound his fist on the bar and holler "I can lick EVERY man in the house!" Just like the way that the great boxer John L. Sullivan would do it. Only Cal used to say it wrong, it should have been "I can lick ANY man in the house!" One night, after too many beers, he uttered the famous words and most of the people in the bar hit him.

When he got back to camp he looked bad, so beat up. He had even been hit at least once on the top of his head with a beer stein. Next morning he had no way of getting up on his feet. When they fell in for roll-call, Force informed Sergeant Matash that Private Gilbert wasn't feeling too good. After inspecting the 'sick' man the Sergeant wondered how he ever got back to camp at all.

Cal was the platoon's bazooka man and Force was his assistant and that night they were going to make a practice jump. Being able to see is one of the important requirements in parachuting, and that's where Cal had a problem. Both his eyes were swollen shut. Needless to say, they made the practice jump but without Cal. Dennis Force took over as the bazooka man and William Martin became the assistant.

By the next night the swollen eyes had opened just a little and Private Gilbert went out on a pass. He had a way of grinning, always good natured, but he couldn't grin that night, although he tried very hard.

Dennis Force continues, "I bought a bicycle for £8 a couple of weeks after my arrival at Quorn. It was a good one. On my weekend passes I went everywhere, usually between Loughborough and Leicester. The bike was popular with the Sergeants during the week on night passes. Staff Sergeant James Robinson of the Second Platoon brought it back one night with one pedal in his pocket and the other bent out of shape.''

''I went on the bicycle one Sunday and rode down the path outside the wall and ventured through an iron turnstile gate into the garden towards the big house. I heard a horrible bark and got a glimpse of a huge bull mastif dog coming for me. He left me in no doubt that I was intruding on his territory. How I got through that turnstile gate at speed without a crash I'll never know. The dog, I found out many years later his name was Wallace, stopped at the gate and I never looked back.''

''On 1st September word was passed that all bicycles were to be put in the field outside the I Company area as we would be leaving Quorn the next day. The next morning we went to the airfield, briefed and issued with all combat rations and ammunition for a jump at Tournai, Belgium. On the 4th we turned in everything and returned to camp, the British in their rapid advance had taken the town and the surrounding territory.''

''Back in Quorn the local citizens were at the camp to welcome us back, but there were no bicycles. All had disappeared. Thirteen days later we went to Holland.''

Out of the replacements, John Lebednick was killed in action in the Ardennes. John Siam was still jumping as a sports parachutist in 1991 and a regular member of the 82nd Old Tymers Jump Team.

It was during the Sicily jump that Staff Sergeant James Robinson, together with an officer, Lieutenant Walter Kroener, were mis-dropped and landed many miles inland. Hiding by day and travelling by night they eventually rejoined the Regiment a week later.

It was the faithful Sergeant Charlie Matash who pulled Dennis Force through a hedgerow to safety and bandaged him up at Fosse, Belgium, after he was hit. As Dennis Force said many years later, ''Charlie was an outstanding man.''

Dennis Force is living in retirement with his wife, Betty, in Bremerton, Washington. They make frequent trips to Europe.

The Division held a review on the airfield at Stoughton, Leicester, on Friday, 11th August, when General Dwight Eisenhower took the salute and thanked the men for their efforts. After three combat jumps, and many casualties, the paratroopers felt sure that the war was nearly over and they would be going home. It was a warm day and to save the paratroopers from discomfort they were ordered to remove their helmets during the speeches.

In his speech Ike said, ''I've owed you a lot in the past and I imagine I'll owe you more in the future.''

These words were heard in silence, and when they realised that they were not going home, helmets started to be thrown down on the concrete runways in disappointment. The helmets hit the ground like a roar of thunder. Somebody remarked, ''This guy is not giving up until we're all dead.'' The officers had to quickly calm down the situation, but Eisenhower had the surprise of his life.

After the Review the senior officers invited Ike and General Lewis Brereton back for tea at their Headquarters at Glebe Mount in Oadby. What surprised General Gavin was the fact that Ike's chauffeur, Kay Summersby, also joined them. "Chauffeurs do not normally join their generals for tea," noted Gavin later.

After their return from Normandy the paratroopers stayed in Quorn for another two months, training replacements that had come to fill their depleted ranks. There were several false alarms when plans were made for a new airborne attack but the ground forces were moving too quickly and the targets were overrun.

A concert was held at the De Montfort Hall, Leicester, on Monday, 11th September and featured Glenn Miller and his band especially for the 82nd. Little did they know but six days later the Division would be in the thick of the action again, and within one month (4th October) Miller would be missing on his way to Paris, although it was not officially confirmed until December.

Jim Coyle received word that his brother, Joseph, who was in the 79th Division, was wounded in Normandy and was in hospital in England. When the Battalion Commander heard of this, he arranged a Jeep for Jim to visit his brother. He was just about to leave when the 505 were restricted and they loaded their equipment bundles for a trip to an airfield at Folkingham.

As Jim said, "I never expected the high command to set up an airborne operation that quickly. I got another shock when I found out where we were going."

On the 15th September, a Friday, they made the journey once more to the airfields for Operation Market Garden, the invasion of Holland. The orders to 'Chute Up' were given on the Sunday morning, the 17th, and at 10 o'clock the C-47's took off and headed east.

In fact, the 505th Parachute Infantry Regiment had only spent a total of a 170 days in Quorn. The impact of those few short days has lasted 50 years and will be talked about for generations to come.

While the 505 had been in Normandy her sister unit, the 504th Parachute Infantry Regiment had been held in reserve and were camped in Shady Lane, Evington. They had been held back in Italy, holding the line on the Anzio Beachhead at the request of General Mark Clark, and at the insistence of the Prime Minister, Winston Churchill. Clark was in desperate need of some battle hardened troops and he was reluctant to let them go, so the rest of the 82nd left for the United Kingdom without them.

Ridgway had pleaded with Clark to release the 504 so that they could be dropped into Normandy along with the 505. Clark's answer was brief and to the point. "Dear Matt," he wrote, "I need them."

Ridgway finally appealed to General George Marshall and he won the day. They arrived in England one month before D-Day, and it was then that Ridgway realised the problem. The 504's casualties had been very heavy and they urgently needed replacements. The Regiment had suffered the loss of 85 officers and 1021 enlisted men either killed or wounded.

Jim Gavin later wrote, "I met the 504 when it returned to the UK and I thought they appeared to be in fine spirits and in good shape. I personally was surprised that General Ridgway did not take them in. It would have made a tremendous difference to the Division. But I believe he had committed himself to the point that if they were not back by a certain time, he could not use them, and Mark Clark reluctantly let them go, but in General Ridgway's mind it was too late.''

Some of the key 504 men were attached to the other regiments for the Normandy invasion. Six of these men were killed in action.

After a two week period of de-briefing they were let loose in Leicester for some fun and relaxation before the retraining of the replacements began. Some of the men were suffering from scabies caught in Italy and it is reported that many Leicester girls suffered the same fate sooner or later.

One practice jump was code-named 'Operation Bumblebee' where a stiff ground wind swept over the drop zone.

Sergeant Albert Clark landed astride a hedge and strained his back. The Medical Officer suggested that an old fashioned hot bath would be the cure. The camp only had showers, but his girl friend, Kathleen, came to the rescue and Albert soothed his aching muscles in a bath at her parents home in nearby Oadby.

Clark returned to Oadby in 1946 and married Kathleen in the village church and took her back to California.

Captain Adam Komosa led his company out of the door of the leading plane. His parachute started oscillating violently in the wind, and he was unable to control it. He hit the ground with such a force that he found that he was completely paralysed from the neck down.

As he lay helpless on the ground the C-47's flew overhead disgorging the paratroopers. Equipment, such as helmets and weapons, broke loose from the jumpers and showered down. Komosa looking up could see the danger, as the other troopers got out of their harnesses the warnings were being shouted.

''Look out! M-1 coming down!'' But there was little he could do. The rifle plunged into the ground a few inches from his shoulder, and buried itself up to the trigger guard.

Adam Komosa spent several weeks in hospital until he learnt that the combat jump into Holland was on. He was not going to be left behind, but the doctors banned him from parachuting for six months. So he arranged to go in by glider, acting as a co-pilot.

When he arrived at the 504 Command Post near Nijmegen, Komosa looking at the situation map discovered that his glider had landed at the wrong landing zone. It was a lucky break as the correct one was in the hands of the Germans and the gliders were machine-gunned as they were landing.

Adam Komosa survived the war to lead his Company down Fifth Avenue in New York for the Victory Parade. He had given his troops strict orders not to break ranks. Marching along he heard his name being called by his former comrades, now civilians, watching from the sidewalks. It was his order, so he did not turn his head to acknowledge. It was a decision he has regretted ever since.

Don McKeage and his wife, Jennie, in England in 1984.

Dennis Force (left) and Richard Tedeschi making a return visit to Folkingham Airfield in 1987 from where some of the 505 left for the Market Garden Operation.

Holland —
the Market Garden Operation

At 13.00 hours on Sunday, 17th September, the 82nd Airborne Division parachuted into Holland near the small town of Groesbeek about one and a half miles from the German border. In all, they successfully brought in 7,467 paratroopers and Glider-borne men.

Gavin had given orders that the paratroopers should land as close to the anti-aircraft batteries as possible and knock them out quickly.

SERGEANT DON McKEAGE, F COMPANY, 505

He writes: "Finally, on Friday, 15th September, we were moved to Folkingham Airfield, Lincolnshire, for the attack on Holland. On Sunday at 10.00 hours the Second and Third Battalions took off in C-47's down the long single runway for a town called Groesbeek."

"The weather was perfect for the jump and it was a great landing. Many years later we learned that the Second Battalion had been mis-dropped. We had hit the wrong target, but it turned out that it was the best misdrop of the war. We took our objective, the flak tower at Molenberg, without much of a fanfare. On 19th September the Second Battalion headed into Nijmegen and the next day took part in the battle for the Nijmegen Road Bridge. It was a very hot fight, but like all the battles we came out on top, although with a terrible loss of life."

"As the men of F Company were heading into Nijmegen, working our way to the park and main highway bridge, we came under heavy enemy artillery fire. Word was passed that Private Arnold Palmer had been killed in the last artillery volley."

"Captain Robert H. Rosen halted the company in front of a Dutch residence. The lady of the house came out, telling Captain Rosen that she had a British flier hiding in the house for many months and that he would like to speak with one of the Americans. The Captain motioned for me to check the house, while this lady wrote down Rosen's name, rank etc."

"I entered this Dutch residence, the dining room table was moved, the carpet rolled up and a floor access panel removed. There hiding in a crawling space was the British flier being only allowed to come out of hiding at night. I assured him that we were in town to stay and within hours we would have the German troops routed. He was very happy and at last he would be returned to freedom."

"I rejoined the Company and we once again resumed our forward progress. Captain Rosen was killed the next afternoon at the park before the bridge."

"Twenty five years later I returned to Holland on 17th September 1969, with the Past President's Club tour. At a little airport just south of Nijmegen we were waiting for four plane loads of Airborne troopers from the Eighth Infantry Division to make a memorial jump. I saw a Dutch lady coming down the line talking to our people, as she came closer I heard her asking if anyone knew Captain Robert Rosen. I stepped forward and told her that I had known the Captain as he was my Company Commander twenty five years ago.''

''She told me how a very young trooper had stopped in front of her house, and while she talked with Rosen the young trooper had talked to the British flier they had hidden for many months under the house.''

''I told this fine lady that I was the young trooper and that Captain Rosen had been killed in the park the very next day. She said that it was wonderful meeting and talking to me again after all these years, but she had always hoped that she might, once again, meet Captain Rosen.''

''One incident that took place while we were on defence out in the dykes east of Nijmegen in October I shall always remember.''

''Private Robert Beckman, the First Platoon Bazooka man, had completely run out of socks. He said he was going back from the front line to a group of houses to see if he could find some socks. These houses were 'off limits' to us.''

''As he was entering one of the houses he was stopped by a familiar voice. General James Gavin had come walking up the road alone, as he so often did. He asked Private Beckman what he was doing back there in an 'off limits' area.''

''Beckman took off his jump boots and showed the General the condition of his feet with the worn out socks. Gavin agreed that something should be done, but looting in an 'off limits' area was not the answer. He ordered Beckman to get back to his platoon on the front and told him that he personally would see that he would receive some dry socks.''

''Early the next morning a Sergeant from Divisional Headquarters appeared at the F Company Command Post with a message and a pair of General Gavin's own mended socks for Private Beckman.''

''I delivered those socks to Beckman. He was later killed in action on 4th January 1945, in Belgium.''

PRIVATE CARL BECK, E COMPANY, 505

After his disastrous jump in Normandy, Beck was looking for a soft landing. He took off in the same plane as Sergeant Otis Sampsom and half way across the North Sea the C-47 lost an engine and the pilot turned back to England. On changing planes they found that they were all alone in the sky. When they arrived over the Drop Zone the area was black with smoke.

''We parachuted in and landed in a big field that had just been ploughed, it was the softest landing I ever made,'' he said later. They were able to rejoin E Company without much delay.

On 19th September, Beck and his buddy, Pete Hable, were working their way down to the Nijmegen Bridge.

''We went into the houses from the front and out the back, over the fence and into another house. Then out the front door, go across the street and into the front of another house. We did that all the way down to the bridge. In a second floor window we set up our light machine-gun on a table and waited for the order to open fire. The Jerries were down in the street.''

''Before the order came a British sniper opened up so we began shooting into a large group of Jerries. This is when I got hit. A shell came through the wall and a piece of shrapnel went into my mouth and came out of the left side of my head, taking everything with it. I woke up in the 119th General Hospital in England, nineteen days later. I didn't know were I was or what the hell had happened to me.''

''I know now that it was my Lieutenant, James Coyle, who saved my life by his prompt first aid.'' His great buddy, Pfc. Earl 'Pete' Hable was later killed in action in the Ardennes.

Forty seven years later Carl Beck still suffers great pain and receives continual treatment for his wounds. Throughout the years he has been fearless of any danger. He completed over 1,500 jumps as a sports parachutist, on one occasion breaking both knees due to a malfunction. He was using a borrowed parachute and found at the last moment he was unable to deploy it. Very near the ground he 'pulled' his reserve, which saved his life.

In 1984, at the 40th Anniversary celebrations in Normandy he had a parachute and jumpsuit specially made in the colours of red, white and blue. He used them both for an exhibition parachute jump in which some of the original 82nd veterans participated. Carl Beck cut a dashing figure and landed in front of a group of press photographers. The next day he was featured on the front pages of all the French newspapers.

Carl's friends were relieved when he packed his chute for the last time and retired in 1986.

CAPTAIN ROBERT 'DOC' FRANCO, 505

''My fourth combat jump was in Holland. I remember it was a glorious day, sunny and warm with no wind. Just right for a daylight operation.''

''The Second Battalion led the 505 into Holland. Colonel Vandervoort told us he wanted his Headquarters Company on the ground first — an unorthodox idea — so his machine-guns and mortars could start operating as soon as possible. The Medical Detachment, being part of HQ Company, shared the honour of jumping early.''

''There were flak towers in many places along the way. We could see people coming out of churches in the small towns. As we neared the Drop Zone there was enemy machine-gun fire from the ground. The jump was smooth, but we were receiving fire all the way down. A man near me, descending at the same speed, was hit. He screamed obscenities at his unknown assailant and promised to get him as soon as he reached the ground — he probably did.''

''Like all good jumpers I considered my chute sacred, but for the first time in my career, with that machine-gun fire whistling and snapping near my head, I stayed flat, got my knife and cut off my chute. By the time I was able to get on my hands and knees, and then move, I saw that our guys had rounded up about forty prisoners or so. Speed was always a trait of the 505, and on that Sunday, 17th September, no time was wasted.''

''The edge of the DZ was also the outskirts of Groesbeek. I quickly rounded up a few Aid men, found an empty house and went to work. I remember a young officer who had the misfortune of being present when a mortar shell containing white phosphorus exploded. He was not badly hurt but particles of the phosphorus imbedded themselves throughout his lower torso and his genitalia. The particles burned and smoldered and the lad was in agony. Luck was with us in the form of a bathtub. The sufferer was submerged in water, which shut off the oxygen, and the burning stopped. It was a bull-by-the-tail situation, and there was no way of letting the victim out without the phosphorus igniting again. Eventually someone found some Vaseline gauze and we were able to blob the stuff on the wounds and evacuate him.''

''Two days later we moved up into Nijmegen itself and prepared to attack the approaches of the bridge. I was in my Jeep moving north up one of those lovely tree-lined roads, now totally jammed with Bren gun carriers and personnel carriers of, I believe, the British Grenadier Guards. In front of one of the houses a group of old 'gaffers' gathered with their brass horns, trumpets, cornets, trombones and a tuba and started to play with the greatest imaginable discord. A young Guards officer in the vehicle in front of mine caught my eye and smiled. 'A bit grim, what?' he said. It was a British understatement.''

''A couple of hours later my driver and I were in the city about one hundred and fifty metres away from the guns on the roundabout on the bridge approach. The tracers from the 88mm guns went down the street just above the bumper to bumper line of tanks. The din was, as usual, terrific. My young driver yelled at me to look. Three British tank men were sitting in the middle of the road around a can of gasoline soaked sand, that had been lit, and they were brewing their tea. This mode of combustion was apparently popular in the desert.''

''I think we took the bridge the next day and many of us went across as soon as we could. We lost quite a number of men in that little footage in front of four 88s, two of them being my Aid men.''

''Shortly after I saw General Browning who had come to see Colonel Ben Vandervoort, and the war correspondent Cornelius Ryan. It was an exciting time for me.''

''I ducked into a small apartment at street level during the fighting and a nice old couple let me use it as an Aid Station. A year or so ago a friend sent a Dutch language book about the battle and I was surprised to find that my name was mentioned in it a couple of times.''

''After it became clear that Arnhem would not be ours, we stayed in the Nijmegen area as occupation troops with some patrol responsibilities. We made many friends. What was sad was the information that after the battle the Dutch people in the German held territory were brutally treated, even more so than before.''

SERGEANT CHARLES KAISER, THIRD BATTALION, 505

There were two Kaisers in the Third Battalion. One was Charles and the other, Major James L. Kaiser.

"We were always getting each other's mail," recalled Charles. "One day the Major came round and told us that Patton had stopped and we could not get any supplies through. We would have to live off the land. My answer was, if the Major was hungry you can come back and have some chicken with us. We had fourteen chickens in the pot. He came back."

"One advantage of having a number of farm boys in your outfit was that they were experts at slaughtering livestock and cutting up the meat. We never went hungry."

PFC. FRANK BILICH, D COMPANY, 505

"Holland for me was full of incidents. I never knew the full story about one of them until many years later."

"When we landed on the Drop Zone our Platoon picked up a bazooka. Across the road there was a house with Germans running all over it. Pfc. George Fotovich shouted to me to put a round through the house window. I put the bazooka to my shoulder and took aim. Fotovich put the round in, tapped me on the shoulder and I pulled the trigger."

"Bullseye, straight through the window — nothing happened — no explosion, nothing. He said, 'Try again.' The second round did not explode either. What the hell's the matter? I didn't know the full story until I met Tommy McClean many years later in New York."

"Tommy McClean, a Lieutenant from our Company says to me, 'Remember those Bazooka shots you put through that window in Holland. You ought to kiss the day that those two shots didn't go off.'"

"His platoon crossed that road to the house to wipe the Germans out but found they had escaped. The house was full of women and children, kneeling and praying. The bazooka rounds had come through the window, hit the soft plaster wall and dropped to the floor. If they had exploded they would have killed everyone in there."

"What a stroke of luck, you just never know what has happened. Was it luck or was it a miracle, you tell me?"

"We moved on into Nijmegen until we hit the stiff German resistance. We occupied a row of houses on the Oude Wertz, the second or third one down, and took over the upstairs rooms. Captain Taylor Smith told us to stay there, nobody was pulling out. 'We are going to hold this position,' were his last words."

"All of a sudden the Germans were all over the nearby railroad track and we were cut off. What we didn't know was, the Company had all pulled back leaving us to our fate."

"There were three of us, myself, Bill McMandon and another guy. With us were three members of a Dutch family, the mother who spoke English and her two young daughters. Around my neck I had my dog-tags and a rosary my mother had given me. The Dutch lady asked if I was Catholic."

"The Germans were getting very close so we went down into the basement from the kitchen. Those houses were built so there was another door and stairs from the basement that came up under the back porch, into a fenced back yard.''

"All three of us were hiding under the stairs as a German officer brought his Platoon into the building. Twice he came halfway down the stairs from the kitchen to give orders to the Dutch lady to fix coffee or something. By then the shooting had died down and it was all quiet.''

"Everytime he came down we thought about shooting him, but the rest would have got us. Her daughters were against a wall — she had only one small light on, and we had not been spotted in the darkness.''

"By about 2.30 in the morning all was quiet. We knew there was a guard on the back porch. If we stayed until daylight they would soon find us. The three of us had a whispered council of war. It was decided that we would make a run for it just before dawn. We talked about who was going first, second and last. The way out would be up the stairs and out under the porch.''

"Again the officer came half way down the stairs from the kitchen and asked for coffee. After he went back we decided that this was our chance, we came up to the backyard and saw a wooden fence with a gate blocking our path.''

"McMandon took off, hit the gate with such a force that it burst open, and went through, I followed. There was a call to halt in German and somebody fired some shots. We were all through the gate and running down the backs of those houses, running until our lungs were ready to explode.''

"We ran across a road and right over an E Company machine-gun position and fell into a ditch. All the E Company boys could say was, 'Where the hell have you come from?' We didn't care, we had made it.''

"Later that day, 19th September, First Lieutenant Waverly W. Wray yelled at Pfc. 'Barney' Silanskis, Pfc. Joe Rajca, Pfc. John Rasumich and Private Jacob Herman to follow him to the railroad track leading to the rail bridge. As Wray raised his head over the track he was killed by a sniper's bullet in the head, fired from a signal tower. Herman was also killed. Silanskis had a bullet ricochet into his mouth off a tank car. He said later that he had his mouth open shouting orders. Luckily its force was almost spent and it bounced off a tooth, turned up into his cheek bone and lodged under his eye, leaving him with a permanent crooked smile to this day.''

"That Dutch family's name was Palmen. The girls were Trudie (or Judie) and Theresa. The next day Charlie Miller rescued three crew members from a British tank that was on fire outside their house. Three times he went into that burning tank and the Germans were shooting at him all the time. He took the wounded men into the Palmen's house. Charlie should have had a medal for that. They said they would write him up for one, but he never heard any more about it.''

"After the battle for the bridge was over we drove out of Nijmegen in trucks, down the main road, and I saw the two Palmen girls on the sidewalk. They recognised me and hollered at me — 'Thank you, Thank you.' Since the war I have made several attempts to find them, without success.''

Frank Bilich (left) and John Siam at The American Military Cemetery at Madingley, Cambridge, in 1989.

STAFF SERGEANT PAUL NUNAN, D COMPANY, 505

"Lieutenant Wray was shot and killed in the railroad yard in Nijmegen on the afternoon of 19th September. I was to be wounded myself a few hours later."

"As I was moving towards the railyard with my Platoon and Lieutenant O.B Carr, our Platoon Leader; Pfc. Frank Silanskis approached me holding a hand over his mouth. Blood was seeping between his fingers. He informed me that Wray had been killed."

"Frank had a large lump on his left cheekbone, but the skin was unbroken. I examined his mouth and saw that the blood was coming from between his lip and the gum. Frank later told me the lump in his cheek was a bullet."

"The Medics made an incision from the outside over the bullet. Apparently the bullet had ricocheted, striking him between the front teeth and the inside of his lip, coming to rest over his cheekbone."

"I was hit later in the day when I tangled with an anti-aircraft gun and its crew. Using a British made Gammon grenade and a Thompson sub-machine-gun, the issue was decided in my favour at the cost of a fair sized hole in my left leg. I was subsequently evacuated by ambulance, truck and hospital train all the way back to Normandy, near where I had landed on D-Day just over three months before."

"I had what we Yanks called a 'million dollar wound'. Bad enough to keep you out of combat for a while, without being permanently disabling."

FIRST SERGEANT JOHN RABIG, D COMPANY, 505

"As we drove out of Groesbeek from the Drop Zone on British tanks the Dutch people were crowded along the sides of the road. The nearer we got to Nijmegen, the fewer people there were. Soon the people just disappeared and we were smart enough to know that the shooting would soon start — and it did."

"Soon we were in the thick of it. I kept behind one of the tanks which was shielding me, I felt safe enough. I began to see crazy Dutch boys, young kids about 16 or 17, with an orange band on their arms, with guns, risking their lives. I tried to get them to go back but they took no notice."

"All hell broke loose on the approach to the bridge. I learnt later that six hundred Dutchmen had volunteered their services to General Gavin, using the weapons from our dead and wounded."

One of those six hundred Dutchmen who fought with the 82nd during those critical days was Agurdus Leegsma, a young man who was living in Nijmegen. He volunteered to join G Company of the 508th Parachute Infantry Regiment as a rifleman and was immediately taken under their wing. Nobody could pronouce his name so the troopers called him 'Gas'.

On 23rd September 'Gas' was wounded during the Company's attack on Thorensche Nolen and was taken to a field hospital for treatment. He soon returned to take his place in the line with G Company north of the river.

Agurdus Leegsma made such an impression with the troopers that President Roosevelt awarded him the Medal of Freedom together with a

Purple Heart. Queen Wilhelmina presented him with a Bronze Cross on behalf of the Dutch Government. This was not to be the end of his military service, for in April 1945 the Dutch Army sent him for officer's training to the Military Academy at Sandhurst, England. Before retiring in 1962 he had reached the rank of Captain in the Dutch Army.

PFC. GORDON A. WALBERG, 80th AIRBORNE ANTI-TANK BATTN

Pfc. Gordon A. Walberg was a member of A Battery of the 80th Airborne Anti-Tank Battalion garrisoned on the Leicester Race Course at Oadby. Instead of horse racing during the war it became a home for various military units.

Just across the road was the house, Glebe Mount, the Headquarters of General Matthew Ridgway. It was one of the duties of the Battalion to supply guards for the Division's Commander.

Gordon Walberg takes up the story. "On Sunday, 17th September, 1944, all plans and briefings were over. For the past two days we had been at an airfield at Balderton, just south of the town of Newark, Nottinghamshire. Our mission was to fly in a CG-4A Combat Glider in Operation Market Garden and land near Groesbeek."

"Our Glider crew included Flying Officer G.W. Fuller as pilot, Corporal Ernie Seddan, Pfc. Robert Hayden and myself. Our cargo was our 57mm Anti-Tank gun and the A-7 Jeep was to follow in another glider, which with luck, we would locate at the same Landing Zone."

Editor's note: Records show that the take-off from Balderton for the 50 C-47's of the 439th Tactical Air Group towing the heavily laden gliders nearly met with disaster. A few nasty moments arose when the 440th TAG aircraft from Fulbeck flew over the Balderton area and caused confusion as the aircraft struggled to gain height. This problem was unseen by Gordon Walberg.

He continues. "I was in one of the first gliders to take off and when the formation was complete we headed out over the North Sea. It was a beautiful Sunday afternoon but there was sadness when we witnessed planes and gliders being shot down over the Walchren Islands and Schouwen Province."

"After three hours in the air we cut loose our three hundred foot nylon rope and the nose of the glider shot straight up. The pilot trimmed it back and we landed at a speed of 94 miles per hour. The impact with the sugar beet field was rough and the pilot released the small drogue parachute on the tail to reduce our speed. We slid across the Landing Zone wrapping fence posts and smooth wire around both the chute and the tail plane."

"We came to a halt with our cargo intact and with caution we crawled out and looked for the enemy. Only a small amount of gunfire was being heard."

"My guess is that we landed in a field not far from St. Antoniusweg and the approach to Klooster Church."

"Our first casualty was Pfc. Charles M. O'Leary when he was killed by gun fire as he left his glider. This would be the Battalion's first casualty of many during our next fifty-nine days."

"We got the nose of the glider unlatched and unloaded the anti-tank gun. Somebody went in search of our A-7 Jeep. By this time the sky was filled with an amazing sight of C-47's, CG-4A's and paratroopers floating to earth.''

''As the Jeep backed up to hook up our 57mm gun I signalled to Pfc. Robert 'Moose' Hayden to search out the small farm house at the edge of the field. As we left the Landing Zone I remember looking back to see if all was still going alright and just thankful to be down safe and sound.''

''In Groesbeek we chased two German Luftwaffe officers into the Locomotief Hotel. Pfc. Kenny Loughman went inside, leaving me by the tall windows outside to block their escape. Kenny fired four or five rounds in the door area and the Germans surrendered.''

Editor's Note: Research has found that it was not the Locomotief Hotel where this incident took place. Gerri Driessen is certain that it was not his hotel. Gerri was about eight years old at the time and was watching the events from a window of his family's hotel. Further enquiries point to the Hotel Pension or, as it was known, the Bond Hotel which was on the opposite side of the road, and on the north side of the railway crossing. This hotel was destroyed in 1944 and never rebuilt. The site is now occupied by a bank.

''On the second day we received word that we could expect the German tanks to come down from Nijmegen to try to cut us off. We set up our anti-tank gun along the highway and had to cut down several trees to give ourselves a better field of fire.''

''In the warm sun of a beautiful day we rested by the gun until I was rudely awakened by a grenade that came sailing through the air. As I stood up to see who had thrown it, an explosion in a tree above me knocked me on my back. I hollered out for everybody to get the culprit but another grenade exploded and knocked me down again. By this time I was getting smart and stopped looking for the enemy and I vaulted over a fence with my rifle.''

''Pfc. Malcolm Neel was with me at that time. Since the war I lost contact with him and forty-seven years later we met again at the All Ohio Day Reunion in Canton.''

''The last grenade explosion set fire to our supplies, ammunition and camouflage net. For a while we were pinned down by the exploding of our own shells. Some of the 505 Parachute Infantry boys came along and helped by smothering the exploding ammunition with sand.''

''Our tactics now consisted of going to wherever we were needed to stop the Germans from mounting their counter-attacks.''

''We knew that we had to hold on to Berg en Dal, the highest ground in the area. As we approached the Hotel Hamer we felt we were being observed and I mentioned this to Herbert Moline, a boy from Chicago. Mortar fire began to fall on us and we jumped into a foxhole that was already dug in the parking lot.''

''The two of us looked very odd in this place but the mortar fire was very accurate and we had no choice. A few paratroopers searched the Hotel Groat de Bergendal and found and killed an enemy observer in the tower. He could see where we were and was able to call for artillery and mortar fire when needed.''

The Hotel Groat de Bergendal and tower were demolished in the 1960s.

''The following morning we heard of another probe by the German tanks in the Beek area. We chose the high ground overlooking the town, facing the German border. As we moved into position we came across a wounded Glider Pilot who had been shot by a machine-gun. I counted at least five wounds in him.''

''The pilot, his voice was very weak, asked if we could help him. I told the Jeep driver, I believe it was C. Perry, to unhook the gun and we carefully lifted the wounded man onto the Jeep and Perry went in search of an Aid Station. We hoped the pilot made it but I was doubtful with so many wounds.''

''We met some local Dutch people by the name of Schretlen and they gave us food and drink.''

''It was decided that if an attack came it would be from the flatlands in front of Beek, so we relocated our gun. Our new location was in front of the Bad Hotel across the street from the Hotel Rusthof. In preparing for an attack we tore the bricks out of the pavement and used the sand to fill one hundred and fifty sandbags.''

''Today visitors would be able to locate our gun pit by the discoloured bricks used to repair the road after we left the area.''

''A British tank came up behind us and the Tank Commander asked us to show him where we thought the Germans were located. He then proceeded to shoot up everything he could and the Germans returned the fire. They had better observation than we did. Their first shot hit a 508th Parachute Infantry Regiment's heavy mortar pit, knocking out the mortar, killing two and wounding another. The next hit was on a British M-4 tank and some of the crew were killed.''

''One round hit the lounge of the Bad Hotel where we had been eating a short time before and blew out part of the heavy glass window. Corporal Ernie Seddan jumped up and finished knocking out the rest of the plate glass window because he did not want more glass raining down on our foxholes. Then our Jeep was hit — which we had tried to hide — and the tyres caught fire.''

''The town of Beek was now in ruins, ringing with the screams of wounded civilians and military. Private Charles E Kidd, one of our crew, said he would move out to the left and see if he could protect our flank. Ernie Seddan and I were wondering how long we could hold out.''

''Ernie, a Normandy veteran, suggested we place two grenades in the front edge of the foxholes along with extra clips of M-1 ammunition. We took our trench knives and stuck then in the ground to our front.''

''About this time a 508 trooper with an asbestos glove on his hand holding a still hot 30 calibre machine-gun came by and told us there was nothing on our left except Germans. I took the firing pin from the 57mm and started up the hill towards Berg en Dal.''

''On the way we located one of the wounded 508 mortar crew. Robert Hayden had picked up an abandoned 45 pistol and as the wounded man was unarmed, Hayden gave him the 45.''

''We knew that we would get our 'ears chewed off' for losing the 57mm gun — and we did. Lt. Colonel Louis Mendez, the 508's Third Battalion

Commander, gave us hell, but backed off a little when we explained that there were only two of us left and without a Jeep were unable to move 2600 pounds of equipment by ourselves. He said H Company, 508, would retake the town of Beek and we were to stand by.''

''At 02.30 we were sent with a Jeep and driver and told to go back into Beek and recover our 57mm gun and anything else we could locate. At the time I told Ernie Seddan that I doubted if the Germans would still be in Beek, and that turned out to be the fact. We pulled our gun out and were then assigned to protect the two Nijmegen bridges across the Waal River from German river craft.''

''On the night of 28th September, or early on the 29th, German frogmen swam down the river and were able to place charges and blow a span out of the railroad bridge into the river.''

''We now know a few names of those German frogmen. They were, Heinz Bretscheider, Jager, Gert Olle, Wolchendorf and Hauptman Hellmer. Out of the original twelve, only two landed safely near Aachen. The other ten were either killed or captured.''

Because of the casualties, Gordon Walberg took charge of a Squad after the first week in Holland. His Commanding Officer, Captain Arthur G. Kroos, previously mentioned as Ridgway's Aide in Normandy, had been shot down in his glider and taken prisoner.

PRIVATE ALBERT 'ABIE' MALLIS, B COMPANY, 505

As the first C-47's flew low over the Drop Zone, Albert 'Abie' Mallis, a young eighteen year old Jewish boy in B Company, jumped out of the door with his Platoon. ''We were so low, about 400 feet, that we hit the ground almost immediately. We must have been in the first five or six planes as I watched the whole Regiment jump above us. Realising the importance of the moment, I took out my knife and cut three panels from my chute and cut off the pilot chute. I folded them up and put them in one of my leg pockets of my jumpsuit. They were going to be the souvenirs of my first combat jump.''

Mallis, 5 foot 5 inches tall, weighed 132 pounds, but when he stepped aboard that aircraft with all his equipment he topped 204 pounds. ''Two guys were holding me up because I was liable to fall over. I carried a folding carbine and as many Clarks chocolate bars from the PX as I could pack. They kept me going for days. I was scared, and worried that my harmonica would break.''

B Company troopers would remember that they were usually conned by a little Jewish guy into carrying heavy machine-gun parts so Abie could play his harmonica, even when marching through the snow in the Battle of the Bulge.

'Abie' Mallis came into B Company in July, 1944, as a replacement after D-Day. B Company had suffered heavy losses in Normandy because they were misdropped, miles from their target. 'Abie' never knew of these Normandy problems until many years later.

''All I knew, these were a bunch of very tough customers. They put me in a machine-gun team as the ammunition carrier. Corporal Edward Haag was in charge. As soon as we landed, Lieutenant Stanley Weinberg and my Platoon were ordered to set up a road block on a hill at Plasmolen. For five days we seemed to be separated from the rest of the Company.''

''We began to receive heavy fire from the 88's and Nebelwerfers, the 'screaming meemies', and around the 20th we had a direct hit on our emplacement. Edward Haag and the other guys were killed. I was the only guy that got out.''

''Stanley Weinberg saved my life on many occasions and I shall be eternally grateful to him for looking after me. He was a quiet, modest man who was always taking photographs. He seemed unaware of the danger to himself as he walked around the foxholes, with shells blowing all over the joint, as he was telling his men to get down.''

''I visited him after the war. He had a haberdashery shop in New Jersey. He died in 1983.''

''When we were not in the line we were billeted in the Groote Muschenberg Hotel in Beek. I remember one day walking back from Nijmegen with John Finnigan, rolling a barrel of Dutch beer all the way.''

''I'll always remember Finnigan's address in New York. It was 7 Central Park West. His father must have been very wealthy.''

''We patrolled into Germany, the fighting was tough and B Company gave no quarter. We had a Sergeant who had been in the Company since its inception, he was Manley Peoples. He was a hard man who took no prisoners. Another Sergeant I remember was Mike Petrillo. After the war he owned a Tavern in Denver, Colorado.''

''I was never really prepared for some of the things I saw. I do recall a situation which involved **** who walked away into the woods with five prisoners. We heard firing and **** walked back alone. Nobody said nothing. It scared the hell out me.''

''When we jumped we only carried enough rations for about five days, after that we had to live off the land. One day I was ordered to go shoot a pig we had spotted. I had to drag it behind me while I was crawling on my hands and knees because I was under fire. Being Jewish I had never eaten pork in my life, so this was the first time — and I enjoyed it. Ever since then I have eaten pork.''

'Abie' Mallas received the Bronze Star for his bravery in Holland.

During the Battle of the Bulge he was wounded in the arm, and while in hospital he had a great idea. ''I obtained a GI fifty gallon can, one with the handles, and filled it half full of fresh snow, poured sugar into it and stirred it around until it had nearly melted. In the K-Ration packs there were small bars of chocolate and I collected scores of them, they were melted, and put in the mixture. That day every person on the ward, about forty or fifty people, was given a cup of 'Abie's' own home made chocolate ice cream.''

''Three days later there was great confusion as everbody had been crapping for two days and there was a great queue for the bed pans.''

What 'Abie' hadn't realised was, the chocolate in the K-Ration packs was Ex-lax, a well known brand of laxative medicine. ''I swear it, I did not know it was Ex-lax, but nobody believed me.''

He returned to B Company but did not fight again. The U.S. Army had issued orders that Jewish troopers who had the letter 'H' (Hebrew) on their dogtags would not be sent forward. There were reports that it had created problems when Jews had been captured, so none were to be allowed to return to the line so near to the end of the war.

Mallis was to spend four months with the Company in Berlin before he returned to the States. "I was just glad be alive every day," said 'Abie'.

****

The 82nd Divisional Artillery Battery had a Private by the name of Malulavich who had never a clear idea of officer's insignias, especially those of the British Army.

While on duty at the Landing Zone as the gliders landed, he yelled to a British Officer, "Let's borrow your field glasses a minute, Joe!" The officer duly handed over his glasses to the GI and when he had seen what he wanted he tossed them back with a "Thanks Pop!"

Malulavich then took off, leaving an astounded Lieutenant General Frederick Browning, Commander of Market Operation, the airborne assault, to put his field glasses back in their case.

FIRST LIEUTENANT JAMES J. COYLE
E COMPANY, 505

This seemed an extremely risky mission to me but Lieutenants were not consulted in the planning. One good element of the operation was that we were to jump in daylight at about 13.00 hours on 17th September. I felt a little better about the daylight jump for two reasons: one, there was no room for night time navigational errors on this operation, and two, we were promised fighter escort all the way to the Drop Zone.

After a day of briefing, going over the maps of E Company's initial mission, we once again loaded our bundles under the C-47s and on a beautiful Sunday morning, 17th September, 1944, we took off for Holland. As we taxied out to the runway, I saw Lieutenant 'Pete' Peterson hobbling alongside the plane waving goodbye.

Our flight into Holland was the most impressive sight I can remember from World War Two. There were over two thousand planes and gliders involved in the fly-in. I could see hundreds of them from my position next to the door of my plane. At one point, we flew under and parallel to a formation of gliders being towed by different types of British bombers that I had never seen before. We were flying slightly faster than they were and yet it seemed like an hour before we passed them.

I could also see American P-38 fighter planes flying around the formations and saw one dive at what must have been an enemy anti-aircraft battery. I could see no anti-aircraft fire, although I learnt later that quite a few C-47s were shot down.

For a long time we flew over areas that were flooded, miles of fields covered with water with the cattle crowding on any high ground that was available to them. I recall praying that there would be no flooded areas near our Drop Zone as some of the men in Normandy had landed in areas which the Germans had flooded and they drowned before they could get out of their chutes. As we flew nearer to Groesbeek, I was relieved to see there was no sign of water.

We were flying at only one thousand feet, and shortly before we came to our DZ we flew over an isolated Convent in the countryside. The nuns had all come out in the courtyard and were waving to us as we flew by. As I waved back, I wondered what they would think if they knew that we would be jumping not too many miles away and the war was about to catch up with them. They made such a peaceful picture as they waved their aprons until I could no longer see them.

A large city came into view which I took to be Nijmegen and we turned in a broad circle to the south. As we swung around to the north again, the red light came on and I gave the familiar commands to 'Stand up' and 'Hook up', etc. As I stood in the door I could see that we were flying over large open ploughed fields and thought that at least we should have a soft landing.

Suddenly, there was a large orange and black burst of ack-ack between my plane and the plane flying right across from us in the formation. I could hear shrapnel whizz past the door over the noise of the engines. As far as I could tell our plane was not hit but there were two or three more bursts between the planes as we flew on.

I could not understand how they could train large guns and follow us at an altitude of only six hundred feet. About the time I was sure that the next burst would hit us, the green light came on and we jumped.

As soon as my chute opened, I looked down and I saw a large tent beneath me which looked like one of our hospital tents I had been in in Sicily. I soon discovered that this was no hospital tent! Enemy soldiers came streaming out of the tent and started running towards 20mm ack-ack guns which were mounted on poles.

My chute drifted away but one of the German soldiers was running right for the spot where I thought I would land. I drew my .45 pistol and tried to get a shot at him but my parachute was oscillating. I was aiming at the sky as often as I was aiming at the ground. I put my pistol back in the holster as I was sure I would drop it when I hit. When I did land I struggled to my knees and drew my pistol again. The German was no more than 15 feet away, running on a hard path that crossed the ploughed field.

Just as I was about to shoot at him he threw away his rifle, then his helmet and I saw he was a kid of about seventeen or eighteen years old. I also realised that he had completely panicked. He just ran past me without looking at me, although I knew that he knew that I had landed almost on top of him. I didn't have the heart to shoot him.

Paratroopers were pretty helpless when they hit the ground and I realised that if he had kept his wits, and kept his rifle, he could have killed me easily. It was a fair trade.

I laid my pistol on the ground beside me where it would be handy if any other Germans that I had seen run out of the tent came my way while I was getting out of my parachute harness, but none did.

Apparently none of them had fired their ack-ack guns and when I looked up I realised why. The sky was full of parachutes. They must have thought that the entire American army had jumped right on top of them, and part of it — E Company 505 — had.

We were able to assemble quickly. Although the DZ was almost a mile square, it was flat and open and one could see it all. I saw one C-47 crash in flames at the far end. We were not able to locate Sergeant Otis Sampson's planeload of men and I was afraid that he and the First Platoon 60mm mortar squad might have been shot down.

The order came to move out to take our objective, the high ground north east of Groesbeek. As we left the DZ we passed near a large concrete flak tower and several men in the Battalion column were taking shots at it, but I am sure there were no enemy troops in it by then.

When I returned to Groesbeek in 1984 I was able to locate the DZ with the aid of a Dutch guide. When I mentioned the tower he told me that it had finally been torn down the year before and showed me the circular foundations which still remained.

As we approached the high ridgeline that we were to attack I realised that it could be a difficult assault. There was some low brush but no cover from any enemy fire that might come down the hill. We moved rapidly, although it was a hard climb with all the equipment we carried.

We reached the crest without being fired on. At the top we found a number of small barracks, all empty, with small fires going and warm food on the stoves. I saw no weapons or combat equipment anywhere. It appeared to me that the troops who had occupied these barracks were from the Todt Battalion, a work group, which had simply fled as we came up the hill.

I could not believe that the Germans did not have a machine-gun or artillery on the ridge. It was the only high ground in the area and they did not defend it.

We set up a Company perimeter on the hill. In a little over an hour Sergeant Sampson came climbing the hill with his mortar squad and the rest of his stick. His C-47 had turned back to England with engine trouble. After transferring the bundles and his men to another plane, they had taken off immediately for Holland again. I was very relieved to see him and the mortar squad, and quite surprised that he was able to rejoin the Company after only a delay of an hour or two.

E Company held this hill position for the night. A railroad line went through the position of one of the platoons. During the night a train went down the line. No one was expecting anything like this to happen and the men were so surprised that they let the train go though without firing a shot.

They were so chagrined when they recovered from their shock that they set up machine-guns and a bazooka covering the tracks. About an hour later another train came roaring along, but this time E Company hit it with a bazooka rocket and stopped it cold. I was glad that the First Platoon was not involved in this because E Company never heard the end of it.

Next day at about 12.00 hours we received orders to attack the city of Nijmegen. We hiked for three or four miles and as we came to the outskirts of the city we met a column of British tanks from the Guards Division. I was relieved to see that the British 30 Corps had reached Nijmegen.

Looking back towards the south, the road was full of tanks and Bren gun carriers as far as the eye could see. This was a reassuring sight. I was surprised that the tanks were American Shermans, but the guns had been replaced by British 17 pounders, a long cannon with muzzle brakes that I had never seen before.

We came into the city like a Victory Parade. The Dutch people lined the roads in crowds that cheered us on our way. Captain James J. Smith, the Company Commander, informed us that E Company was to be the lead Company in the attack on the Nijmegen Bridge across the Waal River, and the First Platoon would lead the assault.

As we moved through the city towards the bridge, a Dutchman came up to me and asked me, in English, for a cigarette. I gave him a few and asked if he was familiar with the area at the bridge approach, and he said he was. I asked him if there were many German soldiers there and he replied that there were a great many in Hunner Park in front of the bridge.

However, when I asked him if there were anti-tank guns in the German defence position, he said there were none. I felt that with all the British Armour, we could handle the enemy infantry. He was correct about the large number of enemy forces in the area, but not about the absence of anti-tank guns.

On approaching the last houses before the open area in front of the bridge, the lead tank began firing its cannon. The roar was deafening and I am sure they were not firing at any particular target but to pin the enemy down. I was moving up alongside the third tank in the column. When I cleared the last house and could see the bridge, I got quite a shock. I didn't expect it to be so large. (I learnt after the war that it was the largest single-span bridge in Europe).

As I moved up the street to the park the two tanks right in front of me exploded and caught fire. The third tank next to me went into reverse and backed up about fifty feet to the houses we had just left. I still could not see any enemy anti-tank guns or troops, but I and a few of my men were left out in the open with no support.

I went storming back to the third tank shouting at the commander to get back with us. He said he was hit — I told him he was not hit as I could not see a mark on the tank. A British sergeant jumped out of the tank and said, "What's that then, mate?" pointing to a large hole on the other side of the turret which I had not seen. I felt about two feet tall. I don't know how the tank took that hit without suffering any wounded or catching fire.

I could see that the tanks were not going to make a move at that point and I was trying to figure a way to get into a position where I could observe the situation without being spotted. Just then an elderly man and woman came out of the back door of one of the houses on my left which faced the park and ran as fast as they could back the way we had come. I realised that if I could get the men in the second floor front rooms of the row of attached houses, we would be able to observe and fire on the enemy.

I moved the platoon quickly into two of the buildings cautioning them not to open fire before I gave the command. I knew that as soon as we opened fire we would receive heavy fire in return. I hoped that we would be able to spot the anti-tank guns and knock them out so the tanks and the rest of the Battalion could advance on the bridge.

The men kept back from the windows so they would not be seen by the enemy and set up their machine-guns on tables near the front windows of two of the adjacent buildings. I could see German soldiers streaming across the bridge from the other side on foot and on bicycles. It was difficult to keep the men from opening fire because I wanted to get as many men in a firing position as possible before we gave our location away.

The Germans had no idea we were there. I knew this for certain when a crew man-handled a 57mm anti-tank gun out of the park and proceeded to set it up in the street not thirty feet in front of us, pointing it up the street to our right where the tanks had been knocked out.

Lt. Colonel Benjamin Vandervoort, the Battalion Commanding Officer, and Captain Bill Harris, the S-3 (Plans and Training), came into the room where I was setting up our position. I explained my plan to him and he approved. He saw the Germans coming over the bridge and the anti-tank gun right in front of us. I told him I knew we could knock out the gun as soon as we opened fire. I told the Colonel I would hold our fire for five minutes. He agreed and would try and move the British tanks forward when we opened up. Then he left to contact the British Commander.

Just before the five minutes were up, someone opened fire from the building next door (I later learned that a British soldier had walked into the room where our men were waiting and seeing the Germans in the street in front of us, opened fire on his own). I immediately had the men in our house open fire with the machine-gun and Browning Automatic Rifle and Pfc. John Keller knocked out the anti-tank gun with a rifle grenade.

We had only been firing for a minute when there was a terrific explosion in the room and it filled with plaster dust, blinding everyone. When it cleared I could see that an anti-tank shell had come through the wall from the room in the house next door on our left and continued through the wall to the house on our right. By some miracle, the only man hit was Private Carl Beck, but he was seriously wounded in the left side on his head and face. We pulled him to the back of the house and some men got him out to the backyard where the Medics could pick him up.

Pfc. Clyde Rickert and I then manned the machine-gun and reopened fire but we could not see exactly where the anti-tank gun firing from our left was located. Just as I realised that tracer rounds included in the ammunition were pin-pointing our position for the enemy, another shell burst into the room from the left, hit the wall on our right, and fell to the floor in the room. We could not continue firing and we moved back out of the front room.

I went to the front room next door where the other squad of my men were to check them out. No E Company men were hit, but a British observer with a radio who had moved into our position without my knowledge, had been killed by concussion when the shell had gone through that room. He did not have a mark on him.

It had now grown dark and we received word that the attack was being held up for the night and that we were to hold our position. Enemy fire had stopped and I placed men in three of the houses on the ground floor to prevent enemy infiltrators from getting into the position.

I was in the upper front room shortly after dark observing the enemy area in front of us as best I could. Suddenly a British tank opened fire across my front from the right and a German tank replied from my left. I don't know how they could see each other in the dark, but a terrific cross-fire of heavy calibre tracers continued for almost five minutes. When the firing ceased, I saw that the tracer fire had set a public building in the park on fire and I could now observe the area to my front by its light.

Next day I saw the German tank, an old French model, knocked out near the traffic circle to the left of our position.

The Company runner came and gave me a message to report to the E Company Command Post located about two blocks behind the First Platoon's position. When I got there, the C.O. asked me to plot my platoon's position on the Company overlay. I had just completed the map when my Platoon runner came in with the information that a patrol was moving in front of our area. The men guessed the patrol was British and had not fired on it, but others thought it was an enemy patrol.

I returned to the Platoon and went to the front of the house where Sergeant Ben Popilsky was observing from the doorway. He reported that two men had walked past on the sidewalk earlier but he thought they were British tankers. Just then the two returned and I could see in the light of the burning building that they wore the helmets and smocks of German paratroopers.

Polilsky and I opened fire with our Thompson sub-machine-guns. One of the Germans went down but the other ran to our left and got behind a tree. He yelled at us in German, and Ben who understood German said he was asking if he could come back and help his comrade. I told Ben to tell him that we would take care of his comrade who was groaning on the sidewalk. When Popilsky yelled back, I realised that Ben was speaking Yiddish to the German.

The German then called us "Verdamt Americanishe Schweinhunts", and we called him a "Kraut Bastard". I wanted the wounded German as a prisoner and I was not about to let the other man come back and pick us off in the doorway now that he knew exactly where we were. He finally ran away, but when we crawled out to get the wounded German we discovered that he had died.

Later that night another German came right up to the window of a building where Pfc. George Wood was on guard, and Wood shot him in the head with a pistol as he started to climb in.

The next day, I took five men through the back yards of the buildings on our left and worked our way to the end of the block where I hoped to be able to spot the anti-tank gun which had fired on us. When we got up into the attic of the corner building, I could see the gun with its crew in the street at the corner.

We opened fire with M-1's from the attic window. The crew could not spot our firing position and when one of their men was hit they abandoned the gun and withdrew to a nearby trench to join with other enemy troops. We continued to fire down on them and hit some. The rest retreated into the park.

While waiting to see if they would reactivate the gun, I sent Private Gill back to the Company Command Post to tell the C.O. where I was and what we were doing. When he didn't return as I had instructed, I sent another man. This man returned immediately and reported that Gill was lying wounded in the backyard next door.

Gill told me that as he started back he had been shot from the back door of the adjacent house. We pulled him to cover. We threw grenades into the windows of the house but the Germans kept firing out of the door. Corporal Thomas Burke tried to rush the door but was hit with machine pistol fire and killed instantly.

While we were firing into the building I saw our Medic, Ralph Hopkins, signal me over the brick wall of the next house. He had heard us firing and had come up by himself from our Platoon C.P. to see if anyone was wounded. He shouted to me that Sergeant Ben Popilsky was lying dead on the other side of the wall. Popilsky had apparently heard the firing from the attack, came to see if he could help and had been killed by the Germans in the house as he climbed over the wall. These had later wounded Gill.

A grenade flew out of a window and badly wounded Corporal Richard Crouse. He later died. Realising we had no cover we had to get out of the yard, and despite all our fire the Germans were in a position where we could not hit them but they could hit us. I pulled the men out of the yard and blew in the back of the house with a bazooka round. Then I took the men back to our original position down the block.

We had knocked out the anti-tank gun. The Germans abandoned it and did no more firing, but we lost three men killed and one wounded.

The next day when the attack on the bridge resumed, the First Platoon was held in reserve in our original position to support the E Company attack, led now by the Second Platoon.

We opened fire as the attack began, but Lt. Colonel Vandervoort came into our front room position to observe the action and told me to cease fire for fear we might hit our own men. The Second Platoon charged into the park with the tanks and quickly overran the German defences and the bridge was taken.

The German artillery had the area well zeroed in however, and immediately began shelling the park. This continued even after dark and E Company had several casualties from the artillery fire.

The following day, E Company crossed the bridge and went as far north as the village of Lent. Here we were ordered to establish a position in reserve as the British tanks attempted to drive north to relieve the British Airborne troops at Arnhem. The 30 Corps were unable to reach Arnhem and later the

British Airborne had to be pulled back across the northern branch of the River Rhine.

In the following weeks E Company was assigned to defend several areas along the narrow corridor from Belgium that had been secured in Operation Market Garden. I cannot remember the order in which we occupied them but they included areas near Mook, Beek and Wyler, amongst others.

In the operation at Mook, E Company relieved a company of the 325th Glider Infantry. We took over ready made foxholes but the first thing I noticed in moving into the position were the one hundred and sixteen bodies of German soldiers lying in the area (I made an actual count). The position was in a heavily wooded area and the enemy appeared to have been killed by artillery tree bursts. I had the First Platoon cover the tops of the two man foxholes with logs and pile dirt over them. A foxhole under a tree is no defence against an artillery burst directly overhead.

On the second day in this position, I had just completed my round of checking the men and returned to my foxhole when a sudden barrage of flat trajectory artillery fire burst all over the area. I could hear the guns going off only a second or two before the shells exploded, so I knew it was high volocity direct fire.

When the shelling ceased I called out to the men to see if any were wounded but got no reply. I was very concerned because when I was making my rounds many of the men were out of their foxholes and cleaning their weapons. I went to check and I was glad to find that they were all down in their foxholes and no one was wounded.

I was only half way back to my foxhole when I heard the guns fire again. I was caught in the open. I hit the ground as the shells burst all around me. I wasn't hit, and as soon as the shelling stopped I got up and started to run for my hole. I heard the guns fire again and knew that I would not make it to safety in time. One of the shells exploded in a tree right over me. I saw a large piece of shrapnel tear up the ground just inches in front of my eyes. At the same time I felt a sharp pain in my leg, I had been hit.

Fortunately it was not a large piece, but I couldn't tell that at the time. I knew that I was somewhere near the Platoon Aid man, Pfc. Tony Jazrowski, and I called out his name to locate his foxhole. When he answered I hobbled over to him, jumped in, and he patched up my wound which wasn't too bad but it hurt a great deal.

When it seemed that the artillery fire was over for the time being, he helped me to the Company C.P. to check with the Company Commander. He put another officer, Lieutenant John Walas, in command of my Platoon.

Pfc. Cullen Clark helped me back to the Battalion Aid Station. There Captain Lyle Putnam, a good friend, examined the wound and said the piece of shrapnel was still in my leg, but it was best to leave it there. He told me it would be alright to return to my Company. I was limping for a week, but it finally healed and I have a souvenir in my leg to this day. (For years it has acted as a barometer; I could always tell when it was going to rain — the scar tissue would itch).

My friend, John Walas, was delighted at my speedy return to E Company.

He was an Assistant Platoon Leader and he told me frankly that his ambitions did not include leading a platoon, his main ambition was to get through the war alive. It didn't work out that way in the end. John later led a platoon in the Ardennes and was killed in action.

In the area near Wyler, the First Platoon had a very rough detail. In a last minute change of assignment, I drew a platoon outpost position instead of a regular front line section which I had reconnoitred in daylight. As a result, I had to take the Platoon into a position I had not seen, except on a map, in the dark.

It was about three quarters of a mile ahead of our main front line and was under enemy observation from high ground. I was very concerned about making a mistake and missing the position in the dark and walking into the German lines. I was very relieved when finally challenged by the troops we were looking for. They had let me reach the front line of their outpost before challenging me. Another one hundred and fifty yards and it would have been the Germans doing the challenging.

This was a nerve-wracking position to occupy. We were there for two weeks and were not able to move out of our foxholes in the daytime. We could not even remove our clothes or boots to wash. Washing consisted of brushing our teeth.

The enemy knew exactly where we were. They sent combat patrols into the position every night. In addition they moved a tank up close to us after dark like clockwork and withdrew it just before dawn. At one point when a couple of men went into a house in daylight to heat their K rations (against orders) they immediately attracted an artillery barrage which blew in the thatched roof and wounded both men, one of whom ran to my foxhole in front of the house.

It was Jazrowski, the Medic who had patched me up the week before. He was hit in the shoulder by shrapnel.

I patched him up, but we had to wait until dark before he could walk back to the Aid Station. The other man was hit in the elbow but ran out of the back of the building so I could not see him. I found out later that he had been given first aid by the mortar squad.

Two days later, a Sergeant from Battalion Headquarters was shot in the head by a German sniper. He was an observer for the 81mm mortars and was in a foxhole with one of our men. Our replacement Medic, Pfc. Calvin Kaufman told me over the sound-powered telephone lines, that were rigged to each squad position, that the chances were he would not survive.

I called back through E Company Headquarters and spoke to Captain Robert Franco, the Battalion's Surgeon at the time. I described the wounded man's condition and told Franco that I thought I could get him out under a white flag and back to the Aid Station. We had allowed the Germans to come out under a Red Cross Flag to evacuate some of their wounded the day before.

The Doc said, however, that it would not be worth the risk, and that there was no hope for the man. He was right — the man died in a few hours and a detail carried his body back to our lines after dark.

Our mission on the outpost was to alert the main line of resistance in the event of a large scale attack. It really should have been manned by a squad and changed every three nights. When we were relieved by a British unit after two weeks, they took one look at the position, mined it, and abandoned it.

While in another defensive position in the Wyler area, I saw two German V-2 rockets launched in the distance. I had no idea what I was seeing and did not even report the first one to Battalion Headquarters. I thought I was hallucinating. No one around me saw it. When the second one went up a night later the British seachlights nearby futilely tried to track it so I knew I was not 'cracking up'.

About this time, I saw my first jet airplane. We had been hearing the sound of jet engines for days, but had no idea what might be making that sound. Eventually I saw the German jet flying very low and streaking home across the German border a few miles away.

I had occasion to take a patrol into the Reichswald, the German forest, on the Dutch border and so set foot in Germany for the first time in October, 1944.

About the middle of November, the 82nd Airborne Division was finally relieved by a Canadian unit. We moved back to a French army barracks at Suippes, near Rheims.

Father Gerard Thuring of Groesbeek greets Allen Langdon who had just made a celebration parachute jump into the original DZ at Groesbeek during the 40th Anniversary celebrations. Langdon was a member of the 505 from Africa to Berlin and wrote the history of the 505th Parachute Infantry Regiment.

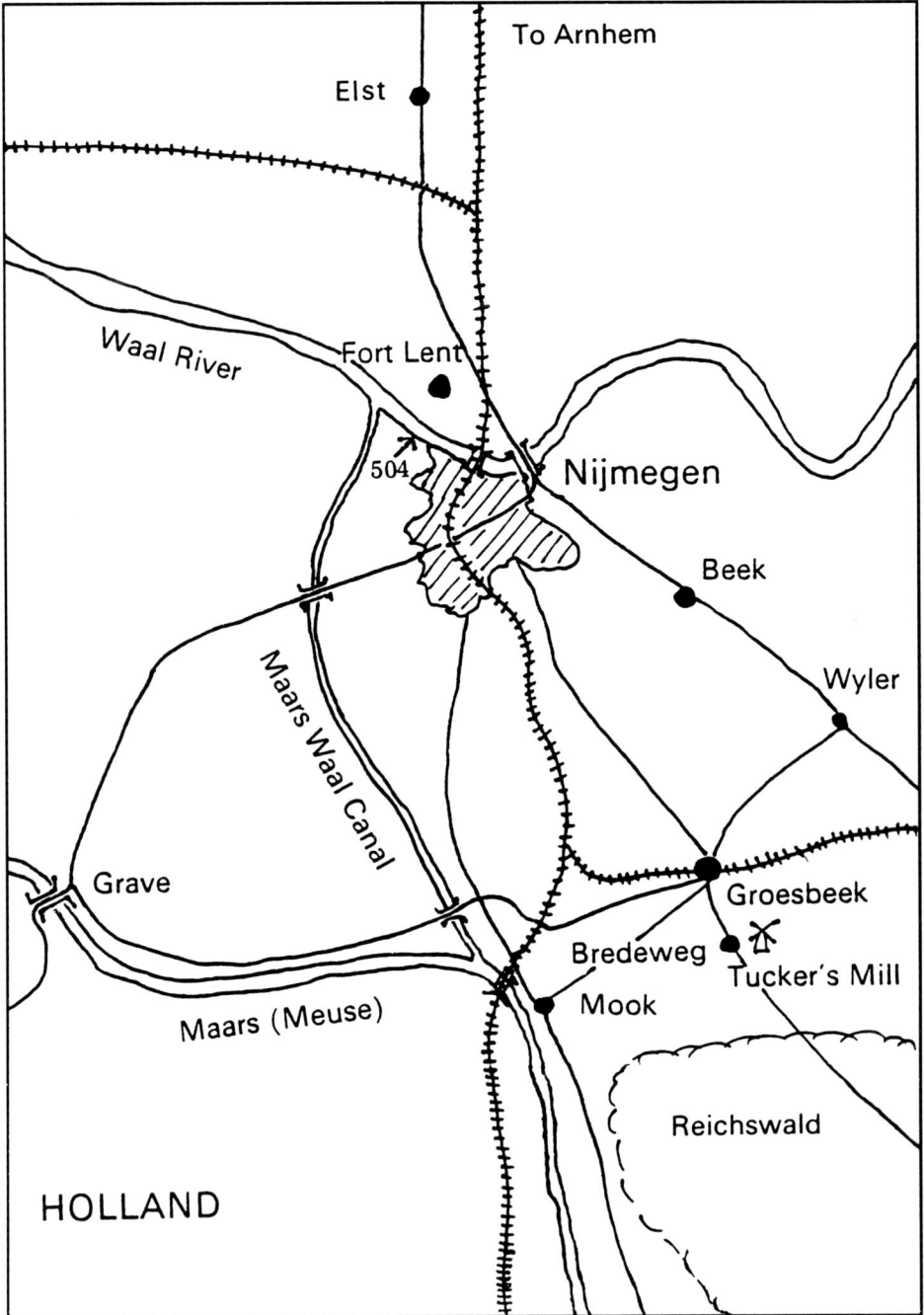

To Arnhem

Elst

Waal River

Fort Lent

504

Nijmegen

Beek

Wyler

Maars Waal Canal

Grave

Groesbeek

Bredeweg

Tucker's Mill

Maars (Meuse)

Mook

Reichswald

HOLLAND

The Crossing of the Waal River

The Waal River was crossed in a dramatic fashion by the 504th Parachute Infantry Regiment on the 20th September, 1944. This action sealed the fate of the German forces holding the two Nijmegen Bridges, one for the road and the other for the railway.

The actual crossing took place to the west of the bridges, near to the power station. Forty years later to the day a ceremony took place at the landing point, Lent, on the north side of the river where the Dutch had erected a Memorial to commemorate the historic attack.

It was an overcast day, almost the same identical conditions that this heroic action took place in. The site was crowded with the local inhabitants and visiting veterans from the 82nd Airborne. Some of those men who made the crossing were there. They included Albert Clark, a Sergeant in A Company, 504, now a retired Highway Maintenance Superintendent from Stockton, California.

General James Gavin performed the unveiling. Afterwards he came to the microphone and spoke in his soft, husky voice and gave a moving account of those first few days in the liberation of the Nijmegen and Groesbeek areas. He used no notes and seemed to be talking from his heart to a gathering of close friends. Everyone of those hundreds of people who listened counted him as their friend. It was not realised at the time but this would be his last visit to Holland before his death in February, 1990.

This was his speech on that day:

"I'm very glad to be here, and that is an understatement! I'm glad to see so many members of the Committee too. I congratulate you, the Committee, for what you have done here in Nijmegen, Groesbeek and the vicinity."

"It was mentioned in the description of the crossing that the young men came a long way — they did. They came seven or eight thousand miles some of them, and they had no idea that they would end up here. And many did give their lives."

"I would like, for the sake of the historical work to impose on you for a few moments, to tell you how we got here at all."

"On 17th September we landed by parachute and glider as you know. Very bad weather in England kept more from coming that we needed for another regiment. So we did not get reinforcements in significant numbers until the 19th or 20th. On the 19th I was joined by the British just this side of the Grave Bridge. They came up from Eindhoven. It is hard to understand this — we were holding this vast perimeter, some forty kilometres around by having two hundred infantrymen into here, a hundred there, a platoon some place else, just fighting by chance from road block to road block."

"We had about half the infantry we needed. But I met in front of the Malden schoolhouse, right on the sidewalk, General Horrocks, General Allan Adair and 'Boy' Browning, Commander of the British Airborne Division. I commanded the 82nd here with very marginal conditions."

"I should inject the word here that our survival depended to a large measure on the help we got from the Dutch — and we got that in an abundance that we shall never forget. Six hundred Dutchmen joined me. All they asked from me were rifles and pistols and weapons of the dead and wounded — expressing a fully worthy commitment to join us in battle on the grounds of knowing the dangers of what would happen if they were caught — and they would have been assassinated of course for they were only wearing civilian clothes with their armbands. They proved to be among the bravest and most patriotic people we had liberated."

"So we had six hundred Dutchmen helping us and that made a big difference."

"So having met on the sidewalk of Malden schoolhouse, General Horrocks said to me, 'Jim, we've got to get on the other side (of the Waal) and get to Arnhem right away!' And I said, 'But we have no way to get there really, but we might find a way.' I asked Browning, 'How bad is the situation in Arnhem?'"

"'Well, I don't know, it is pretty bad. We know they are in real trouble and we have got to get there within 24 hours,' replied Browning. That meant right away as far as I was concerned."

"Within the American Army we have an Engineer Battalion which you can call on when on a mission, such as the 30 Corps was in this case. That means you have bridges and boats."

"So I turned to Horrocks and asked him if he had an Engineer Battalion that would have boats. He turned to his Staff who were gathered in a circle around us and they said 'Yes.' They thought that 30 Corps had boats down the road, perhaps just fifty miles away on this side of Eindhoven. And I asked him when he could let me have them and he said, 'I will get them up during the night.'"

"Well, if you can get them up, I will cross the river during darkness." (said Gavin). "Crossing this fast moving river against some entrenched Germans on his side of the river was in any case very difficult, but at night we had no problem. We were very adept in handling German Infantry having a lot of experience especially in Africa and here."

"Colonel Warren Williams got his orders from me at 11 o'clock at night to make the crossing. He came to my Headquarters near Malden: and so got his orders and we got prepared to go and get the job off around 7 o'clock while it was still dark. At 7 o'clock the boats were not to be seen. So about 10 o'clock I came down to the crossing site at the power plant. Incidentally there was only one power plant then, I notice you have doubled the size of it. It was a smaller size then."

"I came down to look at the crossing site. About a half a mile from the river I ran into a platoon of German Infantry coming along like 'gute soldaten' and they were coming towards me about four hundred yards away. The Sergeant with me, with a lot of combat experience, that was why he was with me, jumped beside the building and gave his covering fire as fast as he could and they were all on the ground in a few minutes.''

''Then I started to get back there to Colonel Warren Williams in his Headquarters to tell his Regimental Commander, 'We do not even have a site where we can launch the boats yet.' He said, 'I will get there as fast as I can.' He was a very tough capable combat commander, Colonel Tucker. He had just come from Anzio with his Regiment where they had some hard fighting. He had jumped into Sicily and he fought the Hermann Goering Division and defeated them.''

''We were ready to go if we could get up there. It was a case of getting up there and getting the boats in the water. He told me to get the boats up at 1.30 hours (pm) at the power plant.''

''At 1.30 I was there at the power plant ready to help him get the thing launched and order support. We were supposed to have air support to strafe the slope, but with the bad weather — like today — they didn't fly. So then the Irish Guards were going to give us artillery support, but the wind was so bad and the smoke blew away.''

''It was broad daylight — What are we going to do? There were two and a half thousand of the British left out of their great combat division of ten thousand. Two and a half thousand left to be killed and sacrificed, and we could not cross the river.''

''We had checked, of course, all along the forest side and under the town. We could not expect the people to swim the river. So finally about 2 o'clock we both went out and we were ready to go.''

''Well, would you believe it, and this is a fact, that we were out to watch the river crossing and at that very moment I had a phone call on the radio from my Chief of Staff up near Groesbeek. He told me we were going to lose the whole area of the Division to the Germans if we did not get back and make some decisions. Molenhoek had just been overrun. This was very important because the only bridge which we had to get tanks across was here at Nijmegen. Furthermore, Beek had just been overrun, so we were being pinched out on two sides, while we were deciding to cross the river here. What could we do?''

''There was only one thing to do and that was to call the infantry to make a supreme effort as they could. This was a tough good infantry. We decided to go ahead. At about that time I went back to Molenhoek it was overrun. In fact the troopers were in the cellars. Anyway they took to the cellars and I sent for the Coldstream Guards to come running from three miles away to save our situation in Molenhoek. And we drove the Germans out of Mook without the Guards being involved — we didn't need them.''

''I captured some German prisoners and talked to them, they were making a counter attack. They were part of a combat team that had a mission of driving through Mook, Molenhoek and joining up with an attack through Beek.''

''So having settled that issue we had to get Molenhoek back and hurry up to beat them off. To get across a ridge I got on my stomach to cross the macadam road and got up there to talk to the troops in the foxholes. There is a very steep hill there and there is a serpentine road going to the bottom. It is still there today. The German armour had got stuck half way up. They could not get up and they could not get down. So all we had to do was deal with the German infantry. That was all right, we liked that.''

"So we dug in, and I talked to the troopers as they were digging the holes. And at that time I made a decision to attack, probably during the night. We got Molenhoek back and we attacked out of Beek towards the flatlands during darkness at about 3 o'clock in the morning. By daylight we were way up by Erlecom.''

"The 82nd Airborne Division's left flank was at Erlecom and the right flank at Molenhoek. In the meantime Tucker crossed here (at Lent). This was described by a British General who had watched as the most gallant action he had ever seen.''

"Well, the praise of the gallantry by the British soldiers, who were themselves very gallant. The bravest of the brave and they made the crossing. They look upon it now with dry humour. And one of them recently wrote to me and signed and verified his name, 'Survivor of the Waal River Regatta'. That's the way they saw it, a regatta that had to be run.''

"This man from the 504th Parachute Infantry Regiment was led by a Captain Burriss, a Lieutenant Megellas, a Sergeant and one Private was with him. Having reached the bank they ran to the railway crossing, saw that they were all right there and then ran to the road crossing.''

"I talked to them about six months ago. They noticed wires on the ground and they decided to cut them, wherever they could find them. They were trained to do that and they cut any wire that was on the ground, whether it was a telephone or something else to be sure to get the explosives. They got the explosives and when the Germans went to fire them, nothing fired.''

"It was a very gallant action, but I must say for history's sake, they suggested we do it. We thought we could do it and the troopers were the ones who did the job that had to be done.''

"Very, very brave men. I myself have never seen anything more gallant and I have seen a lot of good fighting especially with American Parachute troops.''

"Well enough of that. I commend the Professor and Mr Janson for this marvellous monument which you have placed here. And knowing the historical significance of it, I am deeply moved by it. I shall always remember it and I intentionally walked through it as a token of the 82nd Airborne arriving.''

"Now I shall say one word more if I may. The war came to an end and I went back to America and decided to find out about the Atomic Bomb. So I went to the bomb school and learnt how to make the bomb. I went to see bombs tested. I wrote about the bomb and about policy. I opposed the policy of massive retaliation and thus joined the Union of Concerned Scientists in my country. I believed that your country and my country can be defended by the conventional arms, if we are willing to make the commitment. Nuclear weapons should be held in reserve only for in a desperate hour to be used.''

"I mention this in passing though, because I gave you my expertise to combat involvement and now I impose upon you my idea of nuclear things."

"Now I would like to say finally in conclusion, it is wonderful to be back in the Netherlands. I like to breathe the deep fresh air of this great country. To see you people here and know your ways to defend democracy and to the commitments you have made. And your commitment I will never, never forget, to fight beside us in those uneasy, uncomfortable days of 1944."

"Now we have ahead of us peace. We hope we have! We want to give the kind of world we have enjoyed in the past to our children and their children yet unborn, that they may know the fruits of peace and the worries of peace. But always realise the sacrifice we must make to have peace."

"Thank you very much Ladies and Gentlemen......"

* * * * * * * * * * * * * * * * * * * *

On the day of the crossing, the Third Battalion of the 504th Parachute Infantry Regiment was commanded by Major Julian Aaron Cook, a 27 year old West Pointer. 'I' and 'H' Companies were the first to cross, along with 'C' Company of the 307th Engineers.

In the film *The Bridge Too Far*, Cook was shown leading his men across the Waal in one of the boats. This was not really the place for a Battalion Commander, but in the true paratrooper's tradition he chose to lead his men on this dangerous mission.

The two Companies from the Third Battalion swung right and attacked the two bridges, the road and the rail bridges. H Company took the rail bridge and I Company carried on further to the road bridge. The First Battalion followed across and captured the fortifications at Lent. Sergeant Albert Clark was in A Company and he made the crossing with the First Battalion.

The British-built canvas and wooden slatted boats held 16 men and were propelled by paddles. Thirteen paratroopers and three engineers were in each boat. The river was about four hundred yards wide at this point. Of the twenty-six boats on the initial wave only eleven were able to return for the next run. The action started a 3 o'clock in the afternoon, and by 7 o'clock that evening the rail and road bridges were in American hands.

The 504 casualties in this action totalled forty men killed or died of wounds. On the rail bridge alone the German dead numbered two hundred and sixty seven with many others lost in the fast flowing river below.

Colonel Reuben Tucker commanded the 504. When asked what experience his men had in boats, he replied, "It's on the job training."

Tucker was a tough paratroop commander with plenty of combat experience and at that time was held in high regard by General James Gavin. That relationship soured at the end of the war when personal files relating to the misdemeanours of his men during their service in Europe were 'lost' overboard from the troopship coming home.

The Captain Burriss mentioned was Thomas Moffat Burriss the CO of I Company. The Lieutenant Megellas who was with him was James 'Maggie' Megellas of H Company who now lives in Florida. The Sergeant was

Megellas's Platoon Sergeant named Richmond. Colonel Warren Williams was the 504's Executive Officer.

The Sergeant that General Gavin mentions in his speech who fired on the German patrol was Sergeant Walker E. Wood. He was Gavin's bodyguard. Also there, but not mentioned was Hugo Olsen, an officer and trusted confidant of Gavin throughout the war.

The British Coldstream Guards were attached to the 82nd due to the late arrival from England of the 325th Glider Infantry because of bad weather.

Prior to going overseas, Captain Adam Komosa was the S-3 (Plans and Training Officer) of the Third Battalion. Lt. Colonel Leslie Freeman was the Battalion Commander, with Captain Julian Cook as the Executive Officer. Komosa planned, and the Third Battalion executed a simulated river crossing at Coolie Conch Lake at Fort Bragg. When given the river crossing mission at Nijmegen, Colonel Tucker remembered this. Cook, now a Major, was in command of the Battalion and with this previous experience he was accorded the honours of outflanking the Nijmegen Bridges by making this famous crossing of the Waal River.

Julian Aaron Cook was awarded the nation's second highest award for bravery, the Distinguished Service Cross, for his and his Battalion's actions in crossing the Waal River. He died on the 19th June, 1990, at a VA Hospital in Columbia, South Carolina, aged 73.

It was during the battle for Nijmegen that Jim Gavin first met the British General, Brian Horrocks and instantly they became firm, lifelong friends.

Horrocks was most impressed with the 82nd Airborne Division's fighting spirit. As he later wrote: "Without Jim Gavin's 82nd U.S. Airborne, we should never have captured the two great bridges over the River Waal. While the road bridge was being assaulted, and ultimately captured intact by the Grenadier Guards and the 505th Parachute Regiment, the 504th U.S. Parachute Regiment, supported by the fire of the Irish Guards' tanks, crossed the swift-running 400-yards-wide Waal River in British assault boats, which they had never seen before, in the face of vicious German rifle, machine-gun and artillery fire from the far bank."

"This operation, suggested by General Gavin, was the best and most gallant attack I have ever seen carried out in my life. No wonder the leading paratroopers, when they contacted the Guards' tanks, which had captured the road bridges, were furious that we did not push straight on for Arnhem. They felt they had risked their lives for nothing, but is was impossible, owing to the confusion which exsisted in Nijmegen, with houses burning and the British and United States forces all mixed up."

To Gavin's embarrassment when Horrocks asked the troopers what they wanted they said they wanted more to eat. They were missing their American C Rations. Horrocks immediately doubled the rations.

As Gavin recalled later, "When the days grew shorter, and colder in the fall of 1944, and the dampness of Holland seemed to penetrate everywhere, Horrocks's staff enquired about a rum ration — I declined. Finally on our last evening with 30 Corps he sent me a message. 'You will issue a rum ration this evening' — a nice Horrocks touch. We enjoyed it."

The total casualties of the 82nd Airborne for 'Market Garden' were 1,432 dead and wounded.

FIRST LIEUTENANT JAMES J. COYLE
E COMPANY, 505

Within a week of arriving at Suippes after the Division was relieved in Holland, I was given some unbelievable news. Based on time overseas, in combat, wounds, etc., I had been chosen to take the first group of men home for rotation leave. Within two days I was on my way home to spend thirty days leave, after which, I would return with the men to the 505th Parachute Infantry to wherever they might be at the time.

I said goodbye to all of my friends and left with the group of 505'ers for Paris. The weather delayed us for over a week and we were unable to fly to England to board a ship for home. The time was spent seeing wartime Paris and we finally travelled by boat across the English Channel. It was on board the *S.S. Uraguay* in mid-Atlantic when the daily news bulletin informed us of the German attack in the Ardennes. At the time I made no connection between the attack and E Company, 505.

We had hoped to be home for Christmas but the delay in Paris prevented that, and we spent Christmas on board ship.

It was wonderful to see my father, mother, brothers and sisters when I arrived home to Brooklyn, New York. I visited other relatives in Wilkes-Barre, Pennsylvania, my home town, and my sister Margaret in Alexandria, Virginia. I made phone calls to the families of some of the Battalion officers, including Lt. Colonel Ben Vandervoort's father, and visited Bill Meddaugh's family in Poughkeepsie. The days flew by and it soon came time to say goodbye to my family and return overseas. This was very difficult. In my five years in the army, I was only able to get home to see my family four times.

The returning men met on the dock in New York harbour. I was surprised to see Pfc. Rudolph 'Rudy' Oppliger ready to board the *Queen Mary* with the rest of us for the return trip to Europe. He had a serious hearing problem develop while overseas. I had told him to turn himself in at the nearest Army Hospital when he got home to be examined and I was sure that he would not be sent back overseas. He explained to me that he wanted to return to his buddies. This was typical of the kind of men we had in E Company.

When I rejoined my Company I received a shock. The boys had been in very heavy combat in the Battle of the Bulge and there were many missing faces.

Lieutenant John Walas had been killed. Bill Meddaugh was in hospital with pneumonia. Lt. Colonel Vandervoort had been wounded and lost an eye. Half the men in E Company were replacements from the 551st Parachute Battalion which had been disbanded.

I had been able to say that I knew the name of every man in the Company from the North Africa days. I was never able to say that again. The war ended before I got to know all the new faces.

Captain J.J. Smith had been returned to the States with malaria. Bill Meddaugh had been the Company Commander in the Bulge and when he went to hospital he had been replaced by Captain Charles 'Barney' Barnett. I became the Company Executive Officer.

****

In March 1945 the Regiment's newspaper *Static Line* called the first men to be awarded home leave the 'Fortunate Few': while they were in the States the Battle of the Bulge took place. The party consisted of:

Headquarters, Headquarters Company
Sergeant John M. Grogan Jnr
Corporal Charles S. Allen
Corporal Jerome Huth

Regimental Medics
Corporal Kelly W. Byars
Private First Class James J. Kelly
Private First Class Angelo G. Muley

Service Company and First Battalion
First Lieutenant Gerald N. Johnson
Sergeant George L. Bean
Sergeant John D. Bolderson
Private First Class Raymond R. Reichen
Sergeant Otto Opsahl
Sergeant Clyde E. Hein
Sergeant John E. Ragle
Sergeant Marion C. Fabian
Staff Sergeant Frederick Goughler

Second Battalion
First Lieutenant James J. Coyle
Private First Class Rudolph J. Oppliger
Private First Class Denis G. O'Laughlin
Staff Sergeant Louis Yarchak
Sergeant Robert L. Smith
Staff Sergeant Paul D. Nunan
Corporal Jesse B. Shelton

Third Battalion
First Lieutenant George E. Clark
Sergeant Charles A. Knauff
Staff Sergeant Leonard Hodges
Sergeant James McKenstry
Sergeant Armand A. Du Pon
Sergeant Stephen Zaley
First Sergeant Ralph G. Bullard

Sergeant Paul R. Balens
Staff Sergeant James A. Robinson
Staff Sergeant Donald Sutherland

A careful research of the Casualty Lists shows that every man on this list survived the war.

****

First Sergeant John Rabig was another of the lucky ones who, later in 1945, was able to return to the States for his 'rest and recuperation' home leave. After travelling to England he boarded the liner, the *Queen Elizabeth*, in Scotland.

The ship was full of wounded hospital cases returning to the States. He was ordered to help carry the stretchers on board to their quarters. This meant struggling with the patients up and down the staircases between the decks as they loaded the ship.

As he said, ''It was very heavy work and they wouldn't let us use the lifts. During the voyage we were all given one of the wounded to look after if the ship was hit. The guy they gave me weighed about 190 lbs and he was covered in plaster casts which must have doubled his weight. Me, I weighed 150 lbs. I didn't bullshit him, I told him straight. 'If anything happens to this boat, your a ****ing loser. There is no way I can get you up on that deck.' He looked at me very surprised.''

When Rabig got back to his Company they were in Germany. They were all new faces, he didn't recognise anybody, they were all replacements.

General James Gavin unveiling the 504 Memorial at Lent on the north bank of the River Waal in 1984.

John Rabig — one of the great 82nd's raconteurs.

Belgium: The Ardennes

On 18th December the 82nd Airborne hurriedly moved forward into the battle zone from their camp at Suippes, France, to stop the German advance. As 'Doc' Franco recalls:

"I was lucky in that I was able to ride all the way from our base camp to our positions near Werbomont, Belgium, in an ambulance that had a heater of sorts. Everyone else rode in huge open trucks in miserable, wet and cold conditions."

"I remember stopping in a town at dusk, it was snowing and there was the usual confusion. Someone asked where we were. I saw a sign: it said Bastogne. One voice said this is where we are stopping, another called out to continue on. We did."

"We found a farmhouse and I slept on the floor that night in the dry. Many of the troopers were not so lucky. The next day we moved to the Salm River and I set up my Aid Station in a small bakery, about two or three hundred yards west of the river. The old bakery took a number of near misses from what appeared to be 105's, but the little building remained intact and we were able to work and to evacuate our wounded."

"The Allied counter attack on 3rd January was a cold experience. I remember a Battalion Officers' meeting a few days later just before embarking on our final mission to capture the town of Goronne. Lt. Colonel Ben Vandervoort looked at Captain Charles L. Barnett and said, 'Barney, you've got the big company. What's your strength?'"

"'Thirty-seven men, Sir,' was the answer. It was our E Company who were very tough boys, and indeed Captain Barnett was a very tough one indeed. The normal strength of a company was about one hundred and twenty."

Captain Barnett was later killed in action crossing the Rhine when he and another officer, Major William Carpenter, tried to recover a body of one of his men killed on patrol. Major Carpenter also lost his life.

"We had just got the attack under way when we came under fire and shell fragments landed amongst the men. Lt. Colonel Vandervoort was hit, losing an eye. He left us almost immediately, remaining in good health, and later attended several reunions. I always feel flattered when he finds me, steps forward, puts out his hand and greets me warmly. A great guy and a real soldier."

On 20th December Jim Gavin sent a message to his beloved 505th Parachute Infantry Regiment. It read:

Once again Christmas finds us away from home and our loved ones. The year just passed has seen the successful fulfilment of two combat missions of which we should all be justly proud. Through these efforts the ultimate victorious peace has been brought nearer realization. When peace comes and the final blow has been delivered against Nazism, it will mark the end of racial slavery and oppression. Then and then only will the true era of ''Peace on Earth and Good Will Towards Men'' begin. It is to this end that we have dedicated our interests, our efforts and our lives.

While Christmas for us this year may lack the traditional American setting and may not in every respect be what our religious practices decree it should be. It is a Christmas spent like this that will enable us all to look forward to the future, and know that we and our loved ones can enjoy Christmas according to our own dictates and not those of an oppressor nation. It is with this full realization that we share this Christmas here together, and, sharing it with you, I extend to each of you my most sincere wish for a Merry Christmas and a good New Year, with luck and success in combat.

Signed. James M. Gavin,
Major General, U.S. Army.

On 3rd January 1945, all hell broke loose for one of the platoons of F Company of the 505. A detachment of twelve men joined them from the Headquarters Company to make up the numbers. They were machine-gunners and a mortar crew ready for the big offensive.

Shortly after kick off they received a very heavy mortar barrage from the Germans. It landed squarely on the Platoon, severely wounding sixteen out of the nineteen men. Now there were three men left; Lieutenant Harold Case, Sergeant Don McKeage and Private Shuman. The Headquarters men had been completely wiped out.

After pushing the Germans back in the afternoon they were just about to settle down when the Company came on the receiving end of a heavy artillery barrage. In twenty minutes the casualties mounted. Lieutenant John Hamula was killed and Platoon Sergeant John Gore seriously wounded in the back.

Don McKeage took over as First Sergeant, and after taking care of the wounded he finally got his foxhole dug. He had just settled down when Lieutenant Harold 'Casey' Case came along and asked if he could share the hole. The Lieutenant got in first and McKeage sat on his lap. Later Private Shuman joined them and he sat on McKeage's lap.

They had just got to sleep when 'Casey' Case had a nightmare and with his arm around McKeage's neck began to choke him and then finally threw him out of the foxhole. McKeage's first thoughts were that the Germans had got him, but luckily the Lieutenant woke up and all three settled down again for a short snooze.

Two days later Lieutenant Harold Case was wounded and as there were no officers left, F Company came under the command of Sergeant Don McKeage. When Lt. Colonel Ben Vandervoort received the report he sent Lieutenant John Phillips from E Company to take over. Phillips survived the war only to be killed in 1956 on a NATO parachute jump in Turkey.

McKeage's luck held out until 2nd February when he was wounded just as the Company arrived at the Siegfried Line. He rejoined them on the 25th June in Berlin.

As General James Gavin led his victorious men down New York's Fifth

Avenue for the grand parade on 12th January 1946, F Company was represented by three combat veterans: Sergeant Don McKeage, the only combat jump veteran; Lieutenant George Essex who joined the Company in Holland; and Private Henry Quesada who joined during the Battle of the Bulge.

During the Bulge, First Sergeant John Rabig of D Company, 505, was taken ill with a fever and was taken out of the line to a hospital in Brussels. On his discharge he arrived at a replacement centre at Fontainebleau to await his transport back to his unit.

"I was told it would be two days, but then I met Charlie Swan who had been hanging around for six days. We decided to break out of camp and make our own way. We had been issued with an overcoat, helmet and, both being sergeants, a Colt 45 pistol each. There was no ammunition to go with them though. What we didn't know then were the reports of Germans in American uniforms roaming about."

"On the second night we told the guard on the gate that we were going. He would not open the gate at first but he soon got the message. A Frenchman very kindly gave us a lift in his car for about thirty miles towards Belgium. After that we walked until we bedded down in a haystack until daylight. The idea was to flag down an army truck as soon as we saw one."

"We soon realised it was very quiet along the road, there was no traffic. After walking through a village and waving to the locals we sat down on a bridge for a rest. I remember seeing three civilians on bicycles coming along the road from the village. Next time I looked they had disappeared."

"Then without any warning these guys appeared out of the ditches. Two had German burp guns and the other a British Sten. The horrible thought hit me that they thought we were Germans. They couldn't speak English and we didn't know a word of French. We had to talk fast or else I could see both of us shot to pieces. They took our 45's and laughed when they found they were unloaded. What made them suspicious was that we had no Jeep. 'Why are you walking if you are American?' they questioned. To them every American had wheels."

"They took us back to the village, nobody could speak English so we finished up in a cell in the Police Station. Charlie Swan was taken out, under armed guard, to the local store to see if he could buy some food. The girl there could speak our language and she explained our predicament. Help came in the shape of two MP's and before we drove off I realised that they still had our Colts. We got them back."

"The Colonel at the Replacement Centre was not at all happy with us and proceeded to chew our ears off, 'You're under arrest and confined to your quarters,' he ordered. I think he was glad to get rid of a couple of paratroopers as soon as he could. We got our transport back to the 505."

During the fighting in the cold weather it was almost impossible to obtain hot coffee or even fresh water. Frank Bilich still had his supply of coffee powder and his platoon went in search of water.

A source of water was found and heated by taking the pellets from a gammon grenade and lighting them. Lieutenant Lawrence Price smelt the delicious aroma and was invited to have a cup. Price was enjoying the coffee and was interested how the men had managed to make it. He asked how they obtained the water.

Somebody explained that they had broken the ice in the horse trough and used the water. Unfortunately Price had consumed the coffee by the time he realised that the horse trough had been used for washing by the entire Company.

The word had been passed around that the Germans were infiltrating through the lines dressed as American officers. This gave the sentries a great time in thinking up catch questions for all the unsuspecting officers.

Lt. Colonel Edward 'Cannonball' Krause faced an Artillery sentry in this delicate situation.

"What's the password?" challenged the trigger-happy sentry.

"I don't know, but I'm Colonel Krause of the 505."

"OK, we'll go down to the C.P. and check," said the GI.

"No we won't," replied Krause.

The click of a 45 being cocked broke the silence.

"Yes we will," cracked the Colonel.

A few minutes later the Colonel stood waiting as the sentry reported to his Commanding Officer that he had some joker outside who claimed to be Colonel Krause of the 505.

A wild scream was heard from inside the Command Post, "Turn him loose, we've got enough trouble!"

It appears that Krause's reputation was well known outside the Airborne. The Colonel continued on his way.

Germany

FIRST LIEUTENANT JAMES J. COYLE

Within a week or so after I rejoined the Company, we received orders to move up to the River Rhine. Two American armies were encircling the Ruhr industrial area of Germany and the 82nd Airborne was assigned a section of a holding line on the west bank between Cologne and Bonn. E Company held an area at a town whose name escapes me. I should remember it because of an incident which occurred there that I will never forget.

We had been in a defensive position for about a week and it was an easy duty, until one day it was decided (I was never able to ascertain by whom) that we should start patrolling across the river. I was away from Company Headquarters when the first E Company patrol was assigned.

When I returned to the Company, I learnt that Lieutenant Howard Jensen and two men had gone across the river in a civilian kyak, many of which were available along the bank. The patrol had stepped ashore in the dark, right into a booby-trapped minefield. One of the men was presumed killed and Jensen and Pfc. Jim Keenan were trying to get back to our lines, but it had turned light before they could get organised for the return. They were caught by enemy fire on the return trip. They had jumped out of the kyak to avoid the fire but Jensen was shot in the head, and Keenan had to swim the rest of the way to our side.

The next night, Major William Carpenter, the new Battalion C.O., had ordered another patrol to check the body of the man who was killed. I don't know if they wanted the body recovered or if they thought the man might be still alive. They had observed the body with high-powered artillery binoculars during the day without seeing any sign of life. This patrol was assigned to Lieutenant John O'Dea, an officer who had just joined the Company.

I was on the bank with several of the men when O'Dea and one other man paddled off in a kyak. They had only been gone about fifteen minutes when a tremendous explosion lit up the night sky on the other side. It had to be a Teller mine.

We waited to see if anyone would come back from the patrol. Twenty minutes later the trooper who had gone with O'Dea came running along the bank in a state of shock. He said O'Dea had stepped out of the kyak in the dark and had apparently tripped a mine.

Without any discussion, Major Carpenter and Captain Barnett got into a nearby kyak and started for the other side. I didn't understand this move; it was no place for Battalion or Company Commanders.

They had just about gotten out of sight on the river when I heard what I was sure was the kyak overturn. There was some splashing about but no other sound. I immediately stripped to my shorts and started to swim out to them. Carpenter's Jeep driver came in after me. As I swam out I heard their first cries of help and swam towards the sound. Before I reached them the cries had stopped. I called to them but got no reply. When I got to about where I thought they might have overturned, I dove down a few times, but I realised it was useless in the pitch dark.

I also discovered that the current in the river was now much stronger than it had been nearer the bank and I was caught in it. I did not realise this at first until I saw a large boat or barge go close by me in the dark at a fairly rapid clip. My first thought was "What is this boat doing going up the river in the dark?" I knew I was disoriented but had enough sense to finally realise that the boat was sunk and stationary. It was me that was moving rapidly down river.

It was pitch black. I couldn't see the shore but I knew if I kept the current coming from my left I could swim to the bank on our side of the river. I finally reached the bank and then another problem crossed my mind. I did not know how far down the river I had gone.

All I had on was my shorts and dog-tags. It would be just my luck to have some trigger-happy green guy see me come out of the river and think I was a German and to shoot me without first challenging me.

I had barely climbed up on the river bank when I was challenged. I gave the countersign and my name and unit. By the fortunes of war I had been challenged by Staff Sergeant Louis Yarchak, one of the old veterans of F Company, who had gone back to the States on leave in my group.

Yarchak took me to the F Company Command Post, found me a blanket before I got on the phone to Captain Taylor G. Smith, the Battalion Executive Officer. I told him what had happened and that I knew that Carpenter and Barnett had drowned. I said I would be willing to go across the river just before dawn to look for O'Dea, but I was not about to go stumbling around in a mine field in the dark.

Captain Smith immediately told me that Colonel William Ekman, the Regimental Commander, had already been told that Carpenter, Barnett and I were missing. He had stated that no one was to go across that river until further orders.

While I sat shivering in F Company's Command Post, the word came down that President Roosevelt had died. It was 12th April 1945, my 26th birthday.

The next day, Colonel Ekman came to our Company C.P. He was furious over the loss of five men, including a Battalion Commander. He ordered me to write a complete report and forward it to him at Regimental Headquarters.

He then told me that I was to take over as the Company Commander. My elation was shortlived. He broke my heart by saying the position was only temporary; I didn't have the seniority to keep it. His problem was that several higher ranking officers were arriving from the States without assignments. I would have liked to command E Company at war's end, which I knew was coming soon.

Another tragedy occurred a few days later. I had received reports from the Regimental Intelligence Section (S-2) that Germans had been crossing the

Rhine into our areas in American uniforms. I passed the information to the troops in the line, but frankly I did not believe these reports. No German soldier was going to risk getting shot as a spy at this late stage of the game when they knew the war was lost.

I was in the Company C.P. when an emergency call came from the First Platoon Mortar Squad that they were under attack from Germans in American uniforms. I got a Jeep and some men with automatic weapons and we took off for their position.

When I got there the shooting was over. One soldier was lying dead from a head wound and another was in a state of shock. He was standing by an 82nd Airborne Division Jeep parked on a small bridge over the railroad cut where the First Platoon mortar squad had set up a position. These men were living in some wooden box-cars on the track below. Some of their uniforms had been washed and were hanging on lines, strung on the box-cars.

Sergeant John Perozzi, the Mortar Squad leader, came up and I asked him what had happened. He reported that the Jeep had pulled up on the bridge and the two men got out. They started shouting at them in German and opened fire with rifles on his men in the box-cars.

Perozzi told me he did not return fire immediately because he could see the 82nd Airborne identification on the Jeep. He called repeatedly for them to cease fire in English and when they continued to fire he concluded they must be the enemy in American uniforms who had stolen the Jeep.

He gave the order to his men to open fire and with his first shot Private 'Red' Welch hit one of the men on the bridge right between the eyes. This ended the shooting.

The other soldier from the Jeep was now becoming coherent. I asked him who he was and his unit. He told me that they were from Division Intelligence and they had been looking for the 'Germans in American uniforms'. When I asked him what made him think that these particular men were the Germans, he replied that he had seen the uniforms hanging on the box-car and for some reason (which made no sense to me) assumed they had found the Germans they were looking for.

I then asked him if he had cleared through Regiment or Battalion to inform them that they were coming to our area. The answer was, No, they had not complied with this standard operating procedure. He added sadly that he and the dead man had just arrived overseas the previous week.

At this point, Colonel Ekman drove up in his Jeep. I had passed word to Battalion of the supposed 'attack' before leaving E Company's C.P. When he saw the dead man he asked what had happened. I told him that before I gave him the details I wanted him to hear what the Division Intelligence man had to say. The Colonel listened in disbelief to the man's story.

When he had finished I reported that Sergeant Perozzi had held his Squad's fire until the bullets were cracking around his men in the wooden box-cars. He could no longer risk their lives trying to get the men in the Jeep to cease fire.

Colonel Ekman then ordered me to write up a complete report of the incident and forward it to him. The second tragic report in two weeks! He must have thought that I was the biggest jinx in the 505th Parachute Infantry Regiment.

While this was going on, Private Welch was standing nearby in a nervous state. As Colonel Ekman turned to get in his Jeep to leave, Welch grabbed my arm and said, ''Lieutenant, what's going to happen to me?''

I went over to the Colonel and repeated the question. Ekman replied sadly, that under the circumstances, the only thing he could do was to congratulate Welch on his marksmanship. I relayed this information to a very relieved Private Welch.

Two weeks later, Captain Art Miller came down from Regimental Personnel to take over command of E Company. Art was an old friend, but I was sorry to have to give over the command of the Company to anyone.

Once again the 82nd Airborne was attached to the British forces and we moved up to relieve a British unit on the Elbe River. We boarded the old familiar 40 and 8 box-cars, crossed the Rhine at Wessel and moved deep into Germany.

At one point along the route the box-car in which I was riding started bumping and swaying severely, and I realised that we had jumped the tracks. The train finally stopped and I got the men off. When I looked back I saw that the car behind us had tipped over and most of the men in it had been thrown out and had finished up at the bottom of the railroad embankment.

The car was empty and no one was injured except Lieutenant James Meyers from D Company who had been knocked unconscious by the fall. He recovered quickly and was unhurt. The train crew uncoupled the overturned car and we rolled it down the embankment. Our car was then jacked back on the rails and we were on our way again.

We arrived at the town of Blekede on the west bank of the Elbe River. Lieutenant Bill Meddaugh had returned to the Company as Executive Officer, and I was once again the First Platoon Leader.

The orders were to make an assault crossing of the river. This was to be a new experience for E Company. No one in the Company had done this before and I wondered if there were any non-swimmers amongst the men as no life preservers were available.

That afternoon Art Miller, Bill Meddaugh and I went down to the river bank to reconnoitre for a likely spot to launch our boats. We were able to find an ideal inlet with about fifteen foot banks on three sides and an outlet that ran into the river.

When we ventured out to the river to use our binoculars to observe the opposite side we soon came under artillery fire and had to take cover. The fire was later raised and aimed back into the town. We couldn't tell if we had been spotted of whether they were just shelling the entire area. When we returned to Company Headquarters we found that several men had been wounded in the town by the barrage.

Captain Miller issued the order of attack and I learned that my First Platoon would lead E Company in the crossing. My main concern was our inexperience in river crossings. Could we keep the Platoon and for that matter, the Company, together?

The Elbe was at Spring flood, at least one hundred and fifty yards across, with a swift current running. I was praying that we would all land together so we could quickly organise on the other side. The attack would be preceded by a heavy concentration of artillery fire for support, prior to our crossing at 20.00 hours. We were to move our boats into the water under cover of the artillery. Nobody knew what of kind of resistance we would receive from the enemy when we landed.

Shortly after dark we assembled the Company and moved down to the inlet we had chosen for embarking. After spreading the men out in the area, we waited for the trucks to arrive with the boats and the engineers to man them. Exactly on 20.00 hours the artillery commenced firing. It was the greatest barrage I've ever seen. Large calibre guns fired for at least a half an hour and 40mm anti-aircraft Bofors placed direct fire like machine-guns on to the opposite bank.

The problem was that our assault boats had not arrived by the time the artillery barrage had ceased.

It became very quiet. Then a drizzle of rain began which lasted for the next two hours while the men stood around in the pitch dark, waiting for the boats. For the first time in the war, I had a feeling of dread about an operation. The element of surprise was gone. With that amount of artillery preparation, the enemy must surely know that an attack was coming. I had visions of the Company stepping out of the boats and into a minefield, as had happened to the patrols across the Rhine only a few weeks before.

Waiting in the rain for those boats was very nervewracking.

Finally the boats arrived. I can't remember how many hours behind schedule they were. I don't know what kind of boats I expected, but I was unpleasantly surprised to see that each boat would only carry about eight men at the most, with one engineer per boat. We were to do the paddling.

We unloaded the boats from the trucks, assigned the men to their boats and carried these flimsy craft down the bank to the water.

Editor's note: These were a similar type to the flimsy collapsible wood and canvas British assault boats used to cross the Waal at Nijmegen by the 504th Parachute Infantry Regiment the previous September.

We pushed off and I headed the lead boat to the outlet of the little bay towards the river. Just before we were to leave the protection of the inlet and enter the river proper, I heard a lot of shouting behind me. I looked back and saw only a couple of boats were following.

I couldn't imagine how it happened (we had briefed the men on the size of the river), but I could see that the rest of the Company had paddled across the inlet and with the best of spirit, including rebel yells, were assaulting the opposite bank of the inlet!

I put our boats ashore and went back along the bank to stop the premature landing. I started yelling as I approached them, because it had occurred to me that if they thought they were on the other side of the Elbe, they might take me for the enemy. I told them they had not crossed the river yet and we finally got the Company re-organised and headed out towards the river.

By this time the rain had stopped and a fairly bright moon was shining. This was a mixed blessing. We could see the other boats so as to stay together during the crossing, but the Germans could see us coming too.

As we crossed the river we were able to stay in a column despite the current. When we approached the enemy side, I was waiting for the enemy to open fire, but none came. Our boat pulled in near a small jetty and we landed. One of the men told me that he heard Germans talking in a building on a small dock. I told him to ignore it. If they were enemy soldiers, they were not going to fire on us now, they would have done it before we landed. They could be mopped up later.

The First Platoon quickly spread out into a mini-beachhead and the rest of the Company followed ashore. I could hardly believe it, after all my fears and all that had gone wrong, there was no minefield, no enemy in sight, and we were ashore without losing a boat or man. The Company quickly got organised and started moving inland.

The advance was co-ordinated with the other units by radio. E Company was meeting our phase lines on schedule and sometimes ahead of time, occasionally having to wait to avoid advancing too far in front of the regimental line. At one point we had crossed a very large field and when we arrived at the far side we discovered an unmanned 40mm anti-aircraft gun which could have wiped out the Company if it had been fired on us as we advanced.

We could see an enemy artillery battery firing as we advanced, but the fire was high over our heads and falling far to our rear. By the time we reached the point from where they were firing, they had pulled out.

Soon after we finally came on some Germans. The lead scout came back and said they were holed up in a building and a German had surrendered. He said his officers were undecided about surrendering. Captain Miller sent him back to the house with a message that if they didn't come out in five minutes unarmed, we were opening fire. About forty Germans came out of the house and surrendered.

Just before dark the First Platoon was fired on by machine-guns from a small village we were approaching. As I got ready to set up our Platoon for an attack, an artillery officer came up. I had not been aware that he had been moving up right behind us. He was frustrated, he hadn't had a target all day, and if we could wait ten minutes he would call in a fire mission on the area where the enemy were.

It seemed like using a sledgehammer to kill a mosquito because there hadn't been a great amount of fire, but even a couple of automatic weapons could cause us casualties in an attack, so I agreed. In a few minutes a barrage landed right on target and we moved forward without any further resistance. When darkness fell, we were ordered to halt for the night.

There was no resistance next day so we took to the roads and kept marching east. Sometime in the afternoon, Colonel Ekman drove up the column in his Jeep stopping each unit as he passed. He told us that this was as far as we go; for us the war in Europe was over.

As first we could not grasp what he had said. After almost two years of combat, it was over!

We were told that the Russians were closing from the east. Apparently there was a fear that we might start firing at each other by mistake. I can't remember any wild celebrating or cheering. I guess that we just couldn't believe it. We stopped where we were and moved into some scattered houses for the night. It was 1st May, 1945.

Later, I wondered why we had made the Elbe River crossing at all since we met the Russians only about twelve miles east of the river. Why not let the Russians just advance to the east bank and we could remain on the west bank?

After the war, Lt. General Matthew Ridgway, who had been the 82nd Airborne Division Commander up until Holland and then became Commander of XVIII Airborne Corps of which the 82nd Airborne was a unit, published a book in which I found the answer. The British requested our crossing to cover their southern flank as they made a crossing to our north. By this they were able to make a motorised dash across Germany to the Baltic, sealing off Denmark and preventing the advancing Russians from occupying it. The British obviously knew more about geo-political warfare than the Americans did.

On 2nd May German soldiers started entering our lines and surrendering, first in small groups and finally in massed columns with trucks, horse-drawn wagons, field kitchens and ambulances — it was an impressive sight to see. By the end of the day, the entire 21st German Army of 150,000 men had surrendered to the 82nd Airborne Division. They had fought a rearguard action against the Russians in order to reach our lines to surrender.

The next day I saw a few Russian soldiers, but there was not a great deal of fraternising. The higher ranks dealt with the Russian brass and from what I could see there was a kind of no-man's land maintained between the mass of Russian troops and our own.

I was surprised to see women soldiers amongst the Russian front line troops. Also at first glance there appeared to be American Indians in their army, but of course, these turned out to be Mongolian troops.

I had expected the end of the war to bring a little free time and rest, but it was not to be. We started working long hours guarding and feeding the German POW's. I was put in charge of about 10,000 men in a makeshift prison camp in E Company's area at the town of Zeetze. I was assigned as the camp's Adjutant.

Since the Germans had surrendered as units, I dealt with a German General and his staff who we housed in a farmhouse and let them run the administration of the camp. We simply did not have the personnel to handle it in any other way. They were issued with K rations for their two meals a day and we did our best to take care of their wounded which they had brought with them.

The German General and his staff complained to me daily at our meetings. I told them that it was a temporary set-up and that they would be moved back to permanent camps soon. Their Adjutant, who spoke English, was a particular annoyance to me. He was like something out of an Erich Von Stroheim movie: duelling scars, monocle and cane — the whole arrogant act.

One day at our meeting when our new Battalion Commander, Lt. Colonel William Dudley (just overseas from the States) was present, they went into their long list of complaints. Instead of taking a firm stand, the Colonel told me to take notes of everything and with that they began to make demands impossible for us to meet. By the time the meeting was over I was furious, but there was nothing I could do.

When Dudley and I left, I realised I had left my cigarette lighter in the house. I went back by myself. The Germans did not hear my return and when I walked in on them they were laughing uproariously. When they saw me the laughter ceased abruptly and you could hear a pin drop. I picked up my cigarette lighter and then told them in no uncertain terms that we were not a bunch of rear-echelon prison guards, but a front line parachute outfit who had been fighting them all the way from Sicily, and lost a lot of good men in the process. I added that if I were in complete command of the camp they would be laughing out of the other sides of their mouths.

I don't know if there was a similar German expression, but they got the message. There were no more complaints.

The ordinary German soldiers were no problem. One day as I was walking through the camp on inspection, I came on a group of them eating hamburgers. They smelt delicious and when they offered me one, I was just about to accept when I spotted horseshoes on a carcass hanging from a nearby tree. I declined with thanks.

In the camp administration I was using an interpreter, a German Sergeant, who spoke English with a perfect American accent. When I questioned him about it he told me he had been born and raised in Amityville, Long Island, and had been living with his grandparents in Germany at the outbreak of war and was trapped in Germany. I told him to be sure to tell his story to the Intelligence people as soon as he got to a permanent POW camp.

One day the sergeant told me that a German Lieutenant Colonel wished to speak with me. When he translated the officer's request, I couldn't believe him. The sergeant assured me that the German was volunteering himself and about 500 survivors of his paratroop battalion to join our army to fight the Japanese. I thanked the Colonel for his offer but assured him it was contrary to the Geneva Convention.

A few weeks later the POW's were trucked west to a permanent camp. I was then put in charge of all the displaced persons in the area. We grouped them by country of origin, and every country in Europe seemed to be represented. We even had one Chinese seaman who had been interned in Germany at the beginning of the war.

Some were families with children who had been taken from their homes to work in Germany. I felt very sorry for them. We could only house them in barns, but at least they were getting a variety of good rations called 'ten-in-one', each box would feed 10 people for a day. Eventually, they too were moved to permanent camps in their own countries.

Many of the East Europeans did not want to go back but under the agreement with the Russian Government, they were sent back against their will.

When we first arrived in Zeetze, truckloads of survivors of a Concentration Camp at Wobelein, which had been liberated by the 82nd Airborne, were moved through our position. They were all thin and haggard. It was a sad sight. We later learned that the Mayor of the town of Ludwigslust, near the camp, had committed suicide.

While we were at Zeetze a regimental review was held at the nearby town of Vielank at which I was decorated with the Silver Star Medal for action in Holland.

We left Zeetze after several weeks and occupied a number of other small German towns. I cannot recall the names of all of them. The last occupation duty was in the city of Bonn.

One day in Bonn, Bill Meddaugh and I were walking in the town when a little man, who looked like 'Igor' in the Frankenstein movie, came out of a basement flat of a building and beckoned us inside. We had no idea what he wanted but we followed him into a large, dark basement to a room at the far end.

I noticed a peculiar smell as we entered and 'Igor' led us to some large tubs. In one tub, ten human heads were floating in formaldehyde. In another was the body of a woman. The remains reminded me of the survivors of the concentration camp we had seen. Bill Meddaugh was sure we had discovered another atrocity, although when we went upstairs we found it was an abandoned Medical School. Abandoned for a good reason, because I am sure the remains in the cellar were probably from a Concentration Camp.

Eventually the regiment left Germany for France. I was happy to go. From the begining, Germany for me had been tragic, weird and depressing. The whole time had seemed unreal.

We went to Camp 'Lucky Strike' to get ready to ship for the Pacific, or so we thought. After only a few days in this camp, we went to Epinal, France, where we learned that the 505 men with 'high points', i.e. time overseas, in combat, wounds and decorations; were to be transferred to the 507th Parachute Infantry Regiment, 17th Airborne Division. Our places were to be filled by the 'low point' men from the 507.

The 82nd Airborne Division was to be part of the Army of Occupation in Berlin. The rest of us were going home. I was very sad when the day came to leave E Company.

After a couple of months delay in a camp at Rambervillers we moved to the port of Marseilles on the Mediterranean. While there, in August, we heard that the atom bombs had been dropped in Japan and that World War Two was finally over. We boarded the *Queen Elizabeth* and sailed home.

I was sent to Fort Dix in New Jersey for discharge, but while being processed was pulled out of the line because of my medical record of Amoebic Dysentery in North Africa. I was tested as positive for the disease and as a result had to spend two months in Tilton General Hospital at Fort Dix undergoing treatment.

Finally, I was released from the Hospital as cured and discharged with the rank of Captain on 1st January 1946. It was thirty days short of five years since I had entered service in the United States Army.

Editor's note: Just as this book was in its final preparation in August 1991, the news came that James J. Coyle had died of a heart attack at his home in Hicksville, New York. He was 72 years old.

The year before, when he heard that I was writing this book, he sent me his wartime diary. There was one condition. In his own words it was, "Please don't make me the hero of E Company or the 505. I have to face these guys at future reunions. What I have written was really meant for my grandchildren to read after I've gone."

After interviewing many E Company men they all confirmed that Jim Coyle's story was correct in every detail. To them Jim Coyle, holder of a Silver Star, was a great leader, a brave soldier in combat and a fine gentlemen. I am just so proud to have him as a friend and to be able to tell his story.

I have tried to comply with his request, so I have left it to the reader to judge the heroism of Jim Coyle for themselves.

To me he was, and always will be, a great hero.

****

LIEUTENANT CARL CLAWSON, B COMPANY, 505

Lieutenant Carl Clawson rejoined the 505 in Germany, after being released by the Russians from captivity. He was welcomed back by B Company and given the command of his old platoon. His Sergeant was Elmo Jones, known to him as 'the Jones boy'. Elmo went on a lone reconnaissance one day but he was spotted by the Germans and came on the receiving end of a lot of fire power. The only safe way back was along a drainage ditch full of water and Carl remembers, with a smile, that 'the Jones boy' got back soaking wet.

The Platoon's Command Post was in a farm house and from an upstairs window there was a good view of the terrain. One of the lookouts reported a movement in a hedge. "I stood up to get a better view," said Carl. "There was a bang and I was thrown back. Like I fool I was in full view in the window. So the war ended with me in a field hospital — wounded."

CAPTAIN ROBERT 'DOC' FRANCO, 505

As the German Army gave up the struggle, 155,000 of them surrendered to the 82nd Airborne. These were men from General von Tippelskirch's 21st Army.

Captain Robert 'Doc' Franco remembers sitting around a radio with his little group of young medics in northern Germany. They sat sober and silent listening to General Montgomery explaining the war had ended. The 82nd were, not for the first time, under British command. Next day, the final day of the fighting in Europe, this message was delivered:

21 Army Group
Personal Message from the C-in-C
(To be read out to all Troops)

1. On this day of victory in Europe I feel I would like to speak to all who have served and fought with me during the last few years. What I have to say is very simple, and quite short.

2. I would ask you all to remember those of our comrades who fell in the struggle. They gave their lives that others might have freedom, and no man can do more than that. I believe that He would say to each one of them:
"Well done thou good and faithful servant."
3. And we who remain have seen the thing through to the end; we all have a feeling of great joy and thankfulness that we have been preserved to see this day. We must remember to give the praise and thankfulness where it is due: "This is the Lord's doing, and it is marvellous in our eyes."
4. In the early days of this war the British Empire stood alone against the combined might of the axis powers. And during those days we suffered some great disasters; but we stood firm: on the defensive, but striking blows where we could. Later we were joined by Russia and America; and from then onwards the end was in no doubt. Let us never forget what we owe to our Russian and American allies; this great allied team has achieved much in war; may it achieve even more in peace.
5. Without doubt, great problems lie ahead; the world will not recover quickly from the upheaval that has taken place; there is much work for each one of us. I would say that we must face up to that work with the same fortitude that we faced up to the worst days of this war. It may be that some difficult times lie ahead for our country, and for each one of us personally. If it happens thus, then our discipline will pull us through; but we must remember that the best discipline implies the subordination of self for the benefit of the community.
6. It has been a privilege and an honour to command this great British Empire team in western Europe. Few commanders can have had such loyal service as you have given me. I thank each one of you from the bottom of my heart.
7. And so let us embark on what lies ahead full of joy and optimism. We have won the German war. Lets us now win the peace.
8. Good luck to you all, wherever you may be.

    (Signed)   B.L. Montgomery
                        Field-Marshal
                        C-in-C
          21 Army Group   Germany, May, 1945.

'Doc' Franco admits that tears came to his eyes as he read it all those years ago. He writes, "Last week (December 1989) while cleaning out my desk I ran into an old photostat of the message. As I read it through, again I could feel the tears. Regardless of what has been said since those days it is still true that before El Alamein we had not had a victory and after that we did not have a defeat."

Having been in the Army longer than any of his colleagues 'Doc' ended up with more 'points' and was sent back to the States for demobilisation. He returned to his home State of Washington to continue his Medical Practice. As he said, "I saw history being made, I am grateful I saw it through, but even more grateful to have the evidence that I was there."

                    ****

Although there was little contact between the troopers and the Russian soldiers, the senior officers met socially on a number of occasions. When they did, the vodka flowed freely and the Russian officers became very boisterious and ready to show how tough they were.

One such party was attended by General James Gavin and Colonel Charles Billingslea, an ex-504 man but now the Commanding Officer of the 325th Glider Infantry Regiment. During the course of the evening the Russian officers started vaulting over a window sill to the ground below and then would come running back up the stairs.

Gavin not to be outdone 'suggested' to Billingslea that he should follow suit to uphold the honour of the 82nd.

Many years later Billingslea said it sounded like an 'order', he was slapped on the back by Gavin so he duly complied. As he jumped and looked down he realised that he had been on the second floor and the landing area was hard concrete.

As he landed he felt his ankle break, but he got to his feet, waved to the Russians looking out of the window and climbed back up the stairs to the party. Later, when one the Russians saw him with an ankle in a cast and queried why he had returned to the party, Billingslea told him…''that a broken ankle is nothing for an American fighting man.''

Being a famous Division they had their fair share of support and entertainment from the Hollywood stars. They had visits and shows from Bob Hope, Jerry Colonna, Frances Langford, Billy Wilder, Jack Benny, Martha Tilton, Ella Logan, Larry Adler and Ingrid Bergman.

Harmonica player Larry Adler remembers when General Gavin invited him with Jack Benny, Martha Tilton and Ingrid Bergman for drinks at a hotel where the troupe were staying. He recalls, ''I dimly remember a tug-of-Ingrid with General Gavin who, understandably, would have liked to have monopolised the lady. I was having my own troubles with the war photographer, Bob Capa, who was trying to do the same as Gavin.''

Marlene Dietrich came along many times and practically adopted them. While the 505 were in Berlin establishing the occupation, Marlene's mother, Frau von Loesch, a resident in the German capital city, died.

Berlin was completely shattered with little or no public services. There was also a very strict non-fraternization order in force between the Allied servicemen and the local population.

When the problem of Frau Loesch became known, the 505 took over, contacted Marlene who was in Paris, and dug the grave. When Marlene arrived they went to her mother's flat at night and the paratroopers smuggled the coffin down to a truck and took it to the cemetery. Marlene and five people attended the funeral, and when darkness came again the 505 troopers closed the grave. It had to be done secretly as the paratroopers were breaking military orders.

****

Richard Halberstadt with his future wife, Elizabeth, photographed in England, August 1944.

CORPORAL RICHARD HALBERSTADT

Richard Halberstadt from Racine, Wisconsin, tells a story of how General James Gavin played the part of 'Cupid' way back in 1945 and entitles it:
THE GENERAL OKAYS A GI'S AWOL

In the fall of 1945 the 82nd Airborne Division was on occupational duty in Berlin. The war had taken these veterans through from North Africa, Sicily, Italy, Normandy, Holland, Belgium, Germany and on to final victory in Berlin. I was a member of the 782nd Airborne Ordnance Company, 82nd Airborne Division, from 18th January 1944 to 6th January 1946.

When the Division came to the United Kingdom to prepare for D-Day my unit was based in the small village of Oadby, on the outskirts of Leicester. Our billets ranged from Church rooms to a boarded-over swimming pool. During those Spring months we drank our beer in the village pubs, ate our fish and chips and enjoyed the dances and the cinema. This is when I met the love of my life, Elizabeth, an Oadby girl.

Now that we had won our way through to Berlin some of the 'high point' veterans had been deployed to return to the States for discharge. With replacements from other Airborne Divisions the 82nd became America's Honor Guard for the divided city, to fulfil the Potsdam agreement.

Most of the troopers settled in for this choice duty, but all I could think of was my Elizabeth, the girl I had left in England, and to find a way to see her again before returning home. My opportunity arrived when I bid for and received a three week rehabilitation leave to learn Wholesale Distribution in

England. This was to prepare me for discharge and the outside world.

I flew from Tempelhof airfield on 20th October to report to an English Biscuit (Cookie) factory in Redhill, England, where I was to work one week on production, one week in the offices and one week on the delivery van. It was a five day, 8am to 5pm, working week.

The fine English manager was informed of my love in Leicester and gave me leave early on Fridays to pursue my courtship with the stipulation to return on Mondays at my convenience. This was a dream come true.

The first weekend was superb and the second was ecstatic. Returning to Redhill on the second Monday morning I was walking my fiancee down Granby Street in Leicester when I saw General James Gavin standing on the steps of the Grand Hotel. I gave him a proud military salute, which he returned, and I carried on to leave Elizabeth at her place of work. I continued on to the L.M.S. Railroad Station on London Road where I purchased some newspapers to read on the train. Just as I was glancing at them I heard a voice say, "Good morning Corporal, and what are you doing here?"

I looked up into the familiar, beaming face of General Gavin and I nearly collapsed through the platform. I explained my situation and then bodly asked him if it was true that the Division were to return to the United States. He said "Yes." Then I asked him if it was possible for me to remain in England and make my return from here.

He told me to write my request to my Company Commander and the S-1 of the Division and they should work it out for me. If I had any problems tell them to contact him. I thanked him, saluted, and we went our separate ways.

I wrote my letters and finished my third week of work experience on 10th November, but still I had no reply. Should I return to Berlin or be AWOL? Being Airborne I took the initiative and went to SHAEF Headquarters in London to declare my plight. Sympathetic listeners stated they could do nothing and after a half dozen futile attempts found a Captain who had been in the Division and been wounded, who believed my story. He said he would take care of things.

Nearly five weeks passed while I stayed at my fiancee's home, regularly checking with the officer at SHAEF on any progress. I fully enjoyed the leave, but behind it all I could see myself a prisoner in the Stockade. Finally word came to report and be sent home from England on 13th December. I had nearly five weeks of borrowed time with the love of my life.

It was both a sad and happy day when I departed. I was going to be free of soldiering, but it was a long six months before I returned to England in my own time and at my own expense to claim my lovely lady.

We were married in St. Peter's Church, Oadby, Leicester, on 15th August 1946, with the reception in the Church Hall. This had been our Company Mess Hall during our stay in the UK.

Elizabeth and I have now been happily married for over forty years and blessed with three wonderful children. In our hearts we give a multitude of thanks to 'Gentleman Jim' for his compassionate manner in dealing with this unusual situation. We don't know how it happened, we just thank him it did. May God Bless Him!

James "Slim Jim' Gavin

Lieutenant General James M. Gavin of the United States Army died on the 22nd February 1990, aged 82, in a Baltimore nursing home and had been in ill health for some time. He was born on the 22nd March 1907.

To the 82nd Airborne paratroopers he was something special, a unique General. It was not his style to be flamboyant, he did not need the pearl handled revolvers of George Patton as a trade mark. Nor was he an isolationist as Bernard Montgomery, or as publicity seeking as Mark Clark. He led his men from the front and they worshipped him. To them he was a hero. If there was a difficulty or danger, Jim Gavin was there. He was always first 'out of the door' when leading his beloved men on four dangerous combat parachute jumps in Sicily, Salerno, Normandy and Holland.

In combat he dressed in an ordinary trooper's jumpsuit without any badges of rank, except the stars on his helmet and he always carried an M-1 rifle. There was no need for insignias of rank as everybody in the 82nd Airborne knew who he was. They called him affectionately 'Slim Jim'.

At the end of the war when a German General wanted to surrender his army to an officer of equivalent rank, an 82nd Airborne Sergeant brought him to Gavin. The German could not believe that this tall boyish figure was indeed a General. Gavin soon convinced him.

Unlike most he never raised his voice, a quiet word was a command, usually couched in terms of, "I want you to do this." His charismatic leadership and his electrifying presence made him friends all over the world.

Orphaned at a very early age, a local Catholic priest found him a home with a Pennsylvanian coal miner and his family. Joining the Army as a Private in 1924, at 18 he was technically too young to join without his parents consent. When it was learnt he was an orphan the recruiter took him to a lawyer who became his guardian long enough to sign the necessary papers.

Gavin was never to forget that he started his army career as a 'yardbird', an enlisted man.

One of his sergeants persuaded him to take the competitive examinations for admission to West Point. He passed and entered the Military Academy in the Class of 1929. From that start he climbed the ranks to become a Three-Star General. By the age of 37 he was the youngest General in the U.S. Army since the Civil War. In 1942, as Colonel, he commanded the famous 505th Parachute Infantry Regiment, one of the crack regiments in the 82nd Airborne Division. Later he took over from Matthew Ridgway to command the whole Division.

In the film *The Bridge Too Far* he was portrayed by Ryan O'Neal, a choice of actor that Gavin was unhappy with. Nevertheless O'Neal managed to

General James M. Gavin in 1944. At 37 years old he was the youngest General in the U.S. Army since the Civil War and his boyish looks earned him the nickname of 'Slim Jim'.

General James Gavin and his wife, Jeanne, in Leicester in 1984 with the author, Deryk Wills.

convey a good representation of the young, handsome and fearless Airborne General.

Gavin resigned in 1958 when in charge of the Army's research and development at the Pentagon. He could no longer honourably defend the course his country was taking in regard to national defence. Later he was unhappy about the way the Army was being used in Vietnam.

President Kennedy called on Gavin to be his Inaugural Parade Marshal and then offered him the post of U.S. Ambassador to France. Kennedy wanted a soldier to stand up to Charles DeGaulle. Gavin was reluctant at first as he had just accepted a job as President of the Cambridge consulting firm of Arthur D. Little, Inc.

"Are you going to help me out or not?" Kennedy asked, so Gavin took the job which lasted a successful eighteen months.

This writer spent a great deal of time in General Gavin's company during the 40th Anniversaries of D-Day and Market Garden in England, Normandy and Holland. Everlasting in my memory will be the love and friendship which was ever present between the General and the veteran paratroopers of the 82nd. When he entered any room or hall they would give him a standing ovation, such was their lasting affection for this man.

The last time I saw Jim Gavin was in 1986 at a 505th Parachute Infantry Regiment Reunion at Fort Bragg, North Carolina, the 82nd Airborne Headquarters. I was carrying a special message from Prime Minister Margaret Thatcher which I read out at the Reunion Dinner. I finished with the words, "Men of the 505th Parachute Infantry Regiment, Great Britain salutes you." As I walked back to my seat I passed by the General. He caught my eye and with a big smile he brought his hand up to his forehead in a smart military salute in return.

We have lost a wartime hero and I have lost a friend. Many people all over the United States and Europe will be saying proudly in the years to come, "I knew Jim Gavin."

He is survived by his wife, Jeanne, and five daughters.

Medals of Honor

Three Congressional Medals of Honor were awarded for bravery to men of the 82nd Airborne Division during the Second World War.

Pfc. Charles N. DeGlopper of Grand Island, New York, C Company, 325th Glider Infantry Regiment, for his actions on June 9, 1944. It was at La Fiere, Normandy, on the Merderet River where, although wounded several times, he voluntarily made sure that he was seen by a large enemy force, drawing heavy automatic and rifle fire. By this action he helped the withdrawl of an encircled platoon trying to establish the first bridgehead across the river.

Private John R. Towle of Cleveland, Ohio, C Company, 504th Parachute Infantry Regiment for his actions near Oosterhout, Holland, on September 21, 1944. Armed with a rocket launcher he, single handedly and without orders, moved into an exposed position and broke up a German counter-attack of 100 infantrymen supported by two tanks and a half-track. He was mortally wounded by a mortar shell.

First Sergeant Leonard Funk, Jr., of Braddock Township, Pennsylvania, C Company, 508th Parachute Infantry Regiment for his actions at Holzheim, Belgium, on January 29, 1945. After leading his unit and capturing 80 Germans, the enemy, by means of a ruse, captured the four American guards, freed the prisoners and prepared to attack the understrength Americans. Funk, walking round a building into their midst, had a machine pistol thrust into his stomach by a German officer. Pretending to comply with the surrender demand, he slowly unslung his Thompson sub-machine-gun and with a lightning fast motion, shot the officer and led his men in resisting the enemy. Twenty one Germans were killed in the process.

Sergeant Funk had already won a Silver Star in Normandy and a Distinguished Service Cross in Holland.

Besides the three Congressional Medals of Honor, the Troopers of the Division were awarded a total of 78 Distinguished Service Crosses, 1 Distinguished Service Medal, 32 Legion of Merit, 894 Silver Stars, 2,478 Bronze Star Medals and numerous foreign decorations.

****

Tom Porcella (left) and Ed Wenzel at the scene of the battle for Hill 30 near Chef du Pont, Normandy.

A RETURN TO NORMANDY WITH THE VETERANS OF THE 508th PARACHUTE INFANTRY REGIMENT FOR THE 40th ANNIVERSARY OF D-DAY, JUNE 1984

The village of Chef-du-Pont in Normandy is not on the tourist map. It lies about three kilometres off the Route 13, going south out of Cherbourg. It consists of one main street, a square with a hotel, a railway level crossing, a large dairy factory and a bridge across the River Merderet. To the men of the 508th Parachute Infantry Regiment, 82nd Airborne Division, it holds vivid memories. Memories that make them return year after year.

Around this village some of the heaviest fighting for the young American paratroopers took place. Two thousand men from the 508 jumped into the area on the night of the 5/6th June 1944, in the first hours of the D-Day operation. This for many of them was their first taste of combat. In the following thirty three days, 336 men died, 660 were wounded and 165 were missing.

The villagers of Chef-du-Pont have never forgotten the Regiment's sacrifice and their bravery. On each return they come out of their houses to welcome every veteran with kisses and handshakes. Led by the Town Band, parades are held to the 82nd Memorials which are adorned with flowers. Numerous parties are held in houses and local farms that go on late into the night.

Normandy is a land of rivers and swamps. The Germans had flooded large areas leaving only the roads and bridges passable. Whoever controlled these, held Normandy. The Allied paratroopers attack was designed to capture those vital bridges and causeways so that the main landing force could get quickly off the beaches, without interference from the mobile German defenders. Chef-du-Pont, five kilometres from Ste-Mere-Eglise, had one of these vital bridges.

During the main drop the paratroopers found themselves scattered far and wide. Unexpected low cloud made the drop zones hard to pin-point in the darkness. Some men were drowned in the deep flood-water unable to free themselves from their heavy equipment. Others had difficulty in getting their bearings in fields and lanes that looked all the same in the dark. They also had to face fierce German resistance.

Now forty years on they recalled the situations they found themselves in as young men. Most had tears in their eyes as they remembered the friends they had lost. Owen Hill, known to everyone as "O.B.", walked through an orchard where he had been pinned down for hours. The apple trees were ablaze with blossom, just as they had been all those years ago.

Walking down the main street, Charlie Paradise from Connecticut saw a stone wall. He paused for a moment and told me, "The guy in front of me was hit. I pulled him behind this wall. A Kraut was firing at us from that window across the street." Then he said very quietly, "I went across and killed him." Charlie, a tall lean powerful man, just stood there looking. The way he said it was not a boast, just a statement of fact. One thing Charlie has never forgotten was the sound of the bullets zipping through his chute as he floated down.

Joe Kissane, now a tax expert from New York came up. He was in that same street fight and hadn't seen Charlie for forty years.

Just outside the village there is a slight rise in the ground, just enough to bring it above the flood level. It is still known as Hill 30. Ed Wenzel of Pennsylvania and Tom Porcella, a tough little New Yorker, were recalling the fierce fighting they took part in trying to hold this hill. Ed found the crossroads where he knocked out two German tanks. "One of the crew survived," Ed recalled. "And he came down this side of the hedge after me. I saw him just before he fired. He was wearing very thick glasses. I was hit in the stomach. My pals rolled me into the hedge bottom for safety."

"I was there for hours before the Medics found me, at first they thought I was dead." He walked a few more paces searching for words. "It was something I will never forget. I still have nightmares about it and I always see that face, the face wearing those thick glasses." Ed Wenzel spent a long time in hospital recovering, and still has the scars on his body to this day.

Captain Chet Graham was trying to recognise landmarks. He still responds to his radio callsign of that night. It was 'Applecheeks', a nickname which has stuck ever since.

Zane Schlemmer and Pierre Cotelle still trying to solve the mystery of their meeting on D-Day.

One of Chet's platoon was a young trooper from Ohio, Sergeant Zane Schlemmer. Zane landed near a farm which turned out to be the Luffwaffe's Headquarters for the area. ''There was so much flak coming from the two courtyards that I could see the outline of the house and the farm buildings quite clearly. I got my bearings and skirted around the farm, in doing so I found a trooper from the 101st Airborne who was miles off his target. Together we stumbled across a foxhole. The two Germans in it seemed frozen with fear. We tossed in a grenade and finished them.''

Those farm buildings still hold a mystery to this day. It was, and still is, the home of the Cotelle family, Norman farmers for generations. The son, Pierre, fourteen years old in 1944, was out in the fields early that morning checking the cows, when he suddenly came face to face with an American Paratrooper. Beside him was his parachute. They tried to exchange words but nobody spoke the other's language. Pierre, now 59 and owner of the 15th century farm, has never forgotten those few moments.

A party held at the Cotelle Farm, Chef du Pont, Normandy in 1984. Left to right, David Jones of the 508th Parachute Infantry Regiment, Pierre Cotelle and Leonard Giannotti of the 101st Airborne Division.

To this day it is not certain who the trooper was or if he survived. Forty years of research has failed to turn up a name. Pierre still has that parachute and a careful search in 1984 revealed a serial number of MF 42 95 99 47.

Since meeting Zane after the war, Pierre is convinced that he has found his man. In spite of Zane's doubts the two have become firm friends. Every year a party is held on the 6th June in the large dining room of the old farm house. The walls are decorated with draped D-Day parachutes. On the sideboard is a German telephone, still there from when the room was a Luffwaffe office. The tables are laden with food and wine which are all of Norman origin.

Pierre dresses in his Norman farmer's smock and traditional top hat. He darts about like a mischievous schoolboy topping up the wine glasses. The Calvados is something special, distilled on the farm 50 years ago and saved for occasions like this. As one veteran paratrooper put it, "If we ever run out of rocket fuel, I know where to come."

On the road opposite the farm there is a stone momument with a large plaque mounted on it flanked by two flags, the Stars and Stripes and the Tricolour. This plaque reads:

"Into this field in the pre-dawn hours of 6th June, 1944, jumped Sergeant Zane Schlemmer, holder of the American Bronze Star, and heroic trooper of the 508th Parachute Infantry, 82nd Airborne Division."

Zane it still not sure if he was the mystery man. Pierre is certain, to him there is no doubt. The road down to the farm from the main highway proudly displays a large name plate......'Rue Zane Schlemmer'.

Epilogue

As one 82nd Airborne veteran said, "Anybody with four combat jump stars was extremely lucky to survive." Although at any one time there were only twelve thousand men in the 82nd Airborne Division, by the end of the war the rosters show that many thousands of men had been members of this famous outfit.

General James Gavin was to write later, "So we had come to the end of the war in Europe. It had been costly. More than sixty thousand men had passed through the ranks of the 82nd Airborne Division alone. We had left in our wake thousands of white crosses from Africa to Berlin."

When looking through the records it is remarkable to note the number of German and Italian surnames of the American paratroopers. Some of them were first generation sons of immigrants, so therefore their Oath of Allegiance to the United States of America was all important, overcoming all the past national and family ties. They were all proud to be Americans.

There was never any difficulty in finding interpreters for any middle European language in the 82nd Airborne. Typical was Samuel D. Trekur of C Company, 325th Glider Infantry, who was proficient in four languages, English, French, Italian and Russian. He was called upon many times during the war to act as an interpreter. Sam's brother, Steve, also served in the same Regiment in K Company.

The Company rosters are a great source of information. The United States Army liked men to have two forenames and were quite disturbed when they had only one. Alongside the names of these there would be (NMI), which meant 'no middle initial'.

On some occasions when the man had only initials, which is quiet usual for southern families, the Army insisted that he chose a forename to match his first initial.

In 1969, on the 25th Anniversary of D-Day, a group of veterans and their wives made their first organised visit to Normandy. Katie Kaiser, wife of Sergeant Charles Kaiser, remembers walking down a road by herself after a reception in a Town Hall.

"I just couldn't believe the friendliness and kindness shown to us. It was just overwhelming and I began to cry." Katie remembered, "Someone walked up behind me, it was Colonel Krause. He asked if I was alright, and I said I was fine, but I cannot believe I am in this world. Its like being in 'a pumpkin world'. When we go home and try to explain all this, no one will understand. I feel like Cinderella and when I go home the 'pumpkin world' will have disappeared."

Colonel Edward 'Cannonball' Krause took Katie's arm and said he understood. Many years later Katie said of the hardened and sometimes misunderstood paratrooper Colonel, "Such a tender man. We didn't know then he was dying of cancer."

Many years later Bill Tucker was to say of Colonel Krause, "In the end Colonel Edward Krause showed he was a man of heart and compassion. I deeply regret that he was misunderstood and he should have received more historical credit for the capture of Ste-Mere-Eglise. Other 505 officers, such as Gavin, either didn't respect him or just didn't like him. The fact is that he was never relieved from his command and that his Battalion performed its missions with force and gallantry."

The people of Leicestershire still remember the men of the 82nd Airborne Division. There is a memorial stone in Victoria Park, put there by public subscription, which is dedicated to all those who came in 1944, and especially to the men who never returned home across the Atlantic Ocean.

In 1986 this writer was invited to Fort Bragg, North Carolina, to a special 505 Reunion. I was entrusted by the Prime Minister of Great Britain, Margaret Thatcher, to carry a personal message from her to be read out at the Reunion Dinner. The message read:

"I am delighted to send a personal message to you, the men of the 505th Parachute Infantry Regiment, 82nd Airborne Division, on the occasion of your reunion at Fort Bragg."

"The splendid record of the 505th in the Second World War will not be forgotten by the people of Britain. The 505th took off from airfields in the vicinity of my home town, Grantham, for the airborne assault forward of Utah Beach in June 1944. You also fought splendidly alongside the British Guards Armoured Division in the capture of the Nijmegen bridges under General James M. Gavin and fought with distinction to repel and defeat the last great German offensive in the West — the Battle of the Ardennes."

"On behalf of the British people, I send my gratitude and warmest greetings to General Gavin and all the men of the 505th Parachute Infantry Regiment who fought so gallantly in the cause of freedom."

****

In the Preface of his official report of the operations of the Division during the battles of 'The Belgian Bulge', General James Gavin made the following statement about the paratroopers of the 82nd Airborne Division.

"Men fought, at times, with only rifles, grenades and knives against the German armour. They fought with only light weapons in waist-deep snow, in blizzards, in near zero temperatures and in areas where heavy forestation and the almost total lack of roads presented problems that only men of stout hearts and iron determination could overcome."

"The Battles of 'The Bulge', ranking on a par with the brightest victories in the Division's history, also proved again that plans and material are important but most essential of all is the fighting heart, a will to win. To the troopers of the line goes full credit for the brilliant record they made in the name of the 82nd Airborne Division."

****

Part Two

SUMMARY OF BILL TUCKER'S WAR DIARY*

WITH THE SECOND PLATOON, I COMPANY,

505TH PARACHUTE INFANTRY REGIMENT,

IN WORLD WAR TWO

SUMMARY EDITED BY DERYK WILLS

William H. 'Bill' Tucker in 1944.

William H. 'Bill' Tucker was one of the few who survived right through the war in I Company, finishing as a Sergeant. After the war he became an Attorney in his home State of Massachusetts and took an active part in the Kennedy Administration in Washington. He was the instigator in forming a veterans association, the C-47 Club, which embraces all the veterans of the 82nd Airborne Division. As a sports parachutist he made several jumps in France and Holland in 1984 to celebrate the 40th anniversary.

Introduction

This summary was rather hastily put together from a personal diary that I completed in October 1945, covering my life as a soldier begining in 1943. Now Deryk Wills has edited and researched it for his book about the 82nd Airborne Division. Except for ''de-personalising'' these diary excerpts, such as changing — wherever possible — from 'I' to 'Tucker' the material is more or less unchanged.

I have the following observations regarding the content:
* This is not representative of the complete personal diary since I have excluded much material involving my own thoughts, reactions and some activities, including several situations when we were in combat.
* The style and tone of this is still just about that of a young man returning from war to school and writing over 45 years ago. There have been some changes in vision, etc. from that time, but I've left it alone, although in summarising some of the details, a little of that style is lost.
* I'm satisfied that this is an accurate account of what we did and where we were, except for mistakes in the names of places or a particular site in a broad sense of action. It should be noted that my field of vision or knowledge was limited to that of a rifleman, machine-gunner and a Squad Leader over the course of our campaigns.
* One matter must be set aside from the foregoing comment and that is the issue as to whether I Company, or part of it, actually took off by aircraft for Rome on 8th September 1943, and were shortly afterwards recalled to Sicily. One or two historical observers from our outfit have advised me that I Company was not one of the units that did take off for Rome. However, that was my recollection in writing it in 1945 and again in 1986. Several Second Platoon comrades also have stated that they remember it. In fairness, I should point out that I was severely ill at the time with malaria, jaundice and dysentery; that I was evacuated from Maiori to Constantine, North Africa, by hospital ship. I was sick enough to be kept for five or six weeks at a hospital. Despite this feverish period I would have a hard time in 'revising' my then recollection. The 8th September was my 20th birthday!
* I mentioned that the adventures of the I Company's mortar section was a vivid recollection. That was mostly because of our great leader, Jim Downing, and the success — as well as fun — we had working and firing the three '60's' as a battery. Although the Squad Leader's job wasn't all that good when a turn came to repair the wire in an open field, or when Jim, Wallace or I had to spend a couple of nights in some hidden observer spot in front of our lines with the ever wandering Moe Green. Our success in gunnery might have only been exceeded by our excellent cuisine.

* Another observation important to me is that this doesn't contain a lot of material or comment on the fine officers we had in I Company. Most of us will remember that we lost excellent Company Commanders almost immediately after jumps in Sicily and Normandy, the latter having severe effects on the Company's further deployments. When we finally got a commander, Captain McPheeters, who was with us awhile and who worked so well with us through Holland, we lost him too at the height of battle in the Ardennes on 3rd January 1945.

It was Captain McPheeters who set up our mortar section and its uses. I want to point out also, in this regard, that I Company did a fine professional job in Holland, particularly for many days along the Reichswald, near Groesbeek, where we efficiently pulverised numerous attacks. We didn't receive many casualties in Holland since, for one reason, we were not involved in those dramatic and most intense contests such as at the Nijmegen Bridge.

Another reason was that we were able to go through a field campaign with a great Company, with a fine C.O. and officers, and an excellent cast of NCO's and well trained, experienced combat soldiers. We didn't make much noise but did the job.

* Personal Note: I will always remember that on the morning of 6th June 1944, my Father, who taught me pride and to reach for intellect, read the morning paper story that U.S. Airborne troops had been landing in Western France. On his long subway trip to work, he stopped at an old church in Central Square, Cambridge, that morning. I stop there now every few years.

William H. Tucker,
Harwichport, MA
August 1991

Sicily and Italy

Bill Tucker joined the 505th Parachute Infantry Regiment, 82nd Airborne Division, as a replacement when it returned to Africa after the successful invasion of Sicily. Within a few short weeks the Regiment returned, once again, to Sicily. This is Tucker's story.

It was wonderful for the Paratroopers to step from the plane in Sicily and see green vegetation again after so many months in North Africa. They set up camp around an airport and were ordered to dig slit trenches in preparation for any bombing raids. It was almost impossible to dig in the very, very hard ground, especially with their strength being so low in many cases because of their poor medical condition.

They stayed in Sicily for seven days and it wasn't bad, especially when they looked back on their time in Africa. Dysentry was prevalent which made it miserable to walk, bend over, stand up or do anything strenuous physically. It was also very horrible to do any sort of latrine duty, but there was a lot of fruit around, and some girls too, so no one was complaining too much.

Everyone was suffering from loss of weight during this time due to the dysentry, malaria, jaundice and other ailments. Tucker weighed about 135 pounds compared to a usual 185 pounds. When he looked down at his legs they looked like pipes. This was substantiated when Pfc Fred Synold, who had a tongue like a whip but a great guy underneath, said that he looked as though he was walking on sticks.

They had been told that the Third Battalion 505 had been training for sea landings at Bizerte but they knew that they were ready to jump somewhere.

During this period there was a rifle inspection by the Company Commander of I Company, Captain Harold Swingler of St Louis, Missouri. Swingler was a great leader and a very intelligent man who lost sight of a very few things. Nine out of ten guns in the Company were found to be dirty. It was the toughest rifle inspection most of them had ever encountered.

On 8th September 1943, Tucker's birthday, they took off to jump on Rome to seize the airfields in connection with the Italian surrender. They flew over the Mediterranean for a short while and then turned back to Sicily. It was a nice flight while it lasted, but something went wrong in Rome — like Hitler moving in some more Panzer Divisions.

The next day 'blood and guts' Krause (Major Edward Krause) gathered the Battalion together and gave a long speech on security and stated that someone had talked too much so that the Germans were waiting in Rome. He was very sorry about losing the mission — but the troopers were not. His words were, ''Men, last night we had history by the balls,'' then Krause lifted his leg and made a very disgusting comment. Somehow or other it fitted the picture. (Tucker learned many years later from General Matthew Ridgway that it was he who opposed the higher headquarters and ordered the mission to be scrapped).

Right after this there were two big happenings. First, the 505 had to secure the Castelvetrano Airport as the Italian pilots landed to surrender. They lined up along the runway with full weapons. The only thing was that half of them — the Italian flyers — were nuts and deliberately tried to damage their planes when they landed. One pilot got killed and a few of the paratroopers got burnt or hurt.

The biggest event was President Roosevelt's brief stopover in Sicily. His felt hat and his big smile were just as in all the pictures — something never to forget — and a moment of great pride.

(Tucker places this memory in Sicily, but the Editor believes that this was in North Africa while Tucker was convalescing from his illness. Roosevelt was travelling to the first Tripartite Meeting in Teheran in November 1943).

A few more days went by and suddenly the Regiment was alerted to be ready to jump in twelve hours. The drop zone would be behind the right flank of the U.S. Fifth Army which was being badly mauled after landing at Salerno. The 505 were told — as always — that the Hermann Goering Division was there for them to fight.

About eleven o'clock that night they took off and circled north over the Mediterranean towards Sardinia and from there the planes turned east towards the Italian coast. They had not realised it but the Allied plans had all but failed and the landing by the 36th Division was in trouble at Salerno. The only thing that was holding everything up was the great Ranger Battalion fighting in support of the 36th.

Again, during this ride the paratroopers had little fear. They could forget the past and not think a helluva lot about the future. It was a relief to stand up and hook up for the jump. As they passed over the coast they could see many burning ships in Salerno Bay. Finally they were actually able to spot the Drop Zone 'T' lit up by the pathfinder group, and at that point the green light came on. They went out the door.

(As Tucker jumped, he looked up and checked his parachute and noticed he had a malfuction. A line had gone over the top of his chute so that he had, in effect, only two half chutes, this was known as a 'Mae West'. As he was descending too fast he deployed his reserve parachute).

It was a high jump and there was quite a bit of confusion on the Drop Zone since the whole Regiment was jumping into such a small area on a beach.

Realising that they were on the Continent of Europe everybody quickly got their weapons and ammunition in order. It was a very bright moonlight night and I Company managed to assemble itself rather fast. Flight after flight of Battalions poured themselves out on parachutes above them.

Suddenly there was a terrific blast from out at sea. It was miles away but the blast was so severe that they could feel it on their faces. An ammunition ship had been hit by a bomb (as they later found out) and blew up, taking two other ships with it.

After assembling, they quickly moved out to their rendezvous point. From then on Italy was nothing more than hills, sickness, and sometimes when they felt better, great beauty.

In the morning they marched way up to the top of a mountain overlooking Salerno Bay. They were told to dig in and found the ground in Italy just as hard as the ground in Africa or Sicily. It got to be quite hot and the best they could find in the way of food was their own K rations.

Sitting up there that morning they saw a lone Messerschmitt come buzzing in over the Bay. There were British Spitfires patrolling the area at the time, and they immediately got on the German's tail as he flew directly over the 505 spraying the troops with his 20mm calibre cannons. They found out later that only one man was hit in the leg.

While the Messerschmitt was leading the Spitfires a merry chase, a lone Heinkel bomber flew over at about 8,000 feet and dropped a bomb which split a cruiser in two. It appeared that the Germans were pretty tough nuts at that time.

After fooling around for several hours doing nothing, it was decided that they should push on and take up positions on the 'right flank'. They had no idea where the enemy was. All they were told to do was march. The road was hot and as they came down the mountain they came across a motion picture cameraman taking pictures.

The march became unbearable because many were sick. Finally Fred Synold passed out, the machine-gun coming down on his head. Tucker began to have dry heaves and had to stop beside the road — with a few others. Lieutenant John Dolan came up to keep them moving and soon they were able to catch up. I Company had been spread out for a mile or so up the road.

When they reached their destination they found it was along the side of a hill overlooking a very lovely valley. It was a beautiful hill too, but the marching had been hard going.

Sergeant Harvey Hanks set up the First Squad in a defensive position and sent 'new man' Tucker about 200 yards out to the front to act as an outpost. He stayed there for a little while and he began to think it wasn't such a bad idea until it began to get dark. When a little Italian fellow came up to him, he tried to get some information from him about the enemy. He said that the Germans were just over the hill in the next valley.

Tucker was lucky because his Squad moved to new positions and he dug in with the machine-gun crew near a well which had the coldest, sweetest water he had tasted in many months.

They stayed in this position for perhaps three of four days and ate thousands of grapes and dried figs which a little girl brought down from the top of the mountain every day. The only thing that was tough about it was climbing up and down the hill to bring back the rations.

The First Squad by this time had been out on patrol and they later found that they were to move up in reserve to a bivouac area near a river above Salerno. This proved to be quite a nice place. However, there were many details to perform. Sergeant Dey of the Second Squad of the Platoon seemed to run his squad so smoothly and was so respected — even though he didn't look like the All American paratrooper. He was a very disciplined and determined NCO.

(Tucker later described Sergeant Dey as balding, short in stature with a pot-belly, nothing like the dashing image of a paratrooper).

After the Company got settled near the river they went swimming and washed their clothes; or have the Italian women who were around wash them for them.

Tucker could see a town high up on a mountain which overlooked the river. One could not help but notice this little town for it seemed so remote, so far away, so still and so strange way up there in the distance. Sometimes it was even obscured by the clouds. The Platoon was ordered to make a combat patrol up the mountain into the town. It was an opportunity, but quite a march. They had full combat equipment and going up those steep slopes in the dark was hazardous, watching out all the time for the terraces and unmarked precipices.

The town was pitch black and totally quiet. They saw a couple of people in the streets who came out to watch them march through. They were dressed as if they lived 200 years ago and the town had the ancient dirty smell about it that was reminiscent of the old towns of Sicily.

After a few days by the river, Tucker's Company moved down to the beach at Salerno and boarded LCI's (Landing Craft, Infantry) to go up the coast and make a beach landing behind the German lines at a town called Maiori, just south of Naples. It was midnight and pitch dark when the boats headed for the shore. As the boats touched the beach there were gun flashes or lightning flashes, and the paratroopers went into the town with very little opposition. There was a very cold driving rain and they wound up in an old church which gave them some shelter.

Tucker finally succumbed to his illness and was taken to a hospital in Constantine, North Africa, where he stayed for a number of weeks. He did not rejoin I Company until they were in Bizerte where the barracks bags were being loaded for their journey to the unknown. Tucker was put on the loading detail just in time to see an American cargo ship that contained his own precious 'B' bag, sunk.

Before leaving Italy, I Company (as related by Sergeant Howard Melvin) fought its way into Naples on tanks of the British Eighth Army and fulfilled further combat missions given by the U.S. Fifth Army.

I Company was in good shape as it headed to Northern Ireland. The trip took some 21 days through the Mediterranean Sea to the Atlantic Ocean, during which time the convoy was bombed fifteen nights by the German Luftwaffe. The general alarm was sounded countless times, always breaking up the great games of poker and pinochle.

One treasured memory of the river near Salerno remains with Tucker. When they were bathing and washing their clothes in the cool river, someone swam by in midstream at a fast pace with powerful strokes. One I Company guy asked, "Who's that old guy?" Another answered, "That's our boss, General Ridgway." The General must have been all of 46 or 47 years old at the time.

The United Kingdom

Not only was Ireland green, but everybody liked it because it was cool. The Regiment landed at Belfast and I Company was the only company in the Division to be stationed right in the centre of Cookstown, the reason being that it was the only Company in the Regiment which had not had any cases of V.D. in Naples, or so they heard. Each Platoon was billeted in a room that was part of an old hotel, fitted out with double-decker bunks and straw mattresses.

Their stay in Ireland was pleasant after Africa, although the climate wasn't all that agreeable. They made quite a few training marches of eight to ten miles which brought on some very harsh pains in the leg muscles.

It got dark at about 3.00 or 3.30 in the afternoon and didn't get light until after 8.00 in the morning. It was so dark when the Company assembled for reveille, no lights could be used because of the blackout, it made it difficult but everybody was accounted for each morning.

The Second Platoon guys on the second floor were; Scotty Hough, Larry Leonard, Jack Leonard, Bill Laws, Ray Krupinski and Bill Tucker. Life for them in Cookstown did not pass quietly by, there were many memorable or amusing situations. There was plenty of Irish whiskey and beer around so everyone got drunk at times.

Scotty Hough seemed to be a pleasant little guy until one night, as Edwin 'Old Man' Jones and Tucker were sitting on a top bunk playing Casino, when Lieutenant Joseph Vandevegt deposited Scotty in the room, dead drunk. He grabbed a handful of cards off the bunk. Tucker told him to cut it out, but Scotty answered by slugging them both. Scotty was a real Jekyll and Hyde character.

At night most would go to the movies, and after the movies they would stop in some private little restaurant, or milkbar and manage to get some French fries and a steak. A lot of the guys hung around the milkbar down at the corner, most of them with their girlfriends. The girls in Cookstown were few and far between as they had been warned by the priest in their church to stay away from the U.S. Army.

They found that Belfast was quite a town. The first time there, Paul Hill and Tucker met a couple of girls and went dancing. Then surprise, they found out that in the UK the girls did the cutting in. They all got acquainted and the four had some pretty good times together.

Back in Cookstown there wasn't much to do there except get caught for the usual details. There was one, a coal shovelling detail, which was horrible and everybody tried to avoid that. It was hard work getting the drunks back into barracks for the bed check. Scotty was a particular problem and if he hadn't shown by midnight, Larry Leonard would usually go out to get him.

Training continued and they got to fire the machine-gun on a range. One time there was a street parade which was missed because of a coal detail. Leonard, Scotty and Tucker stood on the side of the road, covered with black coal dust while the rest of the Company paraded in full uniform and it proved to be very amusing. From then on the three became known as the 'coal men'.

At night they never got to sleep, somebody always had something to talk about, and Scotty use to analyse everybody, but he had a distorted imagination.

They played basketball while at Cookstown. Gil Mulvaney was about the best player in the Regiment. He and Jim Ritchie were two close friends and there were no better men in the Company. Scotty entered the boxing championship and might have won the welter-weight if he had stayed in shape.

In spite of the almost never-ending darkness, Cookstown was okay — certainly after the sickly, miserable days in Africa and Italy. Tucker kept going to Belfast, met different girls at dances, and even had them visit him in Cookstown at weekends when he couldn't get passes. This was sort of marred by Tucker's constant disagreements and fights with Hill — in Belfast and in Cookstown — arguing over women. In this, Hill was always a step ahead because he was so damn devious.

A lot of guys travelled together, Tucker with Scotty, up to the point where Scotty got drunk. Then it was with Lance Hoffman, Jack Leonard and others from the Second Platoon. Everybody regretted blowing about two months pay at the Savoy Club where they were taken, but not without some struggling. Hoffman was never the same after they shaved off (it took six guys) one side of his big red moustache on the ship to Ireland. It never did grow back right so he quit the moustache and became sort of moody.

Christmas was kind of tough in Cookstown because some, including Tucker, were reported missing for a bed check and wound up doing KP at the Officer's Club. It was good and bad. Good because they ate and drank all they wanted to, and bad because it was tough being on KP at Christmas.

The officers, including Lt. Colonel Herbert Batcheller, had some terrific girls at a party. Tucker had been in the kitchen all day and was stripped to the waist and covered in soot. He was quite a sight, especially when he carried in a bowl of steaming eggnog into the party. The Colonel didn't appreciate Tucker's appearance.

In February the Regiment boarded a train which took them to a Dutch ship in Belfast harbour. This tub, old as she was, managed to get them over to Scotland and for the first time they experienced the punctuality of the English trains. It was very pleasant riding through the Scottish countryside, and from the train they saw something of Edinburgh and Glasgow.

The 505 arrived at their new home base at Quorn, Leicestershire, in the Midlands of England, in the middle of the night as usual. It was snowing and quite cold, but Quorn proved to be a wonderful place as time went on.

The first thing was to get ready for a practice jump. The Third Battalion would be the first of the Regiment to make a jump in England, but before this they got the first passes to go to Leicester. Here Tucker was able to have a hair cut in a real barbershop for the first time in almost a year.

Tucker had a tent with Synold, Sandefur, Hill and a few more. Larry Leonard's tent was just across the way. He spent most of the time over in Leonard's tent but the place always seemed dark. It never had any lights, whereas in his tent, Synold the genius, always had something rigged up. He was a terrific soldier but he talked too much so he never got to be a non-com. Sergeant William Dey, who was in Larry's tent, didn't stay there long because they made him an officer since he was out of the Reserve Officers Training Corps.

The night before the practice jump Tucker's Squad slept in the hangars after chute detail, getting the equipment ready before the rest of the boys came. Captain Harold Swingler was absent being sick with the grippe, so Lieutenant Joe Vandevegt was in charge of the Company. They were at the airfield for two days during which time it appeared that none of the boys carried their grenades, mines or other combat paraphenalia with them as were the orders. Shortly before the jump Major Edward Krause called for an inspection and discovered that 70% of the Company were without their full equipment. He court-martialled all of them.

On the morning of the jump they woke up at 3am and went out to the plane. There was light snow falling and it was very cold on that bleak and snowy field. It was eerie to board a C-47 at night again, it had been a long time since they had last boarded one on that hot night in Sicily.

After take off, the higher they got the colder it got. It was very beautiful to be flying so high up and watch the dawn come up with the snow on the English fields. The idea of jumping into soft snow gave Tucker the idea that it would lessen the chance of getting hurt. About 7 o'clock they jumped, and instead of landing in the soft snow like the others, some of them landed on an icy road.

With a lot of equipment to man-handle it was pretty tough training. They moved out of the assembly area and took up defensive positions on a hill. Everybody was supposed to know what outfit was on either side of each Company, but when Krause, the Battalion Commander came round and asked Dyles who was on the left, he replied, "Stanley Czubernat, who is digging his hole over there."

The Battalion Commander was pretty sore when they assembled for the critique, as he usually was about everything. He commented on the fact that one of the troopers found his static line had been cut, so he had pulled his reserve. Krause thought this was a great thing and made a present of the reserve chute to the guy. The Company was not impressed.

On returning to camp Major Krause ordered I Company to fall in for a dressing down. They stood in parade dress with poor Lieutenant Vandervegt out in front. The Major got up on the Company stump and called them everything from lowdown sons of bitches to a bunch of the rottenest bastards in the U.S. Army. He said they were either the best Company in the Battalion or the worst. They never knew what Krause really thought of I Company.

Most of the paratroopers gradually preferred to go to Loughborough when they could get out in the evening on a pass. They got to enjoy the place just as if it was their home town. They would have a few beers at one of the pubs, go to the movies and maybe wind up getting fish and chips if they got back to Quorn early enough.

It was a lot of fun in the pubs, particularly with the wonderful English people. Their wartime spirit was something of a tremendous reality and substance, it seemed to the paratroopers that they were all in it together. They would enjoy having some of the warm beers in company of whole English families at one of the pubs. Everyone sensed what was coming up ahead but no one talked much about it. There was never a more relaxed time than those evenings in Loughborough.

While at Quorn, Tucker once went down to the south of London on a three day pass to see his old friends in the 506th Parachute Infantry Regiment, 101st Airborne — Tucker's old regiment. The day he got there they were scheduled to make their first night practice jump. When the Company had a roll call the Captain yelled over and asked Tucker if he wanted to jump with them. He didn't, but had no choice but to say — Yes.

It was a pretty black night and he didn't feel too bad about it because he would be jumping without any equipment. Anyway the jump went off but it was so dark Tucker could not see the ground. When he hit, he hit pretty hard, his chin smashed into his knee and just about knocked him out cold.

After a terrible night of pain, Tucker managed to get back to Quorn by the next evening. The problem was that he arrived as the Company was lining up to go out on a night problem and he wasn't in any position to tell the Company Commander or Sergeant Howard Melvin of his injured knee. He met Melvin as he entered the Company street and he was told to get ready. Tucker had one hell of a time struggling through the night problem and finally had to be sent back to the camp.

The training began to intensify and get rougher but they still were quite comfortable and enjoyed everything. Tucker got himself transferred from Sergeant Sandefur's First Squad to Matash's Second Squad to join Larry Leonard's machine-gun team. (This proved to be rather important in the first few days of Normandy and possibly saved Tucker's life).

Quorn was a very beautiful little town and they would not forget the lovely sound of the church clock ringing out the hours at night. Major Krause was always on the warpath for one reason or another. He had staked out, or roped in, a little pebble garden in front of his headquarters. He punished people who walked across it by making them move the pebbles, one at a time, from one side to the other.

On Saturdays they usually played some form of football in a large field near the Third Battalion and had a lot of fun. The weather had turned really good in early May. One day when they were having a game and everybody had big dates lined up that night in Leicester, a shout went up. It appeared that there was some sort of fire in the Platoon's area and they returned to find that Tucker's tent had burned completely to the ground. Apparently Synold, who was always taking a bath, had accidently put a can of Krupinski's gasoline on a hot stove. If the sides of the tent hadn't been rolled up just that very morning a few of the guys might not have gotten out alive.

As they were poking around in the ashes lamenting about their lost Class A uniforms for that night, Krause came up in a terrible rage and told them to get the hell out of there and stop mumbling like idiots. Synold wound up with nothing to his name but his GI shorts.

After a while it dawned on everybody that Krause was worried about having six or eight men with absolutely no equipment with D-Day coming up shortly. The only thing they thought about at the time was that there was no way they could make their big dates that night.

They made one or two more jumps, one which was memorable because it was a bad windy night. When the crew chief opened the door there was a tremendous roar and Leonard said something about what a horrible sight it was in the blackness. There were some casualties on that jump, among them a Lieutenant who everybody respected highly; he broke both legs so badly they never saw him again.

Another time they were scheduled to make an important practice jump that just about involved all the Airborne in the U.K. It was very foggy but were advised that Eisenhower was involved in looking the situation over and the jump had to take place. It was a scary thing in that they were no sooner off the ground and into a heavy fog. The visibility was so bad that the plane came back and landed, as did most of the other planes, without any training exercise taking place.

By this time the Battalions had designated little emblems on their helmets so the Third Battalion had a 'Cannonball' painted on the sides. The nickname of the Company Commander, Major Krause, was 'Cannonball'.

The time for the invasion got close and one day the Battalion assembled to hear from General Ridgway. A week before they had a full dress general field inspection by General Maxwell Taylor before he took command of the 101st Airborne Division. General Ridgway was deeply respected by all and was held in great awe. He always seemed to be the strong man at the top of everything and generated a feeling of confidence, even though they didn't see him too frequently.

Anyway, Ridgway made a short speech which would be remembered by everybody for the rest of their days. He said that it might be hard for them to realise it but they were about to take part in one of the tremendous undertakings in the history of the world. They would be part of a monumental combat effort, that some of them would die and the memories of those would be forever connected and cherished with respect to the mission. Those who lived, would live throughout their days knowing they were part of the necessary, noble and historical effort that their great Division was committed to. He said something like this:

"You men are to take part in a tremendous act in the history of mankind. You may not realise that at this time but you will realise it in the time to come. You will be among the first few soldiers to land in the greatest invasion of history. You are assured by me that you will be on the winning side. All I can ask of you is that you do your best and I will do mine. God be with each and every one of you."

A few days later Captain Swingler called the Company together and gave another talk of somewhat the same nature, except he took it for granted that everybody would all come through it and concentrated on the excellent condition of the Company. By this time everyone was in pretty good spirits, morale was high, and most had seen some combat in Sicily and Italy.

One day they were all suddenly quarantined within the camp at Quorn, and they couldn't even sneak out for fish and chips. At 5 o'clock the next morning they left camp in full equipment and were loaded on to trucks outside the gate.

A few of them remembered at a later time, all the men with all kinds of equipment passing through the gates of Quorn — a full Infantry Company. Their patches were disguised and, as always, they wondered what the few English people who were looking on thought.

The whole Regiment was transferred by truck to the airfields. The Third Battalion was quartered in a huge hangar at Cottesmore with one Company distributed to each corner. By some magnificent effort, each man had been provided with a cot so it was fairly comfortable. They still didn't know where they were going and there was all kinds of speculation that it would be some place like Norway or Holland, etc.

The four or five days they spent there were rather pleasant, particularly in view of the Air Force chow. The procedure for eating was that they left the barbed-wire enclosures surrounded by Military Police, and the MP's stayed with each Company at all times, front, sides and back. No personnel were allowed to come within twenty feet of them. When they went into the Mess Hall they were to say nothing to the cooks. They didn't understand all of this as none of them knew where they were going as yet.

A lot of work was done on the equipment, equipment bundles and getting things ready. Tucker had time to get started on a book, *A Tree Grows in Brooklyn,* and was half way through it before he left.

Towards the end of the stay they were led in groups into the well guarded briefing tent. Everyone was filled with anticipation and there was continual guessing at where they were going. One guess was even Yugoslavia. It was a dramatic moment when they looked at a large table with some mock-up models and large aerial photographs. The first thing that caught the eye was the word 'Normandy', which meant it was France.

The mission was explained by the Platoon Commander and it seemed all very clear as they looked at the mock-up and the aerial photographs. The principal mission of Third Battalion was to seize the town of Sainte-Mere-Eglise. It was the job of Tucker's Company to secure the town and the Second Platoon to lead the attack.

It was easy to see everything on the display table and one of the objectives was to attack and destroy the Headquarters house of the German Commander, which was actually indicated on an aerial photograph. There weren't many questions as everything seemed pretty clear cut and everyone had a sense of confidence that the people higher up knew what they were doing.

As a matter of fact they were amazed in the days to come that they had been so cool about the whole deal. It seemed to Tucker as everybody sweated it out the next day, that he was less worried about this than some of the practice jumps. Anyway, it was like being one big machine and they certainly felt very strong in terms of confidence in what they could do. There was no thought whatsoever of failure and, as always, no one in the Division could even contemplate giving up any ground, once taken, to the enemy.

A great deal of the strength of purpose and acceptance of the duties ahead without question was due to the men's real respect for the Division's leadership. The pride in the Division was above everything, without really saying so, and without throwing around any baloney. The talk they had been given by General Ridgway had probably had much to do with this in the sense that he had given the feeling of involvement in the tremendous historical task that had to be done.

After the briefings they had two more talks by the Commanders. General James Gavin in his confident business-like quiet way, told them that they were well equipped and well trained and ready to do the job with a minimum of casualties. Tucker remembered him saying at the outset that in his area they would outnumber the Germans they were fighting, although they didn't know whether this meant by Battalion, the whole Division or what. He was low-key in his comments, as always, and sort of reeked of confidence.

Then the Battalion had the usual dramatic speech by Major Krause and it did not have a lot of effect. They continued to both like and dislike Krause. The major point of his speech was when he held up the American flag he always had and stated that, "This flag was the first American flag to fly over Gela, Sicily, the first American flag to be raised over Naples, and that tomorrow morning I will be sitting in the Mayor's office in Ste-Mere-Eglise and this flag will be flying over that office."

(Major Edward C. Krause did in fact fly his flag over the Town Hall at Ste-Mere-Eglise in the early hours of 6th June).

Late the next day they began to get packed up and were given detailed instructions as to the loading of each plane with 'jumpsticks' led by each Jumpmaster.

There were countless C-47 aircraft all over the field, so scattered it seemed impossible to count them. As it got late in the day there grew a sense of tremendous anticipation, a quiet feeling in the air, something like when the birds and monkeys in the jungle all stop making noises.

It was about twilight when they finally got all their equipment on, they were more heavily loaded than in any previous jump. All of a sudden there were single files of marching, bent over men, parachutes on and all going in different directions very quietly to various aircraft. It was a real lasting memory for Tucker to stumble along with his load and look around and see so many single files of jumpsticks heading for what none of them knew would be ahead.

There just didn't seem to be any great apprehension, much more a feeling that everyone shared being part of a monumental historic undertaking.

Along with the sight of multitudes of single file jumpsticks marching towards the planes there was a beautiful sunset that would always be in mind. Adding to the scene more than anything else was the sound of the beat and roar of aircraft engines. They didn't waste much time loading, which represented some difficulties because of the heavy equipment they were all carrying, but it went smoothly.

There was one squad from the Third Platoon in Tucker's plane and he remembers that Harry Buffone was sitting right across from him. No one said anything, they were grim but resolute.

The plane started to move, and again the roar of the engines from all over the airfield was tremendous. The roar sounded like drums beating. Suddenly it was their turn and they swung on to the take-off point at the end of the runway.

Tucker got a good look out of the windows as the pilot revved up the engines and held the brakes for the take-off run. What he saw out of the window he would carry with him always. Along each side of the runway there were literally hundreds of people lined up, two and three deep. U.S. and R.A.F. ground personnel, English ATS girls, cooks and bakers — and no one moved. They just stared at the plane, and without moving there seemed to be a tremendous gesture of a salute and perhaps a prayer. They all could feel the spirit of those people with them as the pilot released the brakes and the plane surged forward.

It seemed as if they spent a long time over the coast of England, moving around before starting across what they thought to be the English Channel. In any event, the plane flew pretty low, and their glimpses of the water looked as though it was rough.

It was getting darker by that time, perhaps dark by the time they got well out over the water. The troopers were quiet and the only thing Tucker can remember happening was Harry Buffone being sick — as always in a boat or plane — and he had to use his helmet to throw up. It was real bouncy.

(Harry Buffone always suffered from motion sickness. That did not stop him from being a good soldier. He won two Silver Stars, one in Normandy and the other in Belgium).

The paratroopers kept twisting around to look out of the small windows, trying to see land and the minute they saw the coast of France they went into the clouds and the plane starting buffeting violently. There were gun flashes below but they were more concerned with the C-47 either swerving or being buffeted by the cloud banks.

It wasn't more than a few minutes after they hit the coast that the order came to 'stand up and hook up'. Larry Leonard was number four and Tucker was number five so they had a look out of the door and again the plane started shaking violently. They could see tracers in the air and thought the plane was hit once or twice by ack-ack or machine-gun bullets.

Just before they got the word to 'Go', Leonard turned to Tucker and yelled over the noise of the engines, "Jesus Christ! Tucker, we don't get paid enough for this job!"

With the cloud banks blocking everything out they didn't know where the hell they were or where they would be landing.

Normandy

The paratroopers got the command to "Go" and before they knew it they were in the air with the chutes open. It wasn't a long descent, Tucker could see tracers coming up at a low angle towards him and could hear gunfire. At one point he heard Ray Krupinski yell, "Son-of-a-bitch, I'm hit again."

Tucker hit the ground with a severe jolt in a little field on the outskirts of Ste-Mere-Eglise. The rest of the jumpstick had just missed the centre of the town to land not far from the old cemetery. Tucker was trying to put his gun together and get out of his chute when he saw someone running towards him. He yelled out the password, ready to fire, but it turned out to be Private Everett Gilliland, a member of the Company.

This was pretty much everyone's experience.

The crickets were sounding from all over the place, from the artificial signal cricket they each had, and the gunfire which was hard to pin down by way of direction. The most impressive sight were the C-47's going overhead at a very low altitude after dropping their loads.

The noise was tremendous, the roar of aircraft, the snapping of crickets, the gunfire and yet there were only three or four of the stick who managed to get together and back away from the town. They had to find some way to assemble.

(One C-47 carrying members of I Company was lost, although some on that plane were taken prisoner, others were later found dead or reported missing. Private James A. Rund was found dead near Monteburg and had been stabbed several times by a bayonet — almost mutilated. The possible explanation for this was that Rund looked somewhat like a black, having a very dark complexion. Tucker's good friend, Gil Mulvaney, was taken prisoner and since the war nothing has been heard from him).

Sergeant Robinson took charge of a group from the plane and they kept criss-crossing away from the town, all the time the group kept getting larger. Somehow they lost Robinson somewhere but in the end they had most of the Company together within an hour or so of landing.

It was pitch black and they had never seen anything like the huge mounds of hedgerows running five, six, seven feet high, literally blanketed from the bottom to the top with a jungle of bushes and trees.

An attack formation was started towards the town which was not too far ahead on one of the endless tiny dirt paths between the hedgerows. They kept getting mixed up and frequently stopped, at one point Tucker opened a K ration. This bumbling around went on for about an hour.

During this time there was firing all around them. A machine-gun opened up close on the left and Leonard and Tucker felt very ambitious and started to go after it during a short break. Just as they started to go through the hedgerow a stream of bullets cut the tree right above their heads and they changed their minds rather quickly.

It was begining to get light and they were on some kind of sunken narrow road which was almost covered over with green foliage. It seemed to be kind of eerie. By now there was quite a large group and Lieutenant Walter Kroener had taken command.

They stopped a Frenchman up front and called Tucker up to ask him whether the sunken road would get them to the middle of the town. ''Ou est centre de citie?'' and the Frenchman pointed the way and off they went. Along the way William 'Red the Medic' Barrow stopped a few times to stick a rifle in the ground beside a body.

Other groups from the Company joined in as they moved towards the town. They could see the church and some houses but there didn't seem to be much firing now. Worried looking French people started running past trying to get out of the way. These were the people who were being liberated but they didn't look all that joyful at the time.

Tucker felt kind of happy to see the people, and to know that they were the first troops to liberate the town, especially being the first men in Ste-Mere-Eglise. Tucker remembers shouting to people ''Vive La France!'' but it did not have much effect.

A Platoon from the Third Battalion just before they boarded their C-47 for the D-Day invasion.

Finally they got close to the German truck park and started to attack and firing the machine-gun. Leonard and Tucker ran into the park and set up the machine-gun under a large tree just inside of a five foot wall near the church. It was suddenly all quiet and they felt very strange. Something was moving very close to Tucker so he swung the gun around but didn't see anything until he looked straight above. There was a dead parachutist hanging from a tree right over his head. The parachutist's body was swaying back and forth, and Tucker noticed that he had very big hands. His helmet covered most of his face and had the red diamond on it.

(In 1984 Tucker learned that this man was Pfc Richard K. Buchter of F Company, 506th Parachute Infantry Regiment — a friend from the very same squad that Tucker soldiered in before his transfer to the 82nd Airborne).

All the time it was getting light and they began to carefully look around. The body of another jumper was about ten yards away in the tall grass. All he had on was his jump suit and harness and they guessed that he had cut himself loose from his chute and equipment after being caught in the tree. He must have been shot down whilst trying to get away. His boots were missing.

Then Tucker got a good look at the trees that bordered the park and there were the bodies of several other paratroopers shot by the Germans as they hung there. There were also many empty parachute harnesses.

Major Edward C. 'Cannonball' Krause standing by the C-47 from which he parachuted into Normandy in the early hours of D-Day.

They then ran from the park, right across the square in front of the church. As they passed the church, Tucker and Leonard almost stopped when they saw an empty chute on the ground and ten yards away the body of a German soldier. It was the first dead German they had seen in daylight in France and they would always remember his face. His skin was sort of blue and there was blood running out the corner of his mouth. His uniform looked immaculate and his rifle lay nearby with the bayonet fixed. They guessed that the trooper from the empty chute was a little too fast for the German with the clean uniform.

They kept running and saw other chutes hanging from chimneys and roofs. These were all empty chutes, but they missed the one on the church. They reached the other side of town and guessed that by now Krause was close to sitting in the Mayor's office because Ste-Mere-Eglise was now in our hands. Although they began to wonder just where they were and how many men were around them.

It seemed that the Third Battalion had secured the town, coming in two columns, G and H Companies by the north and I Company from the east, and pretty much intact. Out of all the Battalions in both Airborne Divisions the Third Battalion, 505, had completed their objectives with the most men assembled of any of the Airborne units.

On the south west side, just a bit outside of the town, I Company went into Battalion reserve and they gathered together in a small, closed-in apple orchard. It was the side of town that was farthest away from the beaches.

They stayed there before getting new orders. It got pretty hot and they realised how tired they were and they didn't feel like doing much talking.

After about thirty minutes or so orders came to move out. I Company was to attack the high ground to the south, as the Battalion had been under mortar fire from that direction. Just before they moved someone starting firing at them. Everyone was on the ground, pinned down and it was certainly lucky that no one was killed.

What had happened was an ambitious German soldier — and there were very many ambitious German soldiers in Normandy at that time — had crept along the hedgerow and had fired on them with his rifle from a really good position. Sergeant Clarence Prager had gone down to a well to get some water and as he came back he saw the man at the edge of the hedgerow firing at him. Prager fired a rifle grenade launcher and hit the German in the back and blew him up.

That was something of a lesson - an incident to be remembered — a reason to take their training more seriously.

The attack got started and never in all of the manoeuvres of the past did they chase around a circle so much. On a straight line it was less than a mile. It was a terrible experience during the three hours of walking up and down hedgerows, tearing through hedgerows and thickets. They finally got to the main road with the Second Platoon on the left. The other Platoons were on the right with Captain Harold Swingler leading.

The Second Platoon was in a ditch, alongside in the road, in single file with all their packs and equipment. To this day they don't know why they ever brought their packs into that attack. They were crawling and it was hot as hell. Leonard and Tucker had a difficult time with the machine-gun receiver.

The firing began to get heavier up to the right. Soon Synold's machine-gun was heard banging away, probably seventy-five yards ahead, but no one seemed to move up on Tucker's side.

They were pinned down in that ditch and couldn't even lift their heads up. No one was moving, all of them in a long single line. Finally Ritchie came crawling back with a bullet hole in his left arm. Nobody knew what was happening up ahead and it was awful lying there in the ditch. The group from I Company was stuck.

As it happened, some Germans had got into the ditch on the other side of the road, only eight to ten yards away for a time and threw grenades. The paratroopers got some firing in but the Germans were also firing from the fields to the left. Later they found that Sergeant Howard Melvin had saved everybody from that side by covering the left flank by himself.

There were about nine men in the ditch, including Lieutenant William Gaillard. Jack Leonard kept sticking his head up and laughing, as he always did when things were tough. He was sort of a talker, but was known as a top class soldier. He kept arguing with Lieutenant Gaillard to take off and move somewhere else, but they all wanted to stay and see what had happened to Captain Swingler. As it turned out they were never to see him again. Finally there was no choice but to move backwards in the ditch and find somewhere to cross the road. Clearly, they were outnumbered.

At one particular point there was a hump to get over. As Tucker crawled over it he fell into a deep foxhole dug by the French for protection against U.S. aircraft. The machine-gun receiver jammed into his stomach just as poor Morris Dyles got to the top of the hump. He screeched at Tucker to keep going and all Tucker could do was to haul himself out leaving the machine-gun receiver where it was so as to keep Dyles from getting hit.

Tucker didn't have much choice because he must have had more than ten bullet holes through his pack by that time. All the packs were full and everything had been shot to shreds. Tucker's was all loose cigarette tobacco.

Going back they kept firing to both sides and just at the edge of town they all made a dash across the road into a little sunken orchard near a house.

(Tucker found out later that this orchard was and is, directly across from the house of Henri Renaud, son of the D-Day's Mayor of Ste-Mere-Eglise).

The Platoon stopped for breath but in a few minutes someone opened up from less than fifty yards away with a machine pistol. Tucker and Leonard took a dive over a hedgerow and landed in about two or three feet of pig muck. This was a sort of foul smelling black slime that pigs wallow in. Tucker was in a real mess, now with one trouser leg torn off and his pack in shreds.

They held on for a while and later reached the Company area in the centre of town. By that time things were really humming with fire fights all around. German prisoners were being brought in and they all seemed sort of arrogant.

Larry Leonard and Tucker came across Sergeant Charlie Matash who had a bullet in his shoulder. They later found out that Matash had been up the head of the crawlers in the ditch and had actually run across an open area to draw fire so that others could get across the road.

I Company was again ordered into Battalion reserve at a yard in the middle of the town. G and H Companies were around on line somewhere. It now seemed apparent to all that they were surrounded. Leonard and Tucker started to look for a suitable place to dig in.

Some of the other guys in the squad, Jack Leonard, Bill Laws and others had found some excellent deep holes in the yard which the French had used for shelter in the bombings. In looking around Tucker crossed paths with Sergeant Melvin who had by that time taken actual charge of the Company. He was pretty sore at Tucker for losing the machine-gun, and told him that he and Leonard would both have to go back that night and find it. They all knew that no one would ever be able to move around anywhere in the dark.

With Captain Swingler missing, Lieutenant Vandevegt was now in command of the Company, as he always wound up to be on any operation. It was nearly two weeks later when they heard that Captain Harold Swingler had been found dead in that ditch by the U.S. Fourth Division.

Larry Leonard and Tucker dug their shallow trenches in the back yard of a house in a narrow street. There was an opening to the driveway off to the right. About twenty yards away, towards the street, was a guy from Headquarters Company, 506, digging his foxhole. Melvin yelled that everybody had better dig deep. The thoughts then were about the Germans who might be coming into town that night.

It began to get dark, and the shelling started. G Company was hit hard at first. Two of the 75mm howitzers they had near them were knocked out quickly. Full darkness came at about 11.30 and this was a real dark night. Without any doubt that night in Normandy was a night of hell.

They lay there in the darkness and heard firing fifty yards away in the street behind them. There was an outhouse about fifteen yards to the left and Tucker thought that one of the 505 guys was behind it, but someone was crawling around the side of it. A little while later a man was spotted dragging something from the driveway heading for the hole where the 506 man had dug in. Tucker raised his gun, aimed it and yelled 'Flash' three times but the guy didn't answer. Tucker fired and his target made a leap for the 506 guy's hole.

It turned out to be the 506 man and Tucker had 'tipped' his nose. He had been dragging a board or a log to help cover his foxhole and froze when Tucker yelled the password. Not only did he forget the reply, but couldn't even get a word out — he was lucky.

About 2am Tucker moved about twenty yards to the Company Command Post and started to dig in again. This new spot would allow him to shoot towards the street and to the front of his position, giving him a better field of fire. The problem was that it was not safe to fire unless someone was just on top of you, for fear of hitting one of your own guys.

The dawn came and the shelling started again, and the day brought the worst shelling that they would ever undergo. During the night H and G

Companies had been engaged in a machine-gun and rifle battle with the Germans, so most of the shells landed in Tucker's area.

Before the heaviest shelling they spread out more and Tucker found a hole about four feet deep and about two and a half feet in diameter which he decided to improve. It was beside a hedgerow and Tucker's worry was his right flank. Krupinski was about fifteen yards further back along the hedgerow and twenty five yards back there was a corner where the hedgerows and fences met. At that corner the French air raid holes were being used by Jack Leonard, Bill Laws and a few others. Except for that corner they were spread out and had to be because the shelling was really heavy.

There was no question, a German artillery spotter had them in close sight because that yard became a nightmare. Airbursts went off right over them and they started to lose men early in the day — they were still digging deeper — even with their bare hands.

When things eased up they would pop out of the holes to look around, then the guns would start again. At one time several guys volunteered to pull a 57mm gun out of a crashed U.S. glider about one hundred and fifty yards away to the left. Everyone in the glider was dead. They were spotted and a German 88mm opened fire. Everytime they popped out of a big ditch near the glider the 88 would fire, so after an hour or so they gave it up.

By this time everyone was wondering what had happened to the Fourth Division at Utah Beach because they were supposed to reach Ste-Mere-Eglise within twelve hours after the jump. It was now thirty hours or more. The Third Battalion were surrounded on all sides and there was no way of getting to the beach.

During brief lulls they moved around a little, the street nearby was an unholy mess with a couple of gliders smashed to pieces. It was risky because even though they were the reserve Company here in town, there were snipers about and shots rang out constantly.

One time Tucker saw a bottle in the house and thought it was cognac, so he took it back with him in his jumpsuit pocket. Ten minutes later a shell landed a foot or two away from the edge of his hole. He took the terrific concussion, and felt fluid running down between his legs. He thought he had been hit bad, but the bottle had been broken by the shock waves. It was not cognac after all, it was some kind of vinegar or acid and it burned his legs something awful. It didn't help that one of his trouser legs had been ripped off in the jump. He was practically exposed from the waist down.

About 4pm they got word that there were about two thousand Germans and some tanks heading for the town. Major William Hagen came round to tell them that there were about two hundred men to hold the town and naturally, all would stay until the last man. This was not unexpected because the 505 was an outfit that would never give up.

So they checked around their holes, planning to stay alive as long as they could. Tucker reinforced his position with logs and two pieces of 2×4 he found. Shelves were made in the side for grenades to be handy so that if a tank went over the hole he could shove one at the belly.

A little later the patrol that had been sent out returned with the news that

American tanks were on their way into town from the beach area. Just as this happened H Company encountered the leading German tanks. The paratroopers climbed up in the trees and dropped grenades on them and knocked out two. This held the Germans up, enabling the tanks from the beach to come through and engage the enemy. H Company had done a magnificent job in all this fighting.

There was still a fight on the edge of town that lasted a few hours and the German 88 batteries didn't stop, it just got worse. Tucker's yard was still the main target. A shell hit a tree over the hole that Jack Leonard and Bill Laws were in and he heard screaming and yelling. He ran back to see if he could do anything and saw Jack with his head braced against the side of the hole and his hands clutching his stomach.

Somebody said that he had been hit very badly. The last words he said before he died, which was almost right away, were, "God Damn the bastards, they got me, the hell with it." Bill Laws was out beside the hole and he had been hit in the upper side of his thigh. At the time it was thought he'd be okay but he died five or ten minutes later.

Other guys from I Company behind the ditch had also been hit and seriously wounded. There were many others hit all around by this time from the air and tree bursts. There were wounded men who were still fighting. Men with holes in them like Hughes, Sutherland and Charlie Matash.

The tough ever-ready Sergeant Prager was around boosting morale. Once Prager, Larry Leonard and Tucker had to dive into another big hole and they really crouched in the bottom as shells pounded all around for several minutes. It was not until the sun went down that night that it was realised how rough the 88 guns were and what they could do in battle. They hoped that they would never have another day as they did on that second day in Ste-Mere-Eglise.

It would have been better to get out on the edge of town with H Company and have more targets to fire at. I Company was just isolated and in plain sights of the German artillery observers in town.

It was thought that perhaps when that day was over they'd get a rest but they were immediately ordered to follow up the Germans who had withdrawn from the town and were heading inland. No one knew what happened on the beach but evidently it wasn't such a mess after all.

It was impossible to move I Company that night because every time they stopped they didn't give a damn, they went to sleep. Tucker can't remember all that happened that night, but he does recall there was firing and stopping every ten minutes or so and falling asleep as he walked. Somehow or other the morning came again, the third morning of Normandy.

There were men from other outfits with the Platoon now, including some combat engineers. One of the engineers was a real fatalist, he kept on standing up and looking around when being fired on. Tucker kept warning him to stay low but he'd say, "When your time is up, its up." His time was up about two hours after they met him. He was beside Tucker, behind a hedgerow, when he stood up — and he came down fast, hit two or three times in the face.

This really made everybody think twice about taking chances that weren't necessary. This guy was at least the fourth or fifth one to get shot for no good reason, just supporting the idea that when your number's up, its up. Most didn't buy it by that time.

They moved on with just light firing and found dead Germans around them. Who had killed them they didn't know, but their bodies were on the road and in the fields.

Finally the Third Battalion were ordered to attack the railroad junction at Grainville a few miles away, and secure the left flank. The Second Platoon was ordered to be point. It seemed to them that there was always somebody behind — never anybody ahead, except for well-trained German infantry.

The attack took them to a hilly part of the countryside which they got through without any trouble and they came out on a road not too far from the railroad. Everything looked good until somebody fired from a position on the road ahead, just as they reached a little group of houses.

The Second Platoon were still leading the Battalion's attack. Sergeant Robinson was in command of the Platoon, since Hill had stayed back in the Aid Station with a bad ankle. Larry Leonard led the Second Squad. The First Squad was commanded by Sergeant Felix Sandefur.

They had five or six men in each squad and the Second Squad, included several men from the 506 and the 508, were ordered to go to the left of the road, through the field and attack along the road. The First Squad went to the right, but on the right there was a heavy thick hedge and a hill, so they moved along the roadside ditch. Synold with his machine-gun could not go up the ditch with Sandefur, so Sandefur took six of his men with him.

The Second Squad moved forward through three foot high grass. Arthur Hile was up ahead, and behind him, Tucker had charge of the machine-gun section which comprised of only two other men from the 508. Leonard was there, Krupinsky was to the left in the field with his BAR, and 'Old Man' Jones was on the right, keeping to the hedge.

Although Lieutenant Gaillard was the Platoon leader, Robinson gave the orders. Lieutenant Vandevegt was commanding the Company with the remaining two platoons just to the rear. Gaillard instead of acting as a platoon leader was, as always, out acting as a scout and a one man army looking for Germans to shoot.

The attack started up the fields and through two or three hedgerows which were about ten foot deep and covered in thorns. There were also a couple of the usual pig troughs to negotiate. As they got to near where the road curved they heard some German MG 42 machine-guns firing to the right. It was figured that Sandefur had run into it.

Then suddenly the Germans started firing from the left flank in the field which was covered in irrigation ditches and high grass so it was impossible to see anyone. Before it was known what had happened, Arthur Hile had been hit through the chest and lay dead against the hedgerow ten yards in front.

The Squad were pinned down in the tall grass by the Germans to the left and by a machine-gun in front. There were also snipers in the trees firing

Ray Krupinski, a member of I Company, 505.

down from the hill on the right.

The main body of the Company were two hundred and fifty yards to the rear, near the houses. Vandevegt sent word to move back so something else could be tried. Leonard, Tucker and the two 508 machine-gunners were left pinned down at the front.

They also had a new friend join in, firing a Schmeisser 'spray' gun at them, from no more than thirty yards away. He had the Squad pinned down because they couldn't set up their gun. The only thing to do was to try to get back with the others.

Since they couldn't go round the hedgerows they had to rip their way through. Tucker just tore the branches apart with the thorns and heavy brush ripping his wrists and hands. In no time at all they were bleeding heavily. He finally got through one wide thicket. The German with the Schmeisser was crawling right alongside him in the grass so he had to stay close to the ground, but he still got a few shots in. There must have been several Germans near his team because they knew they hit at least one of them.

One man had stayed in place to cover the withdrawal. That was the reliable Ray Krupinski who was firing his BAR across the field from behind the pig trough. The only way Tucker could get to Krupinski was to crawl through the slime, and it was really slimey.

Somehow they got back to the houses and began to reorganise. They had only fifteen men there as Sandefur and his six men hadn't come back and there was some discussion as to why they went along the road anyway. Everyone was concerned about the First Squad.

Synold was opening up with his machine-gun and then the German mortars began to zero in. An 88 joined in. Vandevegt was waiting for a new plan from Major Krause. All told about two hours was spent at the hamlet protecting the position as best they could.

During this time Larry Leonard and Tucker had another case of cracking up a little. They sat in an irrigation ditch in the water, soaked and very tired. With them they had a bottle of some kind of hard cider; drinking it and sitting there in the ditch they laughed for about an hour. They never knew what made them laugh so much.

There was an old dead tree near the ditch and Zoromsky was about twenty yards away, under the tree with his BAR. An 88 shell hit the top of the tree but miraculously Zoromsky escaped unhurt. This brought back memories of what happened to Bill Laws and Jack Leonard when an 88 shell hit the tree above their hole — so long ago.

Lieutenant Gaillard was still out scouting and sniping and killing the enemy, which is about all he ever did. He didn't seem like much of a platoon leader but he was a terrific scout and could sneak around with the greatest of ease and seemed to be able to hear and spot everything.

Larry Leonard and Tucker were getting more and more mad than anything else and went out to the right where some Germans were begining to move in. They spotted a German about thirty yards away, under a tree. All they could see was his black overseas cap on his head. Leonard had a Kraut sub-machine-gun, Tucker an M-1. Both fired and hit the Kraut. Later Leonard picked up the black cap as a souvenir. About that time 'Old Man' Jones came limping by, he had been hit in the leg.

Lieutenant Vandevegt decided it was about time to try something else, so an attack was organised along the right, through a field. Vandevegt was behind a stone wall with a big radio calling back to Battalion, and he looked in a kind of rough shape. Fred Synold was covering with his machine-gun, and Krupinski led the way across the field.

Following Synold came another combat engineer who had been with them and who was well liked. Tucker came next with Leonard behind him. They had all climbed over a four foot high three board fence. Leonard had just made it over when a shot rang out and the combat engineer was hit right through the head. That left the three prone in an open field.

Other shots rang out and hit the dirt just a few inches from Krupinski's head. There was nothing that could be done except try and get back over the fence since there was no cover and the Germans were on high ground.

Tucker was about fifteen yards away from the fence and Leonard told him to make a dash for it and he would cover. He started firing. He didn't know where to aim but he fired. Tucker made a run for the fence but instead of vaulting it and going over sideways, he climbed up the rungs. Just as he got to the top a bullet went through the front of his jacket and along his chest.

It split the bible his grandmother had given to him into a hundred pieces and little particles from the bible and wool fibre stuck in his eyes and nose. As Tucker was recovering from this experience he looked up and found Vandevegt staring at him as if he were some sort of apparition.

Another new attack was planned. It was still daylight with two or three hours or more before dark. They rummaged around and drank more hard cider. By this time Tucker was in a dilapidated state. He had only one trouser leg left, the front of his pants were wide open. His underwear torn, his combat jacket was ripped across the front where the bullet had gone. His wrists and ankles were bleeding from-cuts from the hedgerows.

'Old Man' Jones had been hit again on the road, a mortar shell had grazed his head. He was last seen struggling down the road, ripping off his equipment, on his way to the Aid Station. It was learned later that he wasn't badly hurt.

Tucker was then told to take a message back to the Company Command Post. When he saw the rest of the Company sheltering and taking it easy in the ditches along the road, he felt a bit screwy about the whole thing. They could have used them in the first three hours of the attack.

When they got a look at Tucker's appearance they figured that the Second Platoon had had a pretty rough time of it.

Back at the C.P. he learned that H and G Companies were moving up and a night attack was planned with tanks. Somebody had realised that more than one platoon was needed.

The firing began to increase over on the right and they began to hear American tanks moving up the hill. Just as it started to get dark the order came for the entire Company to get into a long skirmish line and attack. The plan was to move over the top of the hill on the right and sweep into the positions commanding the railroad junction.

The attack was supposed to go for about a thousand yards and stop. Most of the members of the Second Platoon didn't give a damn for anything anymore, all bayonets were fixed and they moved up the hill. Luckily the tanks cleared a lot of Germans out of their positions. The Second Platoon didn't see many moving, but those they saw were cut down fast.

It was a good attack and carried out well. It was also good work by Lieutenant George Clark who commanded the Company at the time. Tucker remembers someone in the dark on the right yelling to Clark, ''Lets hold up to wait for G Company on the flank.'' Clark yelled back, ''To hell with G Company, keep moving.''

The attack had pushed them right into the position they were supposed to be in earlier on that day, on the curve in the road where Sandefur's squad had gone forward. Leonard and Tucker settled down for the night in a six foot wide and six foot deep former German hole with straw in the bottom. The Germans had used this for a machine-gun to cover the road they had tried to move down earlier. It was right on the curve.

As they were moving around in the dark, someone found some bodies in a ditch about twenty yards from Tucker's hole. These bodies were Sergeant Felix Sandefur and his men all about five to ten yards apart. It was apparent that when Sandy's squad went down the road, the German machine-gunner had fired long bursts from this hole — as 'Old Man' Jones had said earlier — and killed the first six men, and badly wounded a seventh. He was removed that night back to the Aid Station.

After that, they didn't sleep that night even though there was little firing. When dawn finally came they moved the machine-gun across the road to the edge of the field to cover a long stretch of the railroad track.

They stayed in this position at Fresville as Battalion reserve for twenty four hours and succeeded in digging themselves in pretty well. They even tried to play pinochle but they could only think of the guys from the Second Platoon in the bottom of a ditch a few yards away — the remains of Sandy and his squad.

Major Krause was around raising hell with everyone in general, and particularly I Company. He stuck his nose into everything, including firing mortars. One time he gave the command to go three mils left and Moe Green had to tell him that a 60mm mortar shell would never traverse less than five mils. This made him even madder. Lieutenant Vandevegt had recovered and was also back raising hell with everyone in the Company.

There were some prisoners at the C.P. and the paratroopers did some searching of their clothes and took some of their belongings, but not their paybooks. (The paybook was the only means of identification for the German soldier. He was not issued with dog-tags like the Allies). Tucker went back to the Aid Station once for treatment, particularly in regard to all the cuts, scratches and vinegar burns on his legs, stomach and crotch — but they couldn't help much. In fact he couldn't even get another pair of pants.

During the next night the German Air Force was bombing the beach and they thought they could see the anti-aircraft guns and bombs exploding. On the 10th or 11th they moved to new positions so that now the Battalion was pretty well spread out. It was a good spot but there was real heavy fighting to the right at the railroad crossing. There were elements of the 325th Glider Infantry and the Fourth Division trying to move up.

After things had quietened down, Hill showed up. As usual he missed the high spots of the fighting. He seemed to be able to walk up behind anyone, day or night, without being heard. Krupinski was out on the prowl with his BAR and Tucker had the machine-gun set up along a hedgerow.

As yet the Germans had not spotted the new positions although they had many artillery batteries but had done little shelling so far. The weather was bad for standing guard alone during the night. Once Mike Caruso was scared to death when Tucker yelled at him from about three feet away in the dark as he passed by.

In the two and a half days they were there they had a chance to explore the little town on the right. Whilst in one of the houses, some P-38's came over and strafed the town. The French people kept asking, Why do the Americans keep attacking them? They had no answer to give. Tucker did manage to buy a chicken and some potatoes and decided to cook them later.

Leonard and Tucker also found a young blond Dutchman, or at least he claimed he was Dutch. He was about nineteen years old and six foot four tall and in civilian clothes. So they called Prager out to look him over. Prager spoke some German, and when the Dutchman spoke German too, Prager got a little suspicious. He did a job on him with his fists and then hauled him back to the Command Post.

On the way back to their positions, Leonard and Tucker found an old MG-42 German machine-gun and decided to try to out. MG-42's had a very distinctive sound when they were fired. Ray Krupinski was riding a bicycle somewhere over near the C.P. and when he heard the MG-42 go off so close, he dropped the bike and jumped into a ditch.

Later Tucker faced the problem of how he was going to cook the chicken. Finally it was decided to go back about fifty yards, build a fire and cook the chicken by boiling it in a helmet. They were worried about the smoke. The only solution was to have three guys fan the fire to keep down the smoke while one watched.

This worked alright for a while but every now and again somebody would get tired and a big cloud of smoke would go up. As soon as it did they would all scatter for the ditches. The Germans fired at the smoke, once with a very heavy barrage, but no one was hurt.

After about three hours the chicken was cooked. What was left of it would fit into one hand, leaving only three bites each, but it tasted pretty good.

Lieutenant William Gaillard was transferred during this period to the Second Battalion where they desperately needed officers. The Third Battalion didn't need him that much but he was a good man to have around, always out scouting and sneaking after Germans.

In the those two and a half days they didn't lose any men. Things were fairly quiet, even though there was a large German force out in front. Orders came that they were to move back. The move started at 12 noon and they had only gone a mile when the Germans let loose a terrific barrage on the old positions. They felt sorry for the guys of the Ninth Division who had come to relieve them.

The move was back to the Regimental Headquarters in a hilly pine tree area. No sooner had they got dug in they were told to move out again. This time they boarded trucks and headed towards the beaches. It was quite a ride through the southern area of the beachhead. All the way down they sighted crashed gliders, dead Germans and all sorts of debris. There were more crashed gliders than anything else, all over every field.

The destination was a large field which was not enclosed by any hedgerow. They dug in, right in the middle of it, well away from any trees. By that time they were pretty apprehensive of shelling anywhere near a tree.

They got a chance to explore. Apparently there hadn't been any American troops in this area so far and the Frenchmen were still in hiding, not knowing what was going to happen. A visit to a farmhouse produced some food and Tucker went further on towards the river. One Frenchman told Tucker to look over a little hill. He was alone when he found a crashed C-47 with twenty three bodies in it. The C-47 had hit on its nose and flipped over on its back. Most bodies were half burned.

One trooper was a redhead because the top of his skull had red 'dust' patches on it, even after he had burned. Tucker picked out the pilot and the co-pilot by their 'leggings'.

It was a tough thing to see and from that moment on Tucker was through with any great desire of flying about in an airplane.

(In 1984 Tucker found out that this aircraft was carrying troopers from the 508th Parachute Infantry Regiment).

The next morning they moved out on foot. Apparently there was going to be an attack on some town, maybe Pont L'abbe. The First Division, the Big Red One, had already taken the town nearby and they moved into Etienville. Etienville was in absolute ruins, there wasn't a house left standing.

The 507 were on the right and with I Company they were both supposed to be in the reserve of the First Division which was up ahead. I Company stopped by a ruined wall right near a river bridge and they got held up there all day.

There was still heavy fighting going on and the Third Platoon was covering the bridge. The Second Platoon had nothing to do but dig in and eat some more, which they did. During a search around in the ruins of the houses they found lots of U.S. type cookies which tasted pretty good. By now Scotty Hough had found some more liquor and was drunk.

Occasional shelling came in during this time, but on the whole, except for the firing up ahead there wasn't much action. About 4pm Tucker was told to prepare to go on patrol across the river in a boat that night. He was supposed to wear sneakers and a soft hat and it was termed as a long-chance patrol. In other words, he had a fat chance of getting back because of the heavy German concentrations on the other side of the wide, deep river.

He felt sure that this was the end of the road for him. To his good fortune the boat sank when he got about five foot from the bank, so there wasn't any patrol that night.

Shelling started to get heavier and about 7pm they moved out of reserve to join the attacking forces. As they were moving along the road they saw one dead German soldier who had light hair, and he was a dead ringer for Charlie Matash.

There was a lot of stopping and starting as usual. As it was getting dark they made a stop by a hedgerow where there was a dead 507 officer partially covered by a blanket. Tucker exchanged his M-1 rifle for the officer's lighter carbine. The night was spent nearby and luckily it was fairly quiet.

The next morning they moved again and sort of criss-crossed the fields for mile after mile. They must have covered five to ten miles that morning but only moved forward about three. This country was strange to them, they had not had the chance to check it out on a map. During their continual stops they heard constant heavy firing ahead and on the flanks.

It was that morning when it was confirmed that Captain Swingler had been found dead in the road at the hill, just south of Ste-Mere-Eglise.

In the middle of the afternoon they finally got into the assembly area just outside of St-Sauveur-le-Vincomte, the second biggest town in the area. This had been the destination of their original mission and they were thankful they never had to carry it out. The Germans had set up all sorts of obstacles around the town, including poles and sharp stakes in every field. It was now eight or nine days since the begining of the invasion so the Third Battalion would have had a fat chance to hold out even if they had managed to land a concentrated force nearby.

There was a little more rest and some chow from a German truck they found in the assembly area. Finally they were told to move out, attack and seize the town. Leonard and Tucker now had a new plan to carry the machine-gun. Leonard carried the completely assembled gun whilst Tucker looked after the belts of ammunition plus two extra boxes. Lieutenant Kroener was standing by the side of the road and saw this and commented, ''That's the way to carry the gun!'' At this time he was Executive Officer and Robbie (Sergeant Robinson) was commanding the Platoon, and he had a chance of a field commission.

Once underway they came across some tanks of the Ninth Division, and wished the tanks would stay with them but they had orders to stay where they were. The bridge which was further up the road was not safe to carry tanks so the engineers were working on it to keep it from collapsing. It was also under constant fire and many dead bodies were floating on the water.

It was a question of running like hell over the bridge. As they entered the town there was firing from some windows until the open centre square was reached. The only way they got through that was to run behind it. Major Krause was standing on top of one of the roofs yelling at them to keep moving and fire at any window that showed any sort of movement in it.

Luckily they were not losing men, although there was still firing from both sides. Finally they reached the railroad tracks on the other side of town. The area was rather desolate with not much cover, but plenty of good firing positions for the Germans ahead.

I Company was all alone and they shouted for the right flank to be covered. H Company was supposed to be there. They advanced to a banking and a hedge beyond the railroad and stopped.

Krupinski was sent out leading a patrol and they were fired on from a position to the front. So Leonard and Tucker opened up with their machine-gun and fired two to three hundred rounds at the hedgerow about fifty yards ahead, then they charged over the top of their hedge and made a rush for the next one. It was tough breaking through but they finally got into a strong point which was protected by woods and a huge earth bank where they rested. One of them had nailed one young German soldier and they noticed that the bullet had passed right through his face.

They had hoped to settle down there for the night but they got the order that as soon as it was dark they would be either attacking again or on a combat patrol. It was tough because they had enough for one day, but it had to be done. As it got dark they assembled and moved up one hedgerow for about one hundred yards in single file. It was dark as hell. Kroener sent Krupinski out ahead on a one man patrol — Krupinski would be lucky if he ever got back — he did.

Suddenly they ran smack into a German force which was actually going past them on the other side of the hedge. They were less than ten yards apart and everybody started firing in the dark. As they came rushing by, Leonard and Tucker dropped the gun in the tall grass and it hit Tucker on the head when he fell down. Immediate orders were to spread out so they had to move again without the gun. Kroener had a potato masher grenade hit him in the back, but he was okay.

There were three guys, Hill, Leonard and Tucker, sitting with their backs to a tree on that very dark night. The order was to stay still and fire at anything that moved and they knew it was going to be a long night ahead.

Someone started yelling in English, "Americans! Americans! Please help! Please help!" It was Synold who had been shot in the stomach and was out there, somewhere. Many men volunteered to go and bring him in, but the order was again to stay in position. Finally the three got orders to go out on patrol.

In the early morning light they could see figures moving along a hedgerow about forty yards away, which they took to be Germans.

That day Tucker's squad had to guard the Battalion Command Post which had moved into a strong point area. He picked a spot along the hedge and lay there. The German artillery fired at them now and again and the nearest they got was about ten yards or so. Sergeant Melvin came by and saw that Tucker had lost the gun again and gave him hell, as usual.

Suddenly a figure was spotted about one hundred and fifty yards away staggering in, it was Synold. They covered him with their guns but there was little they could do but wait for him. As he got within fifteen yards, the Germans opened up and hit him again and knocked him down.

As planned, Hill immediately dashed out with a Battalion officer so that they would get a Silver Star when there was relatively little risk involved, but he was the quickest to move. The Medics put Fred Synold on a stretcher and as he went by, Tucker saw his face had turned a sort of yellow. He lived three weeks with two holes in his stomach and back.

Things quietened down a little, even though the mortar firing continued, and they began to feel a little more rested as the day went on. There was a heavy German railroad gun firing from the North into the town but the main worry was about getting food.

Those left at the Battalion C.P. now were Goodson, Leonard, Hill, Mike Terella, Zoromski and Tucker. They were the ones who were to live through Normandy from the Second Platoon. They were the ones who got to argue with each other with every day they spent together, and who would probably have as much in common when they were through as any group of men who ever fought together anywhere.

They explored a little bit around the town to find out how the other Companies in the Battalion were making out. With their consciences pricking them, Leonard and Tucker decided to go after the machine-gun and went out with Hill and one other man. They had only gone about fifty yards when they came across the German they had killed the previous night. At this time the Ninth Division were moving through the 505 positions, going out to cut the penins

The   nd the machine-gun where they had dropped it. As they were recovering it they spotted a number of Germans moving across a hedgerow about two hundred yards away. They didn't see Tucker, so he thought it best not to fire on them because they all could have been creamed.

The thing that bothered everybody about Hill, was the type of scavenger he was. They found later that the dead German had some letters and a picture of a girl in his wallet. Hill had taken them.

New jumpsuits had come in by sea and they got the chance to change the gas protecting clothing they had on. It was a relief to take off those hard, crusty, gas protection coveralls. Also it was a relief too for Tucker to wash his hair, but he noticed something was wrong with his scalp. His hair, which was matted and awfully dry, started to fall out. This was because most of the 505 had shaved their heads before painting their scalps black.

The news came through that Cherbourg had been cut off as the Ninth Division had reached the other side of the peninsula. The Second Platoon rejoined I Company a few miles to the west. It was a pretty good area and the chow was plentiful.

The day before they rejoined them they had a brush with some Germans. The First Platoon had been in the lead and had seen about a dozen Germans coming towards them, they set an ambush and killed four.

No sooner had they joined up, the Company was ordered to move out again. This time there was a long march, most of it at night and they had no idea where they were going. At 2am they arrived in a new bivouac area and I Company camped on the side of a hill overlooking a river.

After some sleep they awoke to find that they were on a sort of terrace with quite a bit of green foliage and pine, somewhat similar to southern Italy. The entire morning was spent gathering up all sorts of food and rations for a feast they hoped to have later in the day. A lot of French cheese appeared from somewhere.

Before they could eat it they had to move out again. This time the orders were that pants would not be tucked into their jumpboots. (This ruse was to confuse the German Intelligence as to where the 82nd was, or to make them think it was a new 'green' regiment).

The Third Battalion were ordered to set up strong points in the very thick woods, the Bois de le Mores, as there were supposed to be Germans in the area. No sooner had they entered into the woods after the long march, the leading members of I Company ran into some Germans burying a number of their comrades and there was some firing. This didn't bother anybody at all and only made them sore, all the very tired paratroopers wanted to do was sit down and eat.

The intermittent firing up ahead continued and they all scattered to either side of the road and lay down to wait for somebody to tell them to keep moving. This happened several times. While some firing was going on up head, Zoromski pointed out that Tucker was on one side of the road with the machine-gun receiver and Leonard was on the other side with the tripod. This displeased Zoromski greatly.

Finally Major Krause came down the road looking very disgusted with everyone and told everybody to get moving. They had been just as disgusted as he was and were in no mood to fight — only in the mood to eat.

Things began to get a little worse and there was a lot more firing ahead. Prager came along and told them to move off the road and spread out. For the first time they began to forget about the food. It was getting on towards evening when they converged on an old house, well into the woods. They were still carrying all that food, loaded with ammunition and were not fit physically or morale wise to engage in any fire fight.

As a matter of fact, at this point, they had possibly the lowest morale which they ever had in going into any sort of attack.

Suddenly Sergeant Melvin took over and they heard his booming voice yelling, "Drop that goddam food, form skirmish lines, start firing, let's move!" This brought them to life and they poured through the woods firing every gun and killed or routed any Germans ahead. Melvin was a real leader.

It was pitch black when they reached a crossroads near the end of the woods. There was firing on both flanks. Lieutenant Kroener assembled the Second Platoon and no one, including him, had any idea where or what the position was. Finally Leonard and Tucker got put out in front with the machine-gun to cover the road.

This was a night of nights, a night of terror. They didn't know where they were and had no idea where the men were or who was on the right or on the left. All Tucker and his friends knew was that they were alone.

Hill, as usual, had gone off to find himself a secret place. It wasn't long before tracer bullets were cutting the branches over their heads. They had been spotted early.

They stayed in position and heard firing and occasionally someone yelling. Men were spotted crawling about fifty yards away, they were not Americans, so they opened up. At the same time, about a hundred yards down the road, a heavy fire fight started up. Later they found out this firing was when Geary and Welsh had gone down the road. Pfc Albert Geary was killed and Norman Welsh captured. Another one of the guys got away.

Morning finally came and a line was set up across the main road at the end of the woods. As they were doing this, one of the replacements who had joined them just before the jump was killed right in front of Tucker and Lieutenant Vandevegt. His body was just ten yards out from the line, and they wondered about him. Could anyone remember his name?

(From the records it was Private Joseph J. Przybyla).

Then Robbie took Tucker, Leonard, Mike and Red the Medic (who was still digging holes every time he stopped) on a patrol to make sure the thick woods behind them were clear. It was like a jungle.

Suddenly they spotted a single German moving towards them about fifteen yards away. They froze and when he was ten yards away Tucker yelled "Hande Hocke!" At the same time Robbie emptied a magazine from his sub-machine-gun at the poor guy — and actually missed him. The German just took off like a streak of lightning, leaving his rifle behind. Larry and Tucker were glad because Robbie had no business shooting.

On returning to the cross roads they manned the machine-gun for the next twenty-four hours. The Germans kept wandering singly or in groups along the road towards them, although they held fire to let them come on. Others popped up to see who could shoot someone first. The result was that they wound up alone late in the day, and for one more hellish night with every German left alive in Normandy firing right at their position. The German machine-gun fire was so heavy and close over their heads that Tucker got a headache just from the cracking of the bullets.

About mid-day the Regimental Commander, Colonel William Ekman, came crawling up and talked to them. If he had walked he would have been a dead man. He was in good spirits, a helluva lot better than the men were. They had to move out to the right to extend the line which had been occupied by the First Battalion.

As they moved into the line at this point it was fairly obvious that there had been a terrible fire fight there, especially when they saw how A Company looked on leaving the area. Tucker tried to get the best gun position but the Second Platoon was stuck on the flank. The weakest squad was on the extreme end with absolutely nothing to the right of them. They always worried about the flank, so they set booby traps. There was only part of G Company to the right rear. Leonard, Krupinski and Tucker went back on water detail. The Normandy rain was coming down in torrents and made them very miserable. It was two miles back to the water point and there were no trails in the thick woods.

At the water point they saw Captain John 'Red' Dolan sitting on a water can looking beat. They also heard that when Scotty Hough came in soaking wet after a tough mission, Melvin had hot coffee already for him. The detail got back with the water — even enough for Zoromski who always needed it — and lots of ammunition — but there was no coffee for them.

That night it was decided to stay awake all night and they put a shelter half over their heads, but they were soaked anyway. All they kept thinking of that night was the rumour that they would be here for five or six days.

About 2am the Germans opened up with heavy firing. There could have been a final defence line ahead. Krupinski, Tucker, Leonard and Patino were on the right outpost in a tough spot. During the night a cow tripped the booby trap and Kroener from his C.P. sent Robinson up because Krupinski, even knowing what had happened, fired his BAR just for fun.

Morning finally came and they saw that Hill, as usual, had found himself a pretty good spot. This time he had dug in underneath a dead German who was covered with a little dirt and with a notice displayed on a stick which said, 'Here Lies Fritz'. He figured that no one would bother him if he slept under a dead body. The Squad could smell the stink of the dead man from where they were, about forty yards away. How Hill stood it, nobody knew.

Leonard and Tucker were really sore at each other, but after all they had been through it was no wonder. The outpost wasn't so bad. There were six men, three to stand guard at each hitch, two hours a hitch. One stood on the left side of a hedgerow which cut into it, and two others on the right.

Zoromski had a good hole, dug well into the side of the hedgerow and others could sleep in that when not on guard. Patino was there and was mean and sore as usual. Ray Krupinski was a great soldier but he gets sort of in a frenzy now and then and he readily empties his BAR at anything. Most didn't give a damn because they seemed to be on the edge of some sort of disaster anyway. They encouraged the firing just to upset people behind the line.

These men! Who are they and what will they be? Krupinski was a man who should not be crossed. He won't forgive the people who delayed him from marrying the girl he loved in England. (He did return to Loughborough later to claim his bride). Patino was a mean and miserable person. It didn't make any difference to him who he killed.

The days passed. Tucker went by Hill's place a lot and once when passing by nearly got hit by a sniper. His ankles were covered with open sores from not being able to tuck his pants into his boots. He had been three or four days in this line on the edge of the thick forest during constant rain.

There were a lot of details to fetch water and rations. Zoromski was a man of bravery and a man of character, but when he faced a shortage of water he was in trouble: Red the Medic was digging deeper as usual. The new Lieutenant, James Howall, had really proved himself. Both Chaplains came round to say a quick hello. Major Krause also dropped by. Lieutenant Dey paid a visit and Tucker wondered what he thought after he saw what his old platoon had gone through.

Why can't the paratroopers fight like the infantry? At least they had hot meals in their stomachs and the artillery behind them with replacements coming in every day. This was their eighth day on this combat line and some were beginning to think Bill Laws, Jack Leonard, Sandy and the others who are dead were lucky. In the Second Platoon they had about eighteen men left out of forty-four. The First Platoon had about fourteen left.

Two more days went by, then they got the order for an attack at dawn the next day. Hills 131 and 90 must be taken. Would this be the last job of this campaign?

They had to go back for more ammunition again. It was pitch dark, pouring with rain and they got lost. They went through another bad night thinking that they were in German territory but wound up right behind Stald's hole in the Third Platoon.

The Third Platoon always had a fairly decent setup. Jim Downing had been firing their 60mm mortars all the time, he never quit.

Dawn came up. There would be a forty-five minute barrage before the attack moved out at 8.30am. The outpost men didn't like the artillery barrages in the least. At 7.45am the whole front opened up. The German's started as well and it fast became a nightmare. The Krauts did a lot of firing and the shells landed all around the outpost. This was one of the most deafening barrages they ever experienced.

Hill came crawling up and told them to open fire but they told him to get the hell out of there. He must have forgotten that the Second Platoon of I Company had been protecting the entire right flank of the Allied Expeditionary Force for nine days. Now they forgot and everything landed amongst the Platoon.

The others went back for more ammunition and Leonard and Tucker were left firing all alone. They began to get into the spirit of things and were pretty soon firing like hell. They criss-crossed on all the hedgerows and felt better as they saw the tracers going home. It began to rain hard again and the gun began to smoke like hell.

The others came back with a few minutes to spare before the start of the attack. Leonard and Tucker waited by the embankment, carrying the gun and three belts of ammunition. It was still pouring with rain and they were sure that they would at least scare someone who saw them. They looked bad, with ten days growth of beard, faces black and greasy, pants torn and raincoats hanging down around their ankles.

It was 8.30am and over the hedgerows they went.

The field had good cover and because of the heavy barrage they got to within fifty yards of the Germans before they started firing back. Luckily the Platoon were behind a hedgerow. Leonard's LMG was firing like hell. Zoromski later told them that it was a terrific sight to come up from behind and see everybody all standing there fighting in the pouring rain.

The Germans fired back and their shots got close. Lieutenant Vandevegt was beside them using his radio. The left flank was covered but they still worried about the right. One German dashed forward to surrender and some fool shot him, nailing him with a 45 slug in the leg, but he still was able to get over the top of the hedgerow. Vandevegt managed to get some information from him in either Dutch or German.

There were quite a few Germans fifty yards away across the field. Dey and the First Squad were sweeping their left flank and the Second Platoon had to make a frontal assault. Ray and Mike went over the hedge and were covered with overhead LMG fire. Everyone was doing a good job but one tracer landed right beside Ray, and Vendevegt gave Tucker a dirty look.

The assault carried them forward to the German lines and the paratroopers were all over them. This is when they got into the spirit of things together. They were over the German holes before anybody could get out and surrender. It was like a madhouse. Tucker yelled, "Lets get the bastards out of their holes."

Lieutenant Kroener got one who was trying to run away. In that attack they all acted like nuts. The German artillery fell behind and to the right, so they had to keep moving. The right flank was still wide open and there are booby traps everywhere. They made a stop by a road. Thank God it was raining that day so Pregar could spot the landmines.

Firing was heavy in the 508 sector. They moved on faster. Everything stank around them. They hated the smell of dead cows even more than dead men. The German soldier's uniform always reeked of dead cows so that they could almost smell Germans.

They were fired on again and they stopped behind a hedgerow in the middle of a wide field. Mike Caruso was down the road on the right. There was an explosion and Mike screamed for help. A Medic came running up and Tucker told him to go down the road after Mike. A few seconds later the Medic was blown to kingdom come by a trip wire telemine booby trap.

Krupinski then blasted his way down the road with his BAR and found

Mike with one of his legs hanging off. Then they remembered how Mike used to love to go jitterbugging.

Another rush was made towards a little road, firing all the time. Lieutenant Dey was right there and doing a teriffic job. It felt strange as they had so few men left. Dey warned everybody about the rain and they realised that they were cold and wet, so they started their usual griping.

On they went to another little fire fight. This time they flushed out six prisoners who were very scared. All of them were trembling but they were made to act as ammunition carriers. As the Platoon went through a gap in a hedgerow in single file, a German slug clipped the back of Tucker's helmet, and he started hollering like hell but no one paid any attention to him.

There were dead Germans everywhere. The fight seemed to be getting ahead but there was still heavy fighting on the flanks. They began to sweep the roads for mines. Lieutenant Vendevegt was pleased because Major Krause was pleased with I Company for once.

Finally they stopped at a fairly decent area and dug in. The 508 were still fighting on the left and needed support. It was another long march to reach the top of Hill 90. By that time they noticed that they ached all over from the rain and the cold. they were tired, hungry, and the only thoughts were of how to get out of this mess. There hadn't been many lost so far, but what the hell had they got to lose anyway. They moved on again.

It was eerie country with countless hedgerows and it was well booby trapped. The destination was Hill 131.

Looking back they saw a marvellous sight. Tank destroyers with their 900mm guns were coming up the road behind them. They also saw General James Gavin with his M-1 rifle stalking along the road ahead.

They passed through the 508 men and continued after the retreating Germans. It was getting dark when they finally reached the hedgerow by the highway and set up for guard duty with the First Platoon. It got as dark as hell, but after that day the night was easy.

The morning brought a beautiful day for a change, but the enemy was taking advantage of the good visibility with a railroad gun. Again it was all stopping and starting. Everytime they stopped they dug in because the 88's were firing flat-trajectory. Mike Terella and Goodson had found a good spot so now they all had a chance to talk things over and eat what they could find. While they were sitting there somebody dropped a live grenade and they all made a hell of a dive to keep from getting killed.

Tucker was sent over to a house to talk with two French women and to buy some butter. He was now the Company's interpreter. The houses on the right were explored and they found some water and lots of German equipment inside. They also picked some strawberries.

After settling down for another night, they were awakened to screen the First Battalion who were going to make a raid on the German's left flank. It started to rain and soon turned very foggy. The First Battalion began to come in and it seemed that their raid had been a terrific success with the capture of about one hundred and twenty Germans. These prisoners looked like pretty good men and some of them didn't look too happy to see the paratroopers laughing at them with the rain coming down again.

Hill 131 was finally captured and a move was made towards La Haye-du-Puits. The Company split up. The remaining five in the Second Squad (including the Third Squad too) were sent out to an outpost, but this time they didn't mind. This group was really known as the 'mangy five', Leonard, Terella, Goodson, Hill and Tucker. All they could think of was where could they steal more rations. The outpost was not too bad, except for the fact that it is quite near the German lines and the rest of the Battalion were four hundred yards to the rear.

The new position was on the forward slope of a hill overlooking La Haye-du-Puits. The reasons everyone was stalled at this point were: first, because the 90th Division had failed in its effort to keep up with the 505's left flank making it impossible to enter the town. As a matter of fact some elements of the 82nd Division did enter the town but were pulled back because the 90th Division and the 79th Division on the right flank had stopped.

The second reason was that the 82nd Airborne Division had not sufficient men, equipment, ammunition or anything else at this point to be able to continue the heavy attack. They were at the end of a rope. They were due to be relieved but since the higher command always gets the most out of the 82nd when they can, all they could do was to hold the position so as to make a good cushion for the 8th 'Arrowhead' Division to jump off from.

The 'mangy five' didn't give a particular damn. They dug a few little holes behind a hedgerow on the side of the hill and settled back to listen to the enjoyable sounds of their own 240mm shells as they burst beyond the town — another town flattened like Etienville.

Altogether they spent five days there which were used to castigate and curse at each other; but at the same time reached a depth of common understanding and involvement between five of the most different kinds of people as any group could ever be.

The five were a scurvy bunch. Leonard's problem way down deep was wanting to see his girl friend in the States. Mike Terella looked more wicked than ever. Goodson always laughed and kept his feelings down underneath. Hill was a born survivor. Leonard was a good guy and Mike Terella was a good guy too. All of them were the types of individuals who could, together, make any sort of a concerted effort a success. They were good soldiers for this type of army and for this type of campaign.

Their story of Normandy should be entitled 'Five Survive'. Five survived out of two squads, eleven or so survived out of one platoon.

Things came to a head one day at the outpost. The 8th Division went through to attack La Haye and they were stopped cold. They were scared stiff of snipers even before their attack. The Second Platoon were certainly disgusted since they gave the squad that jumped off through them a lot of good instructions, and much of their ammunition.

The 8th immediately broke up right in front of the paratroopers. On top of that they started drawing the shell fire in. One of the shells killed a damn good Staff Sergeant from Headquarters of Third Battalion. One of the same Division came crawling back unhurt because he was too scared to stick with his outfit. He nearly died of fright when he watched Tucker and the boys pull in a bleeding man and tried to patch him up.

The shelling on the 8th Division got worse and they were trapped out there, and the Platoon couldn't leave.

One day when they were all in the hole and some more shells were coming in, Leonard and Tucker got into an argument. Leonard said, "You can't talk to me like you talk to Hill." Tucker replied, "Do you want to make something out of it?" With the shells falling and the others sort of wild-eyed and wondering whether they were crazy, Tucker and Leonard got out of their holes and started to fight. So life went on at the little outpost.

The 82nd still waited for the 8th to attack but they were being held up everywhere by snipers. One sniper held up a whole Battalion! Tucker gave away most of his ammunition. Patino gave them his machine-gun.

Trips were made back to the Platoon and Company Headquarters and it was found that some of the guys got into La Haye and got drunk. Everybody back there seemed to have a bicycle. As a matter of fact the only ones who were doing any fighting were the five at the outpost.

Kroener had a good Command Post near the road. It was raining when Tucker arrived and there was lots of rations with just the occasional shelling. As usual some people didn't like visitors to come around to draw fire on their C.P.

The last of this campaign seemed misty to all of them. England was far away......

There were four Germans, who had been killed by Scotty with a tommy-gun, on a very eerie dark pathway which was completely covered over by trees and vines. Since they were shot mostly in the stomach, their eyes and faces had become bloated and swollen and the smell was potent. When they went back through there to the rear area with Red the Medic (William Barrow), they were told to guide four new 8th Division men to the Company's C.P. As they went along the little path, Red was eating a can of English beef stew. As they walked by the bodies, Red didn't stop for a minute while everybody else held their noses. The new men looked pretty sick by this time and they didn't seem quite ready to go into combat after that.

It was rumoured that the Commander of the 90th Division had been relieved for failure to keep up with the 82nd.

Vandevegt was now in a happy stage. They started moving back and it meant nothing to the 'Five' that they were just a few survivors. They became coarse — it seemed that something had been taken from them and there was no end. They, the few, had reached the point where they only thought of the next minute, the next hour, and at the most, the next day. The illusion of a sort of glorious end had disappeared.

They stopped at a collecting point on the way back to the beaches so that they could clean up and change into OD's (Olive Drab uniform). The 'Five' in the Second Platoon could still kill each other, but they had a strong bond together and would have killed anyone else much quicker.

It was a hell of a job getting that paint and the black off their heads and faces and trying to look like human beings again. The black paint had taken the oil out of their hair and it was beginning to fall out. During this time they argued constantly. They fought over the loot they had brought back, especially when they found out what Patino had in his backpack.

The trucks made their way to the beaches, through the little Normandy towns where the wonderful people smiled at them. When they passed the graveyards at Ste-Mere-Eglise they remembered that twenty five men from the Company were there. They could not help but feel close to them. They knew that some day they had to return to Normandy: to return to the places where Sandy and his men fell and to the place where Jack Leonard and Laws fell — and to return to visit the graves.

When they reached the beach they found it was crowded with German POW's and all sorts of equipment. The Germans were waiting for boats and it looked as though the Allied force had bagged some pretty good soldiers in Normandy. The 82nd were to find out that the troops they fought against in Normandy, Sicily and Italy were better than the ones they were to face later in Holland, Belgium and Germany.

The LSTs (Landing Ship Tank) were boarded and they found a place to sleep for the journey to England.

There was a band there to greet them on the dock. It was so good, as a matter of fact everything was wonderful as of the moment. Again there was a feeling of the present, no future.

It was wonderful to look at the English ATS girls walking down the street. The men of I Company sat in the park for a longtime until it was time to board a late night train to Leicester. They slept most of the night.

Finally they got off the train at Leicester, very early on a quiet Sunday morning. The trucks were waiting and, at last, they pulled up outside the gates of the old camp at Quorn.

It was some forty odd days since they got on to those same trucks, one hundred and forty four of I Company. Now they only numbered about forty five.

On that early morning as they marched through the gates of the camp, they were older, a lot tougher and a lot stronger. They were awfully proud to be one of those who had lasted in Normandy to come back like this. It hurt also, to come marching past Regimental Headquarters and know how much more of the ground was trod when the Company marched out.

It was still a moment of exhilaration as they silently passed through the gates in columns of twos, not threes as when they left, forty five from one hundred and forty four, and received a salute.

It was a moment of great pride when they swung into the Company street and met the eyes of those who stayed and those who had already returned; it was only those of the Company who could look and appreciate what had happened. They knew.

England was with them again and they will be furloughed! Things were wonderful, the wounded who lived were coming back.

England Again

Tucker had a helluva time in England for the rest of July and through August, with furloughs, girls, Company parties and sports. The Company received some good replacements, but as September dawned, combat began to be planned again.

Without any warning they were alerted and sent to an airfield for a mission. The 82nd were supposed to jump at a place called Tournai in Belgium and link up with the British Second Army which was driving northwards.

It was pouring with rain all the time at the airfield and the mud was ankle deep. After they had been briefed on the job, Tucker sweated it out in the NCO's tent. Some of them had been up since 2am in the morning checking the Squads to see they had the full amounts of ammunition and grenades. The briefing wasn't too long because the problem was a simple one of taking the Belgian town and waiting for the British Army to catch up.

With the rain still pouring down outside, the early dawn found all in the NCOs in a tent moaning and groaning. No one had any heart in this mission, for some reason or other, probably because of the dismal weather and the vagueness of the mission. Just about dawn word came down that the mission was off. The British had driven through Tournai before anybody could even jump. So back to Camp Quorn they went.

Tucker met a guy they called Tommy who was a Lance Corporal parachutist in the British First Airborne Division. He sat in the balcony of a Dance Hall talking to Tommy about the Army and everything in general. There were quite a few people around when suddenly Tommy leaned over and whispered that he knew where the next jump was going to be.

Tucker got a little concerned because nobody was supposed to know. It seems that he had been briefed as a non-com a few days before and the jump had been delayed because of a shortage of gasoline. Anyway, he told him that it was to be a place called Arnhem and it was going to be tough. It was going to be in the next twenty-four hours or not at all.

Back at camp Tucker told the Captain but nothing ever came of it. Only later they found out that two German Divisions were waiting for the British First Airborne Division at Arnhem. Out of 8,500 men who jumped at Arnhem only 1500 came marching back through the 82nd's lines on the road to lower Holland.

The next day the 505 were loaded on to trucks again and left Quorn for the last time. Things were pretty well set up at the airfield and they could tell right away that they were going places. There was that feeling in the air and the weather was good.

Within a day the ammunition was being issued and a briefing took place about midnight on the Saturday night. As they understood it, the jump was scheduled for the next day, Sunday the 17th September.

All the non-coms filed into a large briefing tent with the Company officers and the Intelligence Officer, Sanders, was there to greet them. The first thing Sanders told them was that it could either be a tough or an easy mission. He proceeded to explain that the First British Airborne would jump in Arnhem and secure the bridge over the Rhine opening up the way to the plains of Northern Germany.

The 82nd would jump ten miles below Arnhem at various zones around the city of Nijmegen and secure the big bridges across the Waal River. The 101st Airborne would jump about thirty miles to the south at Eindhoven which was about fifteen miles north of the present British combat line. From that line the British 30 Corps would drive forward through Eindhoven, Nijmegen and Arnhem. In that way they hoped to roll up the entire German lines.

All this sounded pretty good. Sergeant Matash then asked Sanders how many German troops were in Nijmegen for the 505 Regiment of 1800 men to deal with. Sanders answered that there were 4,000 SS troops around the city. At this point Matash asked him how the hell did they expect the 505 to deal with them. "How good do they think we are?" It sounded tough, but they all shrugged their shoulders and went out.

The 17th of September was a beautiful day. Tucker's airplane was way over on the other side of the field, about two miles from the briefing tent and he spent most of the early part of the morning loading up. He went back for breakfast about 08.30 of cheese sandwiches and coffee and was back at the plane again by 09.00. Take off was timed for 10.00.

According to the briefing there was to be at least forty-eight minutes over enemy territory. Lieutenant Richard Degenhardt was the plane's jumpmaster and Staff Sergeant Robinson was No. 2.

About fifteen minutes before loading they noticed a man standing by the tail in a leather jacket and Tucker got talking to him. Everybody thought he was a member of the ground crew because he looked a little shaky. Tucker mentioned the forty-eight minutes over enemy territory to him and at that he nearly had convulsions.

Then they thought, well, he must be the crew chief because he was coming along too. Finally Tucker asked him who he was and he answered, he was the pilot. At that Tucker wanted to trade his No. 22 (last) slot in the jumpstick to get closer to the door. He couldn't make the trade but did manage to put about three flak jackets on the seat underneath him.

With the thoughts and fears of the ride ahead in broad daylight with good visibility, the planes took off and headed east. It was a beautiful day and they couldn't help but look out of the window at England and think that they probably might never see it again.

Holland

They headed east and there were thousands of planes in the sky, including lots of fighters for protection.

The new men were sitting down the ramp in the plane sweating out their first combat jump. As Tucker looked down at the coast of Holland the first thing he saw was two twin guns firing up towards them. A British Typhoon fighter swooped down and it was good to see the flame of his rockets exploding on or near the gun positions.

Their first sight of Holland below showed that the land was flooded. In some places the water seemed to be up to the middle of the first floor windows of each house.

Strangely enough there was ack-ack, but no German fighters. Tucker kept yelling to the men that if they got hit, he would go through the door like at shot, so they had better get ready. Most were sitting on the edge of their seats with the static line in their hands.

Then they spotted men jumping to their rear. The 504th Parachute Infantry Regiment had reached their Drop Zone. Down below they could see German soldiers running. The planes were not very high, maybe seven to eight hundred feet. As they passed over a canal they knew that their Drop Zone was not far away. Lieutenant Degenhardt yelled, "Stand up and hook up!"

So far, this was not nearly as rough going as Normandy. There was only a short time to stand 'in the door'. The plane was not bumping but there were a lot of explosions around and they had seen several planes go down already. Finally the signal came, Degenhardt yelled "Go", and the line started to move forward.

Tucker went out of the door head first and the opening shock of his parachute gave him a tremendous jolt. His rifle butt hit him on the upper cheek and he felt some loose teeth in his mouth. His lips began to bleed.

He landed beside a house, right in the middle of a huge field. The Drop Zone was perfect. Men were running in all directions with gunfire coming from everywhere. The first person Tucker met was Colonel William Ekman, the 505's Commanding Officer, crouched beside the wall of a farmhouse talking into his radio.

Tucker moved to join up with his Platoon. Mike Terella was there, also Howard Goodson and Jack Wingfield. It was the old story, the tough part was over and the biggest part was ahead. The Platoon moved out onto a road at the northern end of the jump field. Terella was in the lead, Leonard joined on the way and they had to collect some of their bundles of equipment. Lots of civilians were going after the beautifully coloured equipment chutes and helping the troopers gather the bundles up.

There was firing as they reached the edge of the woods but not many bullets seemed to be coming their way. They could hear the firing getting heavier from somewhere. The ride had been a long one, the equipment heavy and they were all very tired.

They walked around a little bit to scout things out then set up on a hill. Miraculously enough the jump had been an amazing success on the Drop Zone. All the Company except one squad were pretty well assembled and they were ready to move into position as ordered.

Some were told to go down to the road to help 'Old Man' Jones set up a road block. The road went from east to west and they were facing the German border which was about nine hundred yards away. Jones and Tucker put mines on the road about fifty yards from the position. Jones was to fire if anything came down from the east. Just as Tucker headed back to the rest of his group he heard a loud motorcycle engine. Jones started yelling, then, all of a sudden, a terrific explosion.

Tucker ran back to Jones and found an English parachutist lying on the road with his motorcycle blown to pieces. He had come down in a glider at the German border in the Reichswald and was the lead scout for General Browning who was following in his Jeep.

Jones said that the motorcyclist came down the road so fast that he could not stop him, and besides, the British guy did look like a German parachutist with his round helmet.

The man was obviously dying. His right leg was hanging in shreds and he was peppered all over with parts of the motorcycle. His face had turned yellow but he was trying to smile. He seemed to be in pretty good spirits and he said that he would soon be back in England. Tucker knew that was impossible. All he could do was to give him some cigarettes and leave him to the Medics.

The Second Platoon was now organised. Tucker swapped a tommy- gun for Wingfield's M-1 rifle. On looking around they found that they liked the Dutch countryside. It was really flat and the air was good and not too warm. Apparently this was the playground or vacation area for the Dutch.

As planned, the mortar squads were combined under the command of Downing, Wallace and Tucker. Wallace was an assistant leader of a machine-gun squad who took over the third heavy weapons squad when their Squad Leader went missing.

As there did not seem to be much firing they scouted around. The 376th Parachute Artillery arrived to join the line. They had 50 calibre machine-guns and were expecting a tank attack.

About four hundred yards to the east there was a very large, dark hilly forest area called the Reichswald which marked the German border. The German artillery there had been firing at the jumpers and planes all afternoon. The troopers thought that the Third Battalion must have been the first Battalion to land.

Many planes had been shot down, but not nearly as many as were lost in Normandy. One plane went over the Drop Zone at four hundred feet with both engines smoking. Many men got out before it hit in a ball of fire.

The three mortar squads of I Company set up at a farmhouse. The residents impressed the guys, as did all the Dutch farmers. The man of the house was in his back yard digging a deep trench for his family. Evidently he hoped to stay there in spite of the fighting. He did not foresee that his house would be a shambles within a few weeks and that the battle lines would not move from there for many months.

It was very pleasant to spend the first night after the jump, comparing it with Normandy, sleeping in the barn behind the house and to be able to sneak in every few hours for coffee. It was their first experience of Dutch coffee and it tasted just like German ersatz coffee.

Morning came too quickly and there was firing to the left. The Third Platoon was there, moving along the road towards the forest, and on the right, the First Platoon was moving too. The mortar squads were to follow behind. They were told to expect Halifax bombers to come in towing the gliders carrying equipment so they had to hold the Landing Zone at all costs.

Downing and Tucker scouted ahead for an observation point since the First and Second Platoons seemed to have made contact with the enemy up ahead. They knew that the Third Platoon had been firing and fighting all morning.

Norell Blankenship was hit, others too. Finally Tucker ran into Tony Crineti who told him that Staff Sergeant Clarence Prager had been killed on the road out in front. It seems that Prager was leading the Third Platoon when they ran into a German patrol. He waved a flag to the Germans and hollered to them to surrender. They waved a flag in return and three stepped out on to the road.

Prager went after them, but the Germans jumped into a ditch and opened up with machine-guns. Prager was badly hit, but he kept alive and fighting where he was. He was recommended for a Congressional Medal of Honor for his tremendous action in bringing the Third Platoon down the road and holding the flank.

Staff Sergeant Clarence Prager was posthumously awarded the Distinguished Service Cross. His death was a great loss because he was a soldier without equal. He was a tough guy and everyone was concerned at losing a top man.

(It was later found that Prager's body had been buried in a shallow grave by the Dutch and remained there between the lines until March 1945. His action prevented Groesbeek from being overun by the attacking Germans).

Downing and Tucker were still scouting around for an observation post and came across a deserted farmhouse. By this time they had passed through a big iron gate which separated Germany from Holland. They were in Germany — maybe the first Americans to cross the German border — they'll never know.

In the farm house they found the table set with a roast duck, hot potatoes and vegetables. Evidently they were the first to go into this area since they had strayed away from the First and Second Platoons. The two made themselves comfortable and polished off as much of the duck as they could, carrying the rest of it away.

The firing got heavier. Suddenly about six Me109's appeared and began to strafe. If the Germans had airplanes in this area it was going to be rough. The 505 were in Germany so they were in for it anyway.

The Mortar Squad moved towards the firing, setting up the guns at every opportunity. Bass, Logan, Lester and Intrieri were doing real well for the new men, and Wingfield was Wingfield. He and Tucker decided to go up with the First Platoon to see what was going on.

They saw that the Second Platoon was stuck over on the right and it seemed to be having a fight in a little town. Leo Lopez was the only one who had been hit with a shot through his helmet. It had a hole in it but that was all.

There was a dead man in the middle of the road as they passed by the Second Platoon. It turned out to be young Everett Gilliland who had just married a girl in England who he hardly knew. Gilliland was either shot by a sniper or during a strafing.

The Germans were about three hundred yards away. Finally Tucker and Downing got to the front of the combat line and it happened to be Tommy Thompson's Squad. Louis Russo had a machine-gun in action and there seemed to be Germans in a cluster of houses about two hundred and fifty yards away. They all opened fire.

Gliders were coming in and many were burning, tipping over and crashing. The Second Platoon was still in the town on the right. Tucker got into a deep hole with the Executive Officer, Tommy and a few guys and they all took it easy for a while.

It was getting towards sunset. The firing died down and there was a chance to eat. It got dark a lot earlier here than it did in Normandy.

Just as the sun was going down about a hundred Lancaster bombers came over with equipment bundles. They were released at about six hundred feet over the Drop Zone. The German 88s on the right were firing at the bombers but not one was hit. Their speed was terrific, over two hundred miles an hour and many of the chutes did not open. It was a beautiful sight with the sunset behind the Lancasters as they went over. The 82nd were getting their supplies and the troopers could feel their strength.

Shortly after, Tucker moved over to the left about five hundred yards to set up his own position. The Second Platoon manned a roadblock and the First and Third Platoons were sent to the left and right of the line respectively. However, under Captain McPheeters's plan, which was a good idea, the Mortar Squads were set up right next to the Command Post. Paul Hill and Mike Terella were there and they all dug in. The C.P. had a lot of runners now.

This is where they remained for a while so Jim Downing and Tucker went out again in search of an observation post. About fifty yards in front of the Third Platoon's lines they found a house which had good cover and good visibility in every direction. The cellar was full of potatoes.

They only intended to stay temporarily since it was out in front of the combat lines, but it was such a good observation post they stayed for the entire day. The Third Platoon and Hallahan with his machine-gun was behind them for safety. They ate a lot of potatoes.

The farmer, his wife and six small children were living in a deep hole in the front yard. They too were hoping to stay with their house and land. Tucker felt sorry for them and sympathised with their plight. The farmer was a sturdy character.

(The Wyler family, husband and wife are deceased as of 1985. They had a total of fourteen children. Tucker visited the family several times after the war, in 1970 accompanied by his wife and two children).

The Germans attacked, but not in too much strength. The observation post was the most vulnerable position in the whole line. During the day while some German planes were coming over, Hallahan took the opportunity to cut down a fat cow with his machine-gun. The cow belonged to a rich farmer who lived next door to the Wyler family. The cow's owner did not like it but it was cut up and they gave some of it to the Wylers. It did the guys good to see him get some meat for his kids. He didn't have a cow of his own and as Tucker was eating his potatoes, it was a fair swop.

When night came, Tucker and Downing crawled back to the C.P., as it would have been crazy to stay out there all night. However, Sergeant Melvin told them that since it was a good observation post they had better stay there. Tucker was frustrated but they had to go back. Moe Green came with them and they dug in under the hay and hid. So for the rest of the night the three took turns sleeping under the hayloft, but there was no attack.

It was learned that the Germans had issued an order that the 82nd must surrender or be annihilated. The order was ignored. Still no heavy attack, although the Second Platoon received some pressure. The mortar squad was ordered to move over to the right and support them. The C.P. stayed where it was but Tucker moved out and wound up in an apple orchard which had a greenhouse — a glass greenhouse — in it.

Everybody did a lot of digging in and found a lot of food again. Just behind the Second Platoon there was a windmill. This was to be a windmill of destiny and Tucker took it over as an observation post.

One of them would have to be up at the narrow window at all times, but the first night they were too interested in setting up the guns. So they were not there when the Company Commander tried to reach them on the telephone. Ed Morrissey was on the road block under attack and calling for support. Tucker finally reached the window and fired the guns.

Somehow he got lined up on the wrong target and nearly hit Leonard's position with the mortars. Morrissey was really sore at this and the Captain gave Tucker hell. With the Second Platoon so close the following day Tucker got the chance to go and talk to them. There was no food, no supplies and everything was scarce. While Tucker was talking to Matash, Matash was chasing a skinny old chicken. During the chase, Lt. Colonel Krause came up and told them they would have to forage for food off the land.

(Edward Krause was promoted to Lieutenant Colonel in August 1944 and made the Regimental Executive Officer).

Wallace was now with the Platoon again and they stayed there for another day and did quite a bit of firing. By that time they were well acquainted with the terrain and picked many targets to use.

Just about the time when they were reaching the end of the rope at the windmill, the 325th Glider Infantry Regiment came in to relieve them. Tucker didn't know where they were supposed to go but the news came through that they were going to Nijmegen to help in attacking the bridges.

The Battalion stopped for a rest in a very beautiful pine forest. As it was said, this was a playground for the Dutch people, and it was very beautiful. They made several stops up in the forest and the first time they contacted the Second Platoon they noticed there was something wrong. The previous night the Platoon had sent out a patrol and as it was coming in one of the men had been killed by one of the others, who was immediately transferred out to another Company.

After a long march through the woods they boarded Limey trucks to go north to Nijmegen. There was no firing on the way — just beautiful country. On the approach to Groesbeek they noticed that the rear elements of their outfit had themselves pretty well set up there. There seemed to be plenty of dairy products and everybody had some butter and cheese.

The country from Groesbeek to Nijmegen was not as flat as they thought Holland was. This was more like Germany than Holland. The houses were beautiful, with some of the corners completely covered by glass windows. Most of these windows were broken now but these houses compared very well with the best of houses in the U.S.

By the time they reached Nijmegen they found that both the big bridges had been taken by the 504. The way they took them will go down in history. Both bridges had been under attack. Demolition charges had been embedded in the concrete pillars and Germans swarming over on both sides of the river. These were good German troops too.

The Second Battalion of the 505 were attacking the bridge head on. General Gavin had the Third Battalion of the 504 cross the river in canvas boats where they suffered 50% casualties. They took the far end of the bridges before the Germans had time to blow them.

From both ends they shot down hundreds of the Germans who were in the steel girders of the road bridge. There were German bodies lying all along the banks of the Waal River.

The 504 finished up on the nice flat land to the north of Nijmegen towards Germany and were in constant engagement with the enemy. Fire from 88s was coming down on the bridge and it could not be crossed in safety. All anyone could do was to crouch down on each truck and go like hell across the bridge, one truck at a time.

This I Company did while shells came right over them and exploded. On the other side they started marching in the rain; this time towards the railroad bridge which is about a half a mile to the west. No one knew what was happening and all the troopers seemed to do was to get soaked to the skin, stopping and starting, the old Army way.

They stopped at the north end of the railroad bridge and found they were to be an inner defence core. The mortar squads again joined together and they got their machine-guns back. A good house was found to stay in, right beside the bridge and for a day or two they had a good set-up there.

It was a lot of fun with Boone Crusenberry, he was always finding some kind of old clothes to wear and he was an expert with a little Coleman burner. Boone was always eating like a horse and if you didn't watch your food, he would have it.

There was a two hour guard schedule and in their spare moments they played pinochle in the house. Once in a while German bombers came over and there was a great deal of British ack-ack around the bridge. The Germans couldn't seem to get too close as the nearest bomb fell about a mile away.

In the evening Tucker had a chance to walk around to look things over. He was surprised by the number of Germans being buried. It was a rather mysterious place on this north side of the bridge.

While they were there the remnants of the First British Airborne Division and some of the Polish Brigade marched back through the lines from Arnhem. That is, what was left of them. The GIs' feelings went out to those men as they marched down the road, mostly bandaged and in rags, many of them badly wounded. Tucker got a pretty good idea of what had happened.

Evidently somebody did too much talking because the SS Division hit them hard in Arnhem and they were badly torn up. Only fifteen hundred out of eight or ten thousand men got back. It was guessed that they must have left Tommy in Arnhem, because Tucker never saw him again.

I Company had actually seen the Polish Brigade go in by parachute to help support the British but they were murderously hit by ack-ack and even German fighter planes, so that a lot of them didn't even reach the ground alive.

It was a bad feeling to know that the overall mission had failed, but at least the 82nd knew that its part of the operation was accomplished on time, and with the least men lost.

The next thing that happened was an order to move the Second Platoon onto the railroad bridge to guard it. The orders were to shoot at anything that moved in the air or below the bridge. Everyone was told, from Corporal to General, that they would be broken if anything happened to the bridge.

Tucker's squad and Larry Leonard's squad were at the southern end of the half mile long bridge. They were over the water and there was a gun tower there. There were altogether three gun towers on the bridge. Right beside the Squad's tower there was a swivel pom-pom gun which 'Old Man' Jones and Tucker took over.

They had a pretty good time on the bridge shooting at everything that moved. The men were anxious to fire every time the planes came over. They argued to see who would get in the seat which controlled the German gun and they may have been the culprits who shot down an American B-26 when it flew over. Leo's squad was down underneath the bridge, guarding from below. Leo was drunk all the time, evidently he had found some wine.

Tucker's Squad were on the bridge for two days, during which time he managed to scout around for food and sneak into the city of Nijmegen now and then. It was a beautiful city and still is. For the greater part of it has, like most European cities, clean narrow streets. On the whole the stay in Nijmegen was rather pleasant.

Orders came to move back to Groesbeek as heavy fighting was taking place.

Tucker's Mill at Bredeweg, near Groesbeek, which was totally destroyed during the fighting in 1944.

The first night they had to wait in the woods before going to the old positions. It was just a miserable night. The rain came down through the trees, the wind blew and everyone got wetter than hell. No fires could be lit so they were glad when the morning came and the sun shone again.

Back into the old positions they went. For the next exciting seven days the mortar squads were tied up between the observation post and the Company Command Post. Throughout that time, day and night, they fired continuously as the attacks got heavier. The attacking German troops were not the best they had seen. Wally, Jim Downing and Tucker spent their time shuttling back and forth between the windmill and the Command Post. The windmill, which had a cluster of houses around it, was fifty yards behind the First and Third Platoon lines.

During most of the time it was a lot easier to stay back at the windmill than at the C.P., because there it was under constant shelling, although there was no doubt that the Germans had spotted the windmill being used as an observation post.

The mortars were in such a position that they could fire and hit almost anything that moved beyond the combat lines both night and day. Telephone lines connected the firing positions with the windmill and the Command Post. Various target points were all zeroed in, but at night it wasn't necessary to stay in the windmill because the Command Post called back to the Company and let them know where the targets were.

There were two or three attacks almost every day. After a day or two, numerous German bodies started to pile up in front of the position. The shelling was terrible back at the Command Post. Mike Terella had it good and it was kind of fun for Tucker to be with him and Scotty Hough again.

Tucker recalls several funny incidents. The back yard of the house, where the mortars were, had an old dug-out 'cold cellar' with kind of a narrow door to it. The shells that the Germans were throwing were pretty big stuff and they could be heard coming most of the time. Once, when a shell came in and they heard it coming, Tucker saw Stald and Terella both making a flying dive for the door. They both got there at the same time and with the same velocity that they got wedged side by side in the doorway. Luckily neither of them was hit.

There were several people hit, however, one was Rudy Tepsick and that was quite a loss. Tucker was promoted during this time, as was Jim Downing.

The ammunition kept coming up for the 60mm mortars as there was a road that was well secluded behind the position. Some of the best gun crews were there. Intrieri was a good gunner, and Logan too, he knew no fear, he would stand right out in the open where the shelling was coming in.

There seemed to be enough to eat and there were always plenty of apples. Tucker recalled that it was good to work with Jim Downing and Wally Wallace because they were both nonchalant guys. The trouble was they made him risk his 'ass too many times.

After the first few days the shelling around the windmill began to get tough, there were a few hits and some very near misses. By this time the German's artillery observers realised, only too well, that the only way to drive them out of the windmill was to hit the driveway or doors just beneath it. It was tough for them to do that but they were beginning to get a few pretty close.

The observers were up in the windmill most of the time and on the whole Jim Downing seemed to enjoy himself and so did Wally. Wally fired a few times himself and once when he hit one of the Germans spot on with a mortar shell, he really let out a yell. Just as he was yelling to everybody that he had hit someone, a bullet splattered about a quarter of an inch away from the window on the side of the wall. From that time on it was dangerous to get too near the windows, because the rifle fire was directed towards them.

Jim Downing used to sit up on a table, about in the centre of the windmill, take off all his clothes except for a pair of coveralls, cross his legs, rest his elbows on his knees and peer out with his binoculars and direct the firing. He even took off his boots.

For the first three or four days they did have some other observers. There was the 81mm mortar observer, one for the 75mm guns and some from the British artillery. After things began to get too hot they began to clear out.

Before they all left there was one day when they looked out and saw hundreds of German soldiers in the distance coming through the woods towards the front positions. The British heavy artillery observers called for priority from their control centre. Then, of course, the 82nd 81mm mortar observers stepped up along with the 75mm observers but they could not get priority orders either. Tucker yelled to them to 'step aside' and started firing the little 60s and they did a better job of disbursing, killing and wounding the attacking Germans, possibly better than all the others could have done even if they had put all the big guns on them. The Mortar Squad really had the road from the Reichswald zeroed in.

Jim Downing was usually there during the daytime and lots of times it was impossible for him to get back until after dark because he had to travel across an open field. One cloudy morning, it was the fourth day of this seven day period, there were so many German dead and wounded, a German officer came with a Medic carrying a white flag. Speaking English he asked for a truce to bring in his casualties. He was blindfolded and led to the Command Post. He was rather young looking and even though he was covered in quite a bit of mud, he really looked a soldier. He stood with his hands tied behind his back and a blindfold over his eyes with 'Old Man' Jones guarding him.

Tucker passed the German officer and yelled "Heil Hitler!" The German snapped his heels together and in the perfect example of discipline and soldierly conduct, replied "Heil Hitler!" Whereupon he was immediately hit with the butt of 'Old Man' Jones's rifle.

About the fifth day a squad of Germans broke through the lines in the night and holed up in the cellars around the windmill. Jim Downing and several others were trapped. It was impossible for them to get out of the windmill at all. One 81mm observer stuck his head and shoulders out of the door and took a bullet through his shoulder. At the same time Albert 'Frenchy' Dusseault was leading a squad along the hedge and a bullet went into his lower back, passed through his body and came out of his shoulder. After that

Dusseault was hauled into the windmill and lay beside the 81mm observer.

It seemed that the 81mm observer was feeling pretty good because he only had a shoulder wound. Dusseault was coughing up blood. The observer died about twenty minutes later, but surprisingly, Dusseault lived.

It became increasing apparent during the afternoon that something would have to be done to clean those Germans out. Lieutenant James Howall led the attack from the Company C.P. down the road and tried to out flank them. There was some skirmishing during which time Downing managed to get away from the windmill and across one of the streets. Several men were hit during this fight.

After Howall had led his men into the attack, Tucker started out with Ed Morrissey and a couple of others. On the way they met Lieutenant Degenhardt with some men carrying the wounded. Tucker, together with Morrisey, Downing and the other two men started to cross the open field. The German mortar observer spotted them and started firing mortar shells. Tucker was only a third of the way across, lying alone in the field with the German mortars shells kicking up dust all around. Somehow or other they all made it.

Towards the end of the day the windmill suffered from some very heavy shelling. The doors had been finally blown off and the inside hit by phosphorus shells and was on fire. It was a sort of funeral pyre for one of the most successful defence operations that had ever been attempted. This windmill observation post for the mortars had held off two or three large German attacks, preventing them from penetrating the 505 positions to any depth for a period of a week, night and day.

Tucker couldn't resist taking a last look, so after it got dark he sneaked back. The excuse was to get a map case, a couple of German pistols and some other equipment that he had left behind.

It was very quiet when he arrived. The windmill was filled with smoke, even though there were no flames and it was deathly silent. He picked up the few things and took that last look. To get out he had to climb over the sandbags covering the doorway which a shell had hit. At this point he heard more shells coming in again and Tucker took a big dive over the sandbags and landed on something warm and wet. Reaching out he found he had landed on several German bodies.

(The windmill was destroyed and never rebuilt, but its site is clearly marked today by an elevated square of land. The same family, the Hoof's, still own the site today and they used the old bricks from the mill to build the barn next to the house).

The next day a new observation post had to be found and they still couldn't leave the windmill without a note of regret. For seven days it had been their home. For a week before they went to Nijmegen, it had been even more so. They did find a new post in a house which was about three hundred yards in front of the Company Command Post. This had no combat line in front of it, just bare fields stretching for five to six hundred yards before it reached the woods where the Germans were dug in.

The observers made a little hole in the roof and started taking turns looking out but it wasn't anything like the windmill. They couldn't do much moving around because if the Germans thought they were in there, they would have blown that house off the face of the earth.

For that reason Tucker didn't spend all his time there and there was a chance to get around a little bit and see some of his friends in other platoons. Tucker had a good chance to talk to his buddies, particularly Sergeant Matash. He also went over to G Company and took a look at the Germans from a room which was on the Second Platoon's left flank. While he was up on the roof the Germans attacked G Company and he got a few pot-luck shots at them by firing his rifle. Also there was Richard Cutler with a Browning Automatic Rifle banging away.

On the seventh day they were relieved and went back into the woods and hills overlooking Nijmegen. This became their home on and off during their stay in Holland, perhaps a day and a half at a time and it wasn't so bad. It was an opportunity to practice with the mortars when they weren't actually fighting.

Everybody shared the food and all used Boone Crusenberry's Coleman stove to cook it. Crusenberry was the only man who ever had a stove that continually worked, or perhaps he was the only man who knew how to work it. When he was around there was always a chance of hot food.

Finally, the order came through that the Second Platoon had been picked to attack and clear out the church area in a small town beyond the Third Platoon's lines. The Second Platoon was directed to make the attack because it had suffered the fewest amount of casualties. It didn't turn out to be much of an attack because as they started down the main road leading to the church area things got confused. Eventually they turned around and came back and never found out why this action was stopped.

During one halt they found it interesting to look round at the houses. These were the same houses they saw when they first arrived in Holland and where the people were trying to dig in to save their homes and families. Now every house was just about in a shambles. Not too much on the outside but on the inside there was broken glass, pottery and dirt everywhere.

The civilians had all gone. Tucker couldn't help but remember and admire them for their attempts to hold on to their homes. When he saw those men digging in with their families and little children around them, digging into the ground behind their homes, he knew they could not stay.

During the course of their wanderings they ran across a couple of bicycles and practised riding them. They stayed another two days or so under the trees on the hill overlooking Nijmegen. There were quite a few equipment shelters around in the area and it was interesting to see they contained a large amount of German supplies.

Orders came to move into Nijmegen again. This time the guys were worried because there had been a lot of talk about the 504. It was rumoured that they had been taking quite a beating up there on the east flank, out on the flats and dykes, and the 505 were going to relieve them. Nobody was too happy about that.

On the road to Nijmegen it was interesting to see what changes had taken place. Mostly it could be described in one word — destruction. It was after dark when the trucks arrived in the city. It seems like they sat around forever because it was one of those nights when everybody was very tired and nobody had much idea what was going on. The equipment was heavy, and every time they stopped they went to sleep.

So off they went into the flats to relieve the 504. It was a weird area, anything that was built there or grew there seemed to be completely destroyed. There was an overpowering smell of dead animals and dead men everywhere. There had been some very tough fighting between the 504 and the Germans.

Tucker spent three hours marching. Somehow or other, in his travels, he got hold of a small cart to carry the mortar and some other equipment. As his Platoon got near the the 504 positions the pace quickened and they got lost from the rest of the group.

By chance they did finally get into the spot held by the mortar squad of the Second Battalion of the 504. This was right out on the edge of the battle line and it consisted of a large house enclosed by rectangular woods. It was like an oasis, as all around the house there were shell holes of all sizes.

One look was enough to tell them that this place had been throughly combed by enemy shells. Tucker talked to the 504 just enough to find out how glad they were to leave and long enough for them to point out that anything which moved in daylight was dead. Then they spent the rest of the night going back to look for some equipment which got lost on the journey. It certainly was a relief when it was found.

When the orders came down that there was to be no firing of mortars, Downing, Wally and Tucker thought it was going to be pretty dull. The three grabbed the cellar and decided that they would stay there, the others would have to find foxholes in the back of the house.

It wasn't much of a deal but the cellar felt pretty comfortable. They didn't fire a shot and didn't even stir around the back of the house during daylight. At night they would go out to the Command Post. To do that the route was along a road which was behind the combat lines and this was the most ghostly road they ever travelled on. There would always be swirling mists and fog seeping across the road and every once in a while tracer bullets would fly from nowhere. Here and there would be a broken cart wheel, a dead cow or a German body, pieces of helmets and equipment. Nobody was really anxious to travel that road alone at night.

During the daytime they would go up into the attic of their house along with another observer, who popped up from somewhere, to look around for targets. Of course, firing the guns was out, because if they had they would have been dead men inside half and hour. This artillery observer organised a few shots here and there.

About three hundred yards away in the German lines there was a little black spot which was actually a very deep foxhole occupied by one German soldier with red hair. About 3pm in the afternoon it became very urgent for this German to relieve himself. About that time the observer was in the attic ready to go with his big guns to get this lone redheaded German.

Everybody watched with great anxiety and curiosity every afternoon and the same picture unfolded. The German would make a jump and run about ten yards from his foxhole and there would be a scurry of dirt as a little hole was dug. He would then unfasten his belt and put himself in a rather vulnerable position.

About one minute later he would be back in his hole again and about two seconds later the artillery shells would be landing. While they were there they never got the redheaded German and Tucker just wondered how much he cost the United States in artillery shells.

On the fifth day the Third Battalion went back to a reserve area where they could take it easy for a few days.

The system was going to be that they would stay in the front line for five days and then the Second Battalion of the 505 would relieve them and this would keep going on a semi-permanent basis. Meanwhile the First Battalion was about a mile across an open space to the right at a place called Beek.

It was quite a long walk back to the reserve area but it was well worth while. I Company was billeted in a little hamlet of about ten or twelve houses and each unit had a house of their own. The mortar squads had possibly the best house. Tucker's crew had a bureau to themselves, some blankets and even sheets. On the first morning the owner of the house, who happened to be in the Dutch Resistance Movement, came to pick up something. He certainly wanted them to be comfortable and showed a pretty good spirit about the whole thing.

Lutz and Boone Crusenberry were the cooks and they did a darn good job. Tucker was able to go into Nijmegen in the afternoon and take a shower. The shower rooms weren't bad. This was about all he could do other than take a good look round. It was difficult in keeping Moe Green and a couple of the other boys from taking off for better things.

The day before they were due to go back into the line, Downing, Wally and Tucker got together and decided that if they were going to be of any use to the Company then they must prevail on the Company Commander to accept their plan to get an outpost. Mortars were no good unless the gunners could fire with some assurance of cover. Downing was commissioned to go up with an advance party and scout a new position.

It was a long walk on the return journey and it wasn't as easy as the walk a few days ago. This time the Company had a new position to occupy. In front of them was a dyke about a hundred yards out, but the line was to be dug along a sort of a hedgerow. About two hundred yards behind were two houses. The house on the left was to be the Company C.P., and the other earmarked for the mortar squad.

This was a beautiful setup for them again as it meant they could live in the house, dig in and fire the mortars in the back and still eat steak.

The Command Post, and the observation post for Jim Downing, Wally Wallace and Tucker was an old house which was just behind the Third Platoon's line. When they first got there it was a great problem stringing the telephone wires out because they had to criss-cross several small dykes. Lieutenant Charles Christian had a C.P. about seventy five yards to the rear in an old house. That C.P. was shared with the Third Platoon.

(Lieutenant Charles Christian had been transferred from B Company to I Company. He was one of the original members of the 505 and a veteran of the four combat jumps).

Harry Buffone and some of the others were over to the left. About one hundred and fifty yards beyond Tucker's line, by the end of a dyke, was a cluster of woods that had been ripped to pieces by shells. Here a group of Germans had dug themselves in.

In a short time Tucker didn't like it at all. He fired a few rounds and right away the 88's started coming in. Richard Cutler came upstairs into the attic and said that this was the Third Platoon's property and to get out. Tucker wasn't very anxious to argue about it, so he left.

Again there was trouble with the telephone wires and he had to fix them on the way. Tucker also ran into another live cow and decided to bring it back. That was not as easy as it sounds as he had to run behind hedges and throw things at the cow to keep her from wandering out towards the German lines.

When he got her back to the house, she got away into an apple orchard which was facing the enemy. If she had got out into the open beyond the orchard no one would have a chance to get her as the Germans would surely cut her down. Only a fool would go out there after a carcass.

Three or four of the Squad got at each end of the orchard and started throwing apples which were lying everywhere. Finally Moe Green hit her on the neck and they grabbed and pushed the cow behind the house and out of sight. Anything in front of the house was too dangerous to try.

Those five days weren't too bad. There was no real heavy shelling coming in and there seemed to be a mutual agreement for a time where nobody seemed to try. At any rate the orders were that the Third Battalion were not to start it.

They did however, set up a system of targets so that the mortars could be fired by the map. Tucker couldn't see very well from the top of the house but he could see the woods and the German dyke. Most of the firing was by remote control whereby the people in Platoon headquarters and in the outposts would call back and tell them how they were doing on the targets.

The basic fire points set up were one in the woods and a couple of points along the dyke. There was a system of target codes which were used for each point. One target off to the right, Tucker designated as 'Cicero'. From that day on, Boone Crusenberry and the others used that as Tucker's nickname and for the rest of their relationship in the Army he was known as 'Cicero' by the mortar squads.

For some relaxation they played cards and always managed to scrape up something new to eat. They had steak most of the time and Dikey did most of the cooking. Dikey was Boone's gunner.

On about the third day as Boone Crusenberry finished skinning the cow, the Executive Officer showed up and demanded a hindquarter. The officer and Downing got into a heated argument and Tucker was amazed by the fact that Downing made no bones about telling the Lieutenant that if he was to

(Left to right) George 'Chappie' Wood, William H. 'Bill' Tucker and Prince Bernhard of the Netherlands in 1987 at the opening of the Dutch Liberation Museum at Groesbeek.

get any of the cow, it would not be a hindquarter.

During this time it was rumoured that the Captain played rummy with Sergeant Howard Melvin and lost about a hundred bucks a day.

After the five days were over they returned to the reserve area. Again it was showers and a comfortable bed to sleep in, except for two things. Now there was not enough food around to eat and on two nights they had to man outposts near the hamlet because the Germans were sending patrols down the river behind the lines.

The Commander of the outpost, a Lieutenant, was the new Assistant Officer of the Second Platoon. During the night Leonard and Maglothin, his machine-gunner, picked up a German riding his bicycle down the road and brought him in. He did quite a bit of talking about some buzz-bomb sites behind the German dykes and that the Germans were going to open the dykes and flood the Allies out. After a while they did begin to see the buzz-bombs being launched, but the Germans didn't flood the dykes as yet. The five days on the line and five in reserve continued.

It began to get pretty rough on the line at night and it rained most of the time. The rest area was still the same good deal. Tucker and his friends used to get together at night where Robbie was, talk things over and play cards.

Robbie got a letter from Degenhardt who had been sent back for special duties in England and they never enjoyed listening to a letter so much. Degenhardt told Robbie he had a heck of a deal there and there were all the girls that he wanted, available to have a good time. Lieutenant Richard Degenhardt to all of them was always a good guy.

At night the English bombers used to fly over the position and bomb somewhere in the vicinity of thirty to forty miles away. They could hear the bombs from where they were and it would go on practically all night, every night. Tucker guessed it was a sort of shuttle bombing, like the Wellington's used to do in Africa.

The last time Tucker was up on the line, Doug Roth and Bill True of the 506 came to visit him from the 101st Division. The 506 had been sent north across the bridge and they were on the combat line, probably five or six miles to the left and temporarily attached to the 82nd. They all sat down underneath an apple tree to talk and there was some shelling nearby, but not in their area. Tucker noticed that both of his visitors were pretty jumpy sitting down in the open.

(Tucker, Roth and True trained as paratroopers together in F Company, 506th Parachute Infantry Regiment at the start of their service).

It wasn't uncommon for the Mortar Squad to have guests for dinner. They had a long table in the dining room and Crusenberry used to cook and serve the food. On this day they invited Doug and True to dinner and the two guests were amazed to see that they were eating steak and french fries with silver cutlery and on porcelain plates. Underneath the house was a cellar full of potatoes. Sergeant Melvin showed up and had dinner too. They were really two very surprised guys when they left after having the best meal since they got overseas.

There was quite a bit of activity along the line at night and during this last period they used to have to do some work. The Company was hollering for more men to go out on Command Post duty. That was really tough because every night it was raining and blacker than hell. It got so bad for a while along the line that even mortar Sergeants volunteered to go out and do duty.

They would go out and watch for a while and if they should see a German lighting a match to a cigarette, the guns would get on him pretty quick. Even though they hated to walk along that weird road at night, they did it just to get that feeling.

Ritchie was continually running back and forth from the Second Platoon to the Command Post. From him they got word that the 505 were going to be relieved from Holland in a couple of days by the Canadians. Tucker had on hand quite a bit of mortar ammunition, so he started firing it. The firing had not been going for long when it became increasingly apparent that there were quite a number of short rounds, but that didn't seem to bother Tucker.

While they had been on this line and back in the reserve area they had been receiving whisky and beer rations as per the British Army regulations. The men got rum, and the non-coms got brandy and whisky and there was also a lot of Dutch beer.

The first night after the Mortar Squad got the rum, some of the boys didn't dilute it. A half a canteen cup would just about knock a cow out. After they had been drinking the rum, Fisher and McNary were running up and down the dyke making a lot of noise and firing their 45's. The Germans were very quick at night and the minute there was some movement or light on the American side, they would open up with machine-guns and put some slugs on the spot in no time at all. It wasn't a very sane thing to move around at night.

By that time the opposing forces had got to know each other pretty well, and they knew that the German chow truck used to come in about 2.30 in the morning. For that reason, every night when someone had a little rum inside them, they would go out on the dyke and tie some tin cans together and put some pebbles in them. The tin cans would be tied to the back of a bazooka shell; then fired out of a cardboard cylinder. It made a weird shrieking noise and no doubt upset the Germans during their meals. Anyway, if the GI's had nothing else better to do they would all start firing or doing something else to upset the Germans when anyone heard their chow truck coming in.

The second last day before being relieved from the combat line, Tucker did quite a bit of firing with the mortars. A couple of shells landed near Lieutenant Christian's C.P., so he liked him all the less. Christian had continually warned about firing too much, but there were one hundred and fifty rounds left on the last day and Tucker was determined to give the woods on the left, beyond the Second Platoon lines, a thorough going over.

On top of that, the mortar section captured one full barrel of Dutch beer and everyone drank to their hearts content. Moe Green was really feeling aces on the last day and decided to top all things off with a little experiment.

The first thing the Squad tried to do was fire a mortar at a record distance. So two or three of them got down in the big hole and set the mortar at forty-five degrees, which was lower than safe. Two extra charges were added and the shell dropped down the tube. The result was a sharp compression in the hole, following which Tucker's ears rang for about a year. The shell went harmlessly in the air and exploded about fifty yards from the house. They checked the mortar and found the base plate was cracked and broken. This was about the seventh base plate they had destroyed.

In the afternoon of the last day it was decided to fire the greatest 'barrage' of the war. Each gun was to fire twenty-five rounds in succession into a patch of woods on the left. It was hoped that none of the rounds would be short. Of course one (Tucker) would be in trouble if there was because Lieutenant Christian's C.P. was nearest to where the firing was to take place. Not only that, when they were firing the night before, one of the shells had a hit near the C.P. and set part of it on fire.

Well anyway, they started firing the rounds and there were deafening roars from everywhere. After the guns had been firing for several minutes, calls started coming in that rounds were falling about both lines, particularly near Christian's Command Post.

There was no way to stop it and they finished firing all rounds in the record time of less than three minutes. The woods had probably caught about fifty shells but of the other twenty-five, some had landed near G Company and near the Second Platoon line with about three of them directly on Christian's C.P. They were simply bad rounds, but Christian's C.P. was burning merrily and his gunners had to leave in a hurry in broad daylight and scurry across the fields.

The last night there was spent with some regret, waiting for the Canadians to relieve them. 'With regret' because, again, they found it was a sort of a home, at least in the mortar section, and there hadn't been any real danger to the men. Downing, Wally and Tucker never worried too much about their own skins because they were always too busy to worry.

The toughest job they had to do was to get out and fix those wires. There was always just that little bit of regret leaving a place that you had got used to. It was raining as hard as hell that night as they sat in the barn at the rear of their house with the guns packed and equipment ready, waiting for the Canadians.

Finally, they were ready to leave Holland. Other than the bridges over the lower Rhine not much had been accomplished. It was near Thanksgiving, it was cold and raining very hard. The Canadians were due to relieve them shortly after midnight.

They had raised holy hell for the last day or two, firing all their guns constantly. Tucker was kind of tired of Holland, but in a way he felt a little melancholy as he waited for the relief. The GI's were very much concerned about the number of miles they would have to walk back to board the trucks.

The Canadians did not arrive until 2:00 or 2:30 in the morning. When they got to Tucker he had a chance to talk with them and found out they were pretty damned disgusted with everything. They had been attacking at Walcheren, outside of Antwerp for two or three months and had finally reduced the fortresses held by the Germans on the approaches to the port.

When they came in, their ranks were really depleted from this fighting. Even where the 505 were short on men, they only had three or four to put in the place of about ten or so of the Americans. Tucker felt sorry for them. They said they hadn't had any replacements from Canada for months. The GI's did the best they could to line them up in their positions, wished them well, and then started on the long march back towards Nijmegen.

Tucker stopped and took a last look at the city. The British Army traffic was flowing in and the 82nd were going out, leaving Nijmegen for the last time. Again, there could be said that there was some sort of a melancholy note remembering the hours of comradeship, without too much loss, that had been experienced in this area.

Most men were not in any shape for a long march and it was understood that there was thirty-five to fifty miles to go that day. Not only that, it was cold, damp and raining. All along the road they heard rumours of what Montgomery was going to do by Christmas, but they didn't take much to heart in that because Montgomery hadn't seen much of the German soldiers, and the 82nd had.

It was a long rough day and Tucker can't remember much except that his feet were killing him. All this after a gruelling two months campaign without sleep and proper clothing.

Some time after dark they arrived in a wooded assembly area where they immediately tried to catch up on some sleep under a downpour of rain. A lot of time was spent trying to start a fire but it wasn't successful.

By morning it really was wonderful to feel heat from the fire and get hold of 10 and 1 rations, some hot rum and just sit around and take it easy. They counted their casualites, talked to the Dutch people and had some fun. These areas where they would stop like this and spend a couple of days were very educational in the sense that they could put aside their operations and look around and see the difference in a man's face from just a few months ago.

France and Recuperation

The 505th Parachute Infantry Regiment boarded trucks early in the morning and started off towards the French border. The men had a chance, riding all day, to get a good look at the Dutch countryside.

It was a quiet, grey November day and somehow it had a touch of New England's winter atmosphere about it and what they saw, they liked, although the damage was considerable as everything had been hit very badly.

Another assembly area was reached near the border with Northern France. The nearest town was Maastricht where the 82nd Airborne had buried a lot of their dead in the last two months. There were some tents there but they didn't like the place at all and luckily only stayed a short time.

There was another full day's ride and the more they travelled into France the colder and wetter it got. All the GI's could do was to crouch down in the trucks trying to keep the dampness from sinking in. Nobody cared much for Northern France in winter, it was just cold and damp.

The day before Thanksgiving, 1944, the trucks rolled through the gates of an old French artillery camp which had been re-christened under the name of Camp Suippes. It was to be their barracks and training grounds until the 505 were needed again. As they marched through the inner gates, General James Gavin stood there looking them over. He was wearing a leather flying jacket and he really looked trim.

It was a good set-up with two storey barracks and big halls. I Company occupied the whole second floor of one of the buildings. All the NCO's had their own room, just across from the Orderly Room which was at the head of the stairs.

Outside was the courtyard where the companies could parade. They immediately set to work in making themselves comfortable with bunks and straw mattresses. Jim Downing, Harry Lutz, Larry Leonard, Robbie Robinson, Tucker and all the boys were in the NCO's room. Even Hill came walking in from England or somewhere.

The next day they enjoyed a Thanksgiving Dinner and on exploring they found a theatre in the camp and there were a lot of things to do. The next three weeks were spent doing hard training and some range firing. Parades were held in the courtyard to do some close order drill and as time wore on, day-long training excursions into the countryside took place. In the afternoons they had NCO schools and Harry Buffone tried to skip school all the time.

Colonel Ekman gave talks and V.D. lectures from the stage of the camp theatre. One of his talks was in regard to the looting in Holland and he spoke about the Inspector General catching one of the 82nd men who was nearly executed for the crime. An order had been signed in Holland by General Dempsey stating that the next man caught looting would be promptly hung, so there wasn't any more looting after that.

The mail started to arrive and even some Christmas packages rolled in. As for recreation, they would rush out right after supper. Usually Leonard, Matash and Tucker would go to the movies on Sundays where there was a stage show with striptease girls, acrobats, etc. It was a lot of fun going to these shows, betting to see who could get in line first and grabbing the best seat.

After the first night of passes to the city of Rheims there were no more passes issued. Thirty per cent of the Regiment went that night and it was the last night that anyone went. There were two problems. One was that the paratroopers had been in the field too long and the French people in that area had not really any experience with the American soldier of his type. Another problem was that nobody had any experience of drinking champagne and did not understand that this light frivolous drink could do wonders inside an hour and a half.

When Tucker got back to the trucks about midnight the place was loaded with wild soldiers and MP's. There were men lying in the gutters, dropping off the back of the trucks. Actually, one of the more infamous whore houses in Rheims had been burnt to the ground by troopers who couldn't get in.

Many people had been fighting and there had been killings, a few of which were the result of racial riots. It turned out there were a lot of black soldiers in the Transportation Corps who were going with white girls — and the 82nd Airborne was almost fifty per cent Southern. The city of Rheims was shut to the paratroopers for good. The next day there were many investigations, more restrictions imposed and several court martials instituted.

Leaves to Paris came up and Tucker went with Robinson, Lutz and Leonard. They left in trucks, it was raining as usual and after a long three or four hour ride they got to the outskirts of Paris. This was something really new, it was the first big city they had seen since Belfast.

The outskirts were very large and impressive. The four arrived at the Hotel Republic and spent the first day shopping. It was nice to start out in the afternoon, taking it easy, just walking and looking in the shop windows. The hotel rooms were very spacious and there was a large dining hall. Everything was just right. They wound up in the evening in Montmartre at a big party in a night club which was pretty lively and sat beside some people, including someone who was supposed to be a Countess. She seemed very obliging and when she was dancing with Robbie, he passed out.

At about 5am they decided to go home, they looked everywhere for some transportation because it was about two miles back to the hotel. Finally a fellow with a bicycle pushcart said he'd take them for a thousand francs. It was kind of warm that early morning and he pedalled and pedalled over hill and bridge. They were all so dopey, and when they short changed him, he gave Larry Leonard an argument.

They got back just in time for breakfast and after that they went out to see the sights again, this time taking a camera. It was a beautiful day and Tucker went to the Sacre Coeur and took some pictures of the church.

At dinner that night the violinist played 'Lili Marlene', all in all it was quite an atmosphere, taking the German's place and his song. Later they all got into a bad mood, feeling sort of disgusted with all the dissipating elements in Paris and started drinking cognac in a small café. After that they finished up in one of the places they had been in the night before and ran into the Countess, who had evidently started off last night on a drinking binge and was still on it.

Tucker had a good time in Paris but was a little sick at spending all his money. They all arrived back in Rheims with heavy heads.

Christmas packages started coming in again and they listened to the radios which helped pass the time. Training got to be a little more intensified with a lot of hiking and tackling new field problems. The errors of Holland were analysed and they discussed the problems of the operation to jump across the Rhine in the Spring.

Lieutenant Joseph Vandevegt told Tucker time and time again that he had heard about the good firing the Mortar Squad had done in Holland. Captain McPheeters gave a lot of lectures, as did other officers, on various subjects.

Some of the guys managed to beat the rap at the court martials for the night in Rheims because of the excellent defence work of Lieutenant George Clark.

The best thing about the Camp was the NCO's room. All the guys in that room were good men in the field and good men in training. Especially Jim Downing and Wallace.

There were a few radios up there and they spent a lot of time listening to the music. The BBC used to play songs like 'I Walk Alone' and 'I'll Be Seeing You' as much as ten or twelve times a day. Somebody usually had a recently arrived package of goodies to hand out. Every once in a while they would get a chance to spend the afternoon in the sack. The training didn't hurt any because the food was pretty good. There was a chance for sports, movies at night and the stage shows on Sunday afternoons.

On the night of 16th December 1944, Tucker and his friends were at the movies and every once in a while the show would stop and a Captain, Major or Colonel would be called out and told to report to Headquarters. They began to get a little apprehensive as to what was going on as they returned to the barracks and went to bed.

At 2am Rudy Tepsick started banging on Tucker's door. He told him to get the squads ready to move out by 8am with full equipment. He explained that the Germans had busted through in the Ardennes in Belgium.

Everybody bitched and raised hell in general but started to get the squads ready. They all had a devil of a time running around and scurrying up equipment and ammunition. Even (new) First Sergeant Elmer Ward was looking for equipment. After the return from Holland they had all put in a petition for Sergeant Howard Melvin to be promoted to an officer. Nothing happened in regard to that because Colonel Krause still hated Melvin's guts. However, Sergeant Ward, the Regimental Sergeant Major wasn't getting along in the Regiment Headquarters so he had been sent down in place of Melvin, and Melvin was now the Sergeant Major. This wasn't as good as having Melvin, but Ward was the next best thing. He did his best and helped the squads to move out.

On the radio was heard lots of broadcasting in German and English as to the confusion of what was going on at the breakthrough. One thing was certain, the 505 were going to engage the enemy pretty quickly and they had to get all their equipment and be ready to go. They did!

By 8 o'clock in the morning every man in every squad in the Company was ready, standing in the backs of huge Diamond T Trailer trucks waiting to head for Sedan, France, as the initial point for the new mission.

It was raining quite hard and the paratroopers were very reflective and silent. It was a very long all day ride that took them through the old First World War battle grounds. They noticed that there were still some of the debris from it in the fields, together with a lot of momuments along the road.

It was kind of cramped, sitting on the floor of those big Diamond T Trailers. Each carried about fifty or sixty men. Still it was better than stooping over in the back of a two and a half ton truck. They amused themselves by singing their favourite songs on the way up — 'I Walk Alone' and 'I'll Be Seeing You'.

****

(Left to right) William H. 'Bill' Tucker, General James Gavin and Elmo Jones in Leicester in 1984 during the 40th Anniversary celebrations.

Belgium — The Ardennes

Just at sunset the trucks passed through a small town called Bastogne where there was a single 82nd Military Policeman directing traffic. They didn't take much notice of the town, but after they had passed it, about ten minutes later, they heard gunfire and screaming mimmies coming in from the east. They knew then that the Germans had cut the road behind them. There wasn't much to worry about to where they were or where the road was cut, they just kept going east.

After it had become quite dark, they reached a rather quiet place, stopped and got off by the side of the road and relaxed amid the trees and shrubbery. It gave them a chance to eat and scurry around as usual. No one seemed very nervous since no one knew anything.

The order came to move out in the darkness and they passed heavy U.S. artillery pieces, but there was no firing and very little organisation. The impression was that no one knew where the enemy was. After walking a mile or so they set up a defence for the night.

It was a very hilly area with some deep narrow valleys. After the usual fooling around and arguments with Matash and Leonard as to whose squad was to have what in the defence line, Tucker settled down for the night. It was good to have Matash back as one of the squad leaders. It seemed funny that Matash, Leonard and Tucker started off as a machine-gun team years ago and were now the three squad leaders in the Second Platoon.

It was very cold and so far there seemed nothing to worry about. At daybreak and with something to eat they were ready to move. Just before they started to move out, Tucker noticed that the 376th Artillery had begun to dig in. Near those guns there were several Command Posts and a lot of confusion.

They guessed that they were still in Belgium as they walked along the road for a mile and passed through some elements of various Infantry Divisions. They looked pretty confused and didn't have much to say; neither did the 505.

There were a few burnt out and wrecked vehicles along the road but not much evidence of any foxholes or defence positions. After more walking in this hilly country they took a break near a farmhouse on a hill overlooking the road. Directly opposite, on the other side of the road from Germany was another hill. The road seemed to run in a valley all the way to the distance. This was a good place to set up a defence line.

The Belgian people at the farm were very scared. Some of the Medics set up a casualty station there. Doc Hanson of the Third Battalion reckoned the 505 would be back in France within a week. It was a matter of wild conjecture on how long the campaign — or whatever it was they were mixed up in — was going to last. The reason for so much conjecture was that the guys had not yet resigned themselves to having hard fights with the Germans since they were supposed to be in barracks at Rheims for a rest.

A good part of the afternoon was spent trying to find out where to go and where to get food. When the order came, all the NCO's reported to the C.P. and found that the Regiment was going to make a night attack. Further up the winding road in the valley there was a small town. No one knew if the enemy were there but it was going to be a night march and an attack to clean out any Germans.

The town was some miles away and they started off in the darkness with I Company in the lead. As usual they always hated to leave a good spot. The attack was timed for about midnight, but who knew where the enemy was or what was going on?

The area was a beautiful hilly forest with an air of mystery about it. The road ahead looked like a mountain pass with very high peaked hills and a mountain to the side of it. I Company were strung out on each side of the road and the First Platoon formed a point with the Second Platoon in the middle. It seemed to get quite warm as the step quickened and a break was taken after about five kilometres. Just to the left of where they stopped was a smashed and burnt-out Jeep. Ten yards away they discovered a dead American in a crawling position just off the road. It was figured he had been surprised by the German advance within the last day or so. He must have been trying to reach a small building about ten yards further on when he had been cut down. The paratroopers gathered in the shadow of the small building and tried to snatch a smoke.

After many more stops and false alarms they reached the town without mishap. The advance party had made no contact with the enemy so they warily entered the town, stopped right in the middle and found there wasn't a soul around. At one house it was noticed that there was little chink of light under the blackout curtains and they went to investigate, hoping to find food rather than Germans. The people let them in and several of the guys clowned around a little and were rewarded with some Belgian coffee and bread.

Tucker's French was pretty good with the Belgians, at least they managed to understand each other. They said that the Germans had passed with tanks on a road about three kilometres north, parallel to the one the 505 were on, on that same day.

Whilst in this house, for some reason or other, one guy pressed the trigger of a tommy-gun and fired a couple of bullets through the floor. He claimed it was an accident.

Orders now were to dig in around the edges for the night. The town was formed like in a saucer with a ridge running round the edge. It wasn't very high and about every ten yards or so there was a wire fence or a hedgerow. The Second and Third Squads were on the ridge but the mortar squads stayed back at a house on the outskirts, where they could fire the 60mm's if they had to. Tucker's Squad got in the barn first and then the people let them in the house where they gave out coffee.

They sat around and talked through part of the night and for the rest of it slept out in the yard. It was cold as hell out there. In the morning things were still quiet. After some more coffee they ate inside with the family.

All the local people were wondering what was going to happen. This was the 20th December. Like Normandy, but unlike Holland, the GI's were continually trying to figure out what they were supposed to be doing and where the enemy was.

Actually they were quite willing to settle down in this town. However, as it got dark orders came down to be ready to advance by truck. It seemed the only time they moved anywhere in this country was when it got dark. The Company assembled in the main street and waited for the trucks. They had to wait for a hell of a long time during which they noticed that the Command Post had been established, as always, in a very lush place. When the trucks arrived they began again to go in the direction of Germany. It was a ghostly ride in the back of a two and a half ton open truck. After about ten miles they got off at a deserted farmhouse on the side of a hill.

I Company wandered around for some time until they finally came down to a railroad track with a sunken roadbed and followed the course of the track. Orders finally arrived to the squad leaders and it seemed that the mission was to keep going until they came to a large cement bridge. About fifty yards east of the bridge there would be a river, called the Salm.

Over the river at that point would be a wooden bridge and I Company were to cross and set up a bridgehead on the other side. Again, nobody knew if the enemy would be there.

They reached the bridge and found that General James Gavin had already been there. No contact with the Germans was made, but there had been some small arms fire along the way so everybody was extra careful. Tucker slept that night on the gravel in the railroad pit and it was awfully cold and uncomfortable. In the morning they all started to swap food and argue like hell again.

The new position was on a very steep hill on the west bank of the Salm River, but still no men had been put on the other bank. The road on the far side went winding up a hill past quite a few homes, on this side the road did the same and about half way up there was a block of houses running along a ledge. By the first house a 57 anti-tank crew were digging in. All the time Tucker was looking for the most useful place for his mortars. (This was the Belgian village of Rochelinval.)

Lieutenant Christian and Tucker went on patrol. Things seemed pretty deserted. There was a little wooden footbridge up to the left which they crossed and went up the steep hill with the winding road. Half way up they met a Belgian citizen, who fortunately again, Tucker got along good with in French. He told him that there was strong enemy armour at a town about five kilometres away. This was enough for the patrol to hear at the present time so they scooted back across the bridge. The I Company Command Post was also up on the hill and they had good coffee there, brewed by Scotty Hough.

Things were begining to move. Hallahan and two other guys were on patrol and had gone about two thousand yards across on the other bank. The C.P.

was supposed to be in radio contact with them but all they could hear was a lot of static.

There seemed to be heavy attacks at Trois Ponts a few miles to the north against the Second Battalion and the Germans were reported to be heading south towards I Company. Christian was wondering about his defences, when he was ordered to move the Second Platoon across the river and hold in a delaying action. The attack was expected to shift from Trois Ponts down to the bridges.

It was then decided to go over and see what was doing across the river. Tucker found Willis Maglothin with the machine-gun cursing everyone at his luck in having to carry all the heavy equipment. Just about that time a German tank appeared round a bend in the road about one hundred yards away. Maglothin opened up with his gun on the tank which was loaded up with wild men in black uniforms and things started. The huge German tank swung its gun turret and as the gun fired, Tucker made a flying leap into a ditch and escaped unhurt.

Maglothin had been hit in the leg and as they tried to get him back across the river they ran into Major James Kaiser. He said that they were being hit by a battalion of the First SS Adolph Hitler Panzer Division. The only way to bring Maglothin in was through the water, which was four to five foot deep: his leg looked in shreds.

Christian pulled all the Second Platoon back across the river. It was quite dark and they got ready for action. At the same time the C.P. was trying to contact Hallahan on the radio and bring him in. Finally, when they did hear him he was told to move south down the river and come through the 325 or the 508 lines.

Unfortunately he came through into the H Company area and Norell Blankenship got shot by an H Company BAR man. Everything was confused now but at last the Platoon were back across the river with the wounded. This meant they could open fire when they were ready. The Germans made a rush for the wooden bridge and I Company fired from all over the hill and the German 20 millimetre guns returned the fire. Matash was down at the bridge and they blew up a tank or half track as it tried to cross.

The American fire increased and Tucker's mortar shells were dropping in the right places. He could see flashes and it was a wonderful sight in the darkness below where the Germans were. They were pretty wild. The mortar was so high up on the hill they could not elevate their 88's on the other tanks up towards it, even though its position was only about one hundred and fifty yards walking distance from the bottom of the hill. All they could do was to fire their 20mm guns.

Herbert Bass and Tucker were lying in the back of a wooden shack and the 20mm shells were ripping the roof off. They kept telling Emelio Intrieri to fire away. After a while the Battalion Commander sent orders to cease fire. Things quietened down considerably and the NCOs went to the C.P. where Major Kaiser and Captain McPheeters were trying to figure things out.

(McPheeters was a very wealthy man and a member of the family that owned the Cincinnati Reds baseball team).

Tucker then went down the hill with Scotty and helped bring Maglothin up. He was cursing the Germans loudly, but he lived. Willis Maglothin received the Silver Star for his actions.

During the night the biggest worry was how much artillery the Germans would bring up in the morning and how open the lines were on both sides of the Company.

Towards dawn the valley was very foggy and the 82nd artillery started coming in and landing across the river, but the GIs were still sweating it out, waiting for the German artillery to start. Then the morning of 22nd December arrived, and with it they saw that the enemy had finally pulled back a couple of miles instead of digging in.

Across the bridge a patrol found a half-track loaded with Germans in American uniforms, and with American cigarettes. Rudy Tepsick and Matash went on patrol and the rest of the day Tucker spent running around checking the flanks. A lot of the mortar shells were falling short and he worried about the bad ammunition.

There was concern again about the night because in the very open positions the Germans could infiltrate through easily. The Second Platoon grouped around the house up on the hill, behind which they had the mortar and kept in contact with the C.P., about fifty yards below. The Germans did infiltrate through the positions on the left, but the guys survived another night.

There was quite a bit of firing during the next day. On the enemy hill opposite there was hardly anything to see except two or three small hamlets. Every once in a while there was a glimpse of a black uniformed German darting between the houses. Tucker's mortars fired at a range of about one thousand yards and the hits seemed good, but some of the rounds were bad and fell short. One landed close to Rudy Tepsick and there was hell to pay. This one was a dud and he was lucky. Orders now were to take the serial number on the cases which held the short rounds and turn them in.

Frequently they wondered how the First and Third Platoon mortar squads were doing and who was left but they were too far away. Tucker missed working with Jim Downing and Robert 'Wally' Wallace and couldn't help thinking how strong they felt in Holland when they were all together.

There were rumours of the 101st Airborne being engaged in heavy fighting to the west at Bastogne. Tucker's teeth which had been hit with the rifle butt in the Holland jump were hurting, they were extremely painful.

The combat lines were wide open but they were not sending up the cooks or supplymen to help fill the gaps yet. With these problems facing the Platoon they were all constantly bickering with Lieutenant Christian. Time was running out for I Company that day of 23rd December and night was coming. With it, scattered firing started and there was great apprehension about what would happen that night.

During darkness they were ready to fire at anything. At one time Tucker went by a hedge and spotted a German crouching a few yards away. He was frozen but managed to empty his gun at him. Oddly enough 'he' turned out to be an old automobile tyre that had rolled into the side of the hedge: so the battle went on.

Morning came again, the day before Christmas. After fooling around and hearing the rumours that were going down the line, Tucker got permission to go to the Battalion Aid Station and get his bad teeth yanked.

There were some Signal Corps cameramen hoping to get some motion pictures of the boys in action. The enemy as usual was not in sight during the daytime. The Signal Corps men were quite willing to undertake the venture and they suggested that the guys should start firing at anything that might be the enemy.

It was about three miles through very dark, thick and eerie woods to the Battalion Aid Station. Tucker had a feeling of deep apprehension that day walking through those woods, as if he was being watched all the time — a real sense of dread.

When he got there they were topsy turvy with rumours of a withdrawal. Captain 'Pete' Suer, a dentist, finally pulled Tucker's two bad teeth out with the aid of a pair of medical pliers and a flashlight. Tucker then started the three mile walk back at a pretty fast pace going through those woods which, with the coming of evening, were getting darker. The pines made it so dark along the road and it was so silent that the noise from his boots on the snow sounded like thunderclaps.

(Two days later, on the 26th December, Captain Alexander P. Suer was seriously wounded by a mortar shell and died of his wounds).

The orders were to make the first withdrawal which the 505 had ever experienced with the 82nd. They were told that the holes in the flanks were miles wide and that the enemy were infiltrating through to the left and right, The withdrawl, to straighten the line, was to start at midnight.

Part of the Second Platoon were to be left as a rear guard until 5am, and then to blow the bridge. The beatings in Normandy and other places were catching up with I Company's good luck in Holland. Some of the Second Platoon pals would die for sure on this Christmas Eve.

Shortly after dark, heavy firing started on the left, near the First and Third Platoons. Then the word came that an entire German Battalion had attacked them from the rear. The Germans wanted to get back across the river to their side and they had to come through the 505.

Two Germans had been taken alive, an officer and a sergeant. They were wounded but were not treated until they revealed that they were part of a Panzer Battalion of five hundred which had been to the Third Battalion's rear, hiding in the woods. They were low on ammunition and waiting for Christmas Eve to make their move. Later it turned out that this was the SS outfit that shot the one hundred and fifty prisoners at Malmedy. In the attack the Company lost Gavin Edgerton and Moe Green. They were apparently prisoners in the woods with the rest of the German Battalion.

Shortly before midnight the Third Battalion were under way in attack formation. That Christmas Eve in 1944 was snowy, cold and clear; a beautiful evening. The green pines were laden with the heavy snow. It was probably a typically beautiful German Christmas, but the column was burdened by the snow. The Jeeps and anti-tank guns had to be pushed and there were frightened artillery and supply people with the Company going through those strange woods that Tucker had taken earlier to get his teeth pulled.

Suddenly there was the sound of machine-guns and rifles as the point was fired on. Everybody dropped to the ground and in the darkness around them there were flashes everywhere. The point up front kept calling for machine-gun fire on the flanks and the mortar battery to fire ahead of the column. After a short while they pushed on.

All kinds of firing split the night on all sides and lots of mortar shells were laid down to the front. The Third Squad of the First Platoon at the point pushed on, even with all the firing no one seemed to get hit.

A strange yell was heard as Edgerton and Moe Green dashed out from the trees and joined the column, and now they learned more about the remnants of the German SS Battalion in the woods. There was no place to go except forward.

(As evidenced later from Moe Green, the Germans were the remnants of Colonel Pfiefer's SS Battalion. During the lonely walk by Tucker through the woods they had been on both sides of the road, watching him, and let him go through. They didn't want to take any more prisoners, or kill anyone who would be missed. Being low on food and ammunition, they were preparing for their withdrawal and did not wish to create any 82nd patrol activity).

Downing was up there with the Captain directing fire to the sides of the road ahead. The mortars were set up to fire at one hundred to two hundred yards in front of the point. After each thirty rounds the point was pushed forward with all the automatic weapons firing. Finally they broke through the Germans.

This had been one of the best fights they had ever been in and it was not even planned. It was an accident that the two forces were withdrawing through each other at the same time. Through the confusion Major Kaiser said over the radio, "What help can I send you Archie?" The Captain answered, "Just send that guy to the three forks and we'll get through."

(It appears that the path through the forest split into three and this radio message was to make sure that a guide was at the 'three forks' to be sure that they took the right path).

The Third Battalion finally hit daylight as they left the thick woods. After about twenty minutes the remainder of the rear guard arrived and then they all pushed on a few miles until they were halted. This was on the road which was at the base of a long line of hills and it was understood that this would be the new defence line.

It turned out to be a beautiful Christmas Day, especially there in the snow covered hills of the Ardennes. They had been praying for the guys left at the bridge at the Salm River who had to come through the enemy infested woods. While the troopers were eating their rations, the rest of the men came in. They had suffered casualties. John Lebednick and Frank Federico were hit at the railroad tracks — Lebednick had been killed. They were all very tired and as proud of their actions as everybody was. Soon after the column had left the railroad pit they were attacked by superior German forces moving south along the rail bed, but they held out.

The new defence line was set up on the hill. It looked like good country and the view certainly did command the road and the terrain for a thousand to two thousand yards east. There were heavy dense woods across the road at the base of the hill. The mortar squads were ordered to group together for the defence and they were working together again.

Again Tucker found a wonderful house at the rear of the hill, around which they set up the mortars. Immediately he arranged the usual kitchen duties and put the boys to work digging in the guns; Downing, Wally and Tucker went out to the front to set up an observation post.

It was snowing but they were lucky to find a big hole right with the First Platoon. They dug it deeper and the snow made the work a little harder, but Tucker didn't mind. His Second Platoon riflemen were up to the right in reserve, where they should be after that tough fight at the bridge.

This was the beginning of five days in this position. Five days and five nights including New Year's Day which did not go by without some excitement. Downing, Wally and Tucker established a routine of taking turns at the O.P. They found it very cold sitting up there watching the road but the hole was deep and they felt some security.

On the second day, about a company of Germans attacked. The guns opened fire and managed to catch them as they were running back into the woods across the road below the hill. All the guns were firing and probably hit many of them in the woods. However, one gun was at the wrong angle and nearly killed Patino and Tommy Thompson in the First Platoon. Moreover, some of the shells were wasted and the holes in the snow where they had hit could been seen. Lieutenant Christian saw them and told the Captain.

That was the climax of Tucker's running disputes and, of course, brought things to a head with Lieutenant Christian. Downing and Tucker had been brazenly open towards him as he requested more of the men, time and time again. At one time they both complained to the Captain about this.

On the third day, after Tucker heard about the complaint of his firing, he went up to see Christian to bitch. He forgot that the Second Platoon was in reserve and that Christian had been taking out all the patrols, which is pretty tough on the nerves. Tucker found him sleeping in a hole by some pine trees behind the defence line of the Third Platoon.

He bent down and checked him, and as Christian started to shake his head and get awake, Tucker started to bitch. Christian staggered towards Tucker, his hand was on his 45 holster: he cursed him, threatened him, and Tucker thought that he would kill him until he tactfully withdrew. From then on Tucker stayed clear of Lieutenant Christian.

In those five days, life at the house was good. The top floor was used for sleeping but it was pretty hard getting to sleep because they used to figure that if a shell hit the roof, Stald and Tucker would be the first ones to go. A three man guard was put on at night, one in the house and two outside, sitting in a hayloft right behind the house.

Wally and Tucker used to sit in the hay together on guard. They had to watch carefully because the rear was the left flank of the line and there was really no contact in the gully with H Company. The Germans were infiltrating through there all the time. They had the guard duty there on New Year's Eve, which again was a beautifully clear and cold night. It was one of those nights when they found time to think a few things over. Mostly of England, a little of the family and perhaps a little of the girl friends. It was strange because they sort of forgot the U.S. and probably had more warmth for England and the life they had there than anything else. Home and family seemed a lifetime behind — they were with their buddies.

There was a lot of pride in their own self-reliance, and the respect which it had all achieved. It was due to the tremendous power of the 82nd Airborne Division's front line combat troops, in their individual dignity, mutual respect and the exhausting actions of deep comradeship and pride. So most of them had those thoughts on that beautiful New Year's Eve and those thoughts have stayed with everybody throughout the years.

During this time there was much to do in the day. Tucker explored the Second Platoon's area and once stood on an open hillside in the Third Platoon area to direct fire upon the enemy four hundred yards away. During those five days they all grew up some more.

On the 28th or 29th December the men went back in relays to the Company Command Post for a belated Christmas dinner. This was the only hot meal they had in the battlefield in two years in Europe, Africa or Sicily. With a good meal and the warmth of the C.P., it was tempting to stay around and talk about what you had done, but the C.P. was only interested in what they were doing and they had more men to take care of.

Casualties were light in that period, but a piece of shrapnel had gone through Ed Morrissey's head and put his eye out.

Robbie took out a snow-capped patrol at one time. Finally a heavy attack was stopped on the east flank and planes were dive-bombing and strafing the enemy a thousand yards away.

Every day they could see the bombers go over at twenty thousand feet leaving their beautiful vapour trails in the sky, surrounded by flak from the German anti-aircraft guns.

On the evening of 1st January 1945, the Third Battalion were ordered into reserve and all the GIs were thinking of home or what would be next. The 517th Parachute Infantry Regiment would be taking over the combat line. At midnight they came into the postions and the 505 started to slowly move to the rear with all their equipment.

It was a very long march with so much equipment and thoughts were that combat really got you out of shape. They finally pulled into a large snowy grove of pine trees and settled down for the night. This was about four miles behind the lines and for some reason they let them light fires.

It was wonderful to sit around the fire with the guys and get warm. After the coldness of combat, it seemed to bring out expressions of the feelings which they had been sharing in the field as good friends and comrades.

In the morning they found that the Second and Third Battalions had been practising tank attacks in the area, and that day there was a practice rifle grenade firing at trees. The day went by quickly and with it came the first mail in many weeks.

With Tucker's mail came a big box of chocolate cookies, without a dent in them, from Mrs Morrison (a neighbour and mother of one of Tucker's school friends). Then came the news that an attack was planned at dawn the next day, the 3rd of January.

After much finangling around as to who would sleep where, the fires were lit and they stole from fire to fire, talking to each other and feeling the warmth. No one else could be involved in the history that they shared. Everyone had one of the chocolate cookies. A group with Tucker sat around the best fire and talked half the night. They did not seem to worry about tomorrow. The sense of camaraderie gave them the greatest strength they ever had. Lieutenant Degenhardt talked a lot that night. He was one of the best, the most regular officer they ever had. Perhaps the guys knew he would die tomorrow. They finally turned in for a few hours sleep.

With the dawn of 3rd January came a new day which would bring with it disaster for the old Third Battalion, and the old men from Africa who survived Sicily, Italy, Normandy and Holland. The first order was that all men should be in proper uniform for the attack. Overcoats were to be left behind and all they had to take were guns, ammunition, belts and harnesses. It was Bill Hallahan's turn to stay behind with the equipment but he wanted to be in on the attack and so he swapped places with someone.

Tucker didn't mind the loss of his overcoat. He was the only man in I Company who didn't wear long underwear as the cold never bothered him. They moved out after breakfast. It was dawn when they spread out along the road and found that they were to reach the initial point Command Post outside of Basse-Bodeux by 08.25. The attack would start at 08.30 and progress back towards the Salm River and towards a town called Fosse, up in the hills.

It was very grey and cold with the snow turning to slush under their boots along the road. The temperature was such that one minute the slush was freezing and another minute you sweated enough to make it miserable. During the first break, an officer and a NCO were killed by artillery. The 82nd artillery started to open fire and short rounds were heard landing dangerously close. They kept marching and the American guns kept firing short until Louis DiGiralmo lay dead at the side of the road.

Downing and Tucker had fought to employ the 60mm mortars together in the attack, but today they were to do that only under the Captain's orders. In the meantime all Platoons were to attack at parallel courses to each other.

By 08.25 the initial point was reached and five minutes later the attack moved off, going up a fire lane on the big hill to Fosse. No enemy were encountered at first.

It was uphill in single file, all the way to Fosse and their tails began to drag. For about half an hour they had no trouble as they climbed the hills in the snow. The 325 and the Third Battalion were attacking to the right and the 508 were behind in reserve. The whole front was moving forward in a major attack. Was it to be all the way to Cologne?

As the summit of the biggest hill was reached they proceeded slowly with great caution. The Company was sort of wound around the side of the hill.

The First and Second Platoons pushed for the high points. Suddenly they were fired on by machine-gun posts at the left rear, which they had passed but were closer to the top of the hill than them.

The paratroopers ran up to the next level of the hill to get a line on the German machine-guns. Part of the Third Platoon sheltered behind a ledge. This hill had probably six or seven ledges all the way up to the top.

The German machine-gun fire was now steady and heavy, coming from the left flank and the front. The Second Platoon was ordered to double back and attack from around to the right. The enemy firing continued, but it seemed to be coming from both sides now. Apparently the Germans were dug inside the town of Fosse and had set up strong machine-gun posts at the crest of the hill to the left. These could look down into the valley and I Company were in between the outposts and the town.

Captain McPheeters was at the head of the First Platoon attack and was killed by machine-gun fire from the top of the hill. Hallahan started to move that way too and was shot through the head.

Lieutenant Degenhardt moved forward when the Captain went down and was also killed by the machine-gun fire. Richard Cutler, a veteran from Africa on, died leaving a wife and children. The GIs could only move by crawling and finally had to lay flat where they were in the snow.

They knew now that they were really pinned down. The German artillery was screaming in and crunching all around. It was terrible, the troopers wanted to dash forward at the town, but others had tried to and were killed. The operations sergeant, Sergeant William F. Reynolds, crawled up ahead and was killed.

The guys that were nearest the town were safer from the artillery. They couldn't move back or they would lose the attack, and if they moved forward the machine-gun posts could nail most of them.

A group from the Second Platoon tried to move up to another ledge to open fire. Three died: bullets through the neck partially ripped Nick Cavallaro's head off. A bullet hit Tucker's rifle and it ricocheted into his left shoulder. The same burst of machine-gun fire hit Dennis Force badly in the face and arm.

Another bullet went into the rear of Tucker's helmet, ripped through the liner and tore a big hole out of the front. He fell to the ground and seeing the holes in the helmet, asked Stald if the top of his head was still there.

They rolled themselves, the wounded and the dead down the side of the hill away to where there was cover. Somebody had to do something, try something new.

This was war and the fighting that one reads about. The thoughts they had were that they could tell this story for a hundred years and few people would believe it. They probably could never understand it as it actually was. The noise was terrific. The artillery was wiping the men out slowly, nobody could move.

The remainder of the Platoon, having failed in its attack on the outpost, rejoined Tucker on the lower ledge of the hill. The First and Third Platoons were still out in front, fifty yards from the town and pinned down.

They moved on again, up towards them, staying along the side of the hill.

There was a little path going up to the town and to the right of it was a big haystack. Some of the guys were behind that haystack. The German shelling was getting worse. Tucker pressurised Christian for an open assault on the town because of the increasing losses from the shelling. Everyone was flattened in the snow.

About the only moving around they could do was to crawl over to the haystack and sit there with Rudy Tepsick for a few minutes and then crawl back, all the time arguing with Christian about what could be done. There was no Company Commander, and a decision could not be made until they got word of what was happening on the flanks.

Rudy Tepsick was a good man, big and strong, above all he had brains.

The front of their combat suits were frozen with occasional patches melted from the body heat. Hill came by, lumbering along and holding on to a wound in his neck. The Company had lost at least forty men on the hill.

Bullets were whining through the area at waist height as Tucker sat with Rudy behind the haystack. He seemed to feel a little secure but he still knew what a machine-gun could do if they decided to shoot the haystack.

Suddenly as they sat there they saw H Company moving in, about three hundred yards away along the valley, to give them a hand. The Germans saw this too and in a moment H Company was under a murderous artillery barrage.

After ten minutes they gave up on them. Tucker and Tepsick were pressing for an attack and assault on the town. They did not know what they were waiting for, they couldn't even dig in.

Along the road was spotted a large body of men coming up, moving too closely together. Tucker had to get them to turn back or they would have everybody killed. He ran to the road and yelled to their Captain to get the hell back. Larry Leonard was on the ground nearby with some men.

Then the end came. The German artillery zeroed in, right where they were, and the shells exploded all around. Nearby two men were blown apart. Larry was hit and was bleeding from a head wound. The Captain who had led his men up the road had disappeared from sight.

Tucker ran out and ordered every man back behind the first ledge. The explosions around them were terrific. A shell landed between Oscar Harris and James Brown — close friends — and two more African veterans of the 82nd were lost forever.

There was a wire fence along the top of the six foot deep ledge. Logan got over it, Intrieri got over too and he dropped down. The last man, Tucker, was about to fall over the fence when he heard the whine of a shell. As he fell back he saw a shell hit Intrieri in the back. Tucker was then rammed into the fence as he was hit in the knee.

About three hundred yards back along the ledge there was a First Aid Station collecting point. Many were there including guys with bad leg wounds. Lieutenant Christian had a head wound which Tucker bandaged for him, and told him he was hit really bad and was probably done for. The Lieutenant looked serious and agreed. They were strange men now, but Tucker and Christian were finally friends at the Aid Station.

Tucker then wanted to go back into the line but Christian said "No, you are too badly hurt for that." They had to make a run for it in a Jeep. One guy was afraid and gave Tucker his 45 which he tucked into his jacket and he sat beside a pale faced man on the Jeep who was dying with a bullet through his head. Life could certainly go fast.

On the way Christian and Tucker had to get out to hack down fences. His knee really hurt and the swelling was stiffening it up. His arm was also frozen where it was hit.

At last they reached the town of Basse-Bodeux which they had left several hours ago in peace with few prospects in mind. Tucker was not sane after two shots of morphine and for some reason, as they drove into town, he fired the 45 into the air.

At the Regimental Headquarters the ground and the buildings were littered with dead and wounded men. The Surgeon gave him sulfa and quick bandages. Men were dying. Tucker's wounds felt small by comparison as he looked around at the others. He told the Surgeon that he didn't want any help and he was told to go in an ambulance with the other wounded.

He hung around the yard awhile. Colonel Krause, now the Regimental Executive Officer was pacing up and down. Tucker said to him, "Well Colonel, the old guys got it today." Krause stopped, gazed at him and beyond him. It seemed that there were tears in his eyes. An ambulance pulled up and Tucker slowly climbed into the front seat beside the driver. The morphine still made him feel a little high and it was pleasant to ride along.

All along the road were trucks, tanks, guns and more equipment slowly pushing forward. On seeing this Tucker knew that they were winning the war. It was a strange thing but when he was back lying on the field before Fosse, he could not realise how a war could be won with so few men in the front line and so many at the rear. But as he looked at this long line of equipment, he could see that the rear just pushed at the front and what burned out at the front was quickly replaced from the rear.

Regiments replaced regiments. Battalions replaced battalions, but no one could replace the men and the friends that Tucker lost on that day.

After one night in Fosse, the attack of the 82nd continued to roll eastward. I Company went on to the Ruhr battle, where Tucker rejoined them in late February together with some officer replacements. He found a little more than a third of the men who attacked Fosse on the 3rd January were left.

The Company completed its missions along the Ruhr and the Rhine but 3rd January had broken its back and driven a terrible blow into its spirit and camaraderie.

After patrolling the west bank of the Rhine, there came a duty in Bonn, searching house by house. Tucker didn't find anything but the schnapps was good. Along the Rhine they lost Lieutenant William Dey on a river patrol — a great I Company soldier and a fine person.

Near the end, as I Company crossed the Elbe in attack formation they lost their wonderful member of the Downing mortar section, Wally Wallace, who was the last of the old men to die who had started in Africa over two years earlier.

MEMBERS OF I COMPANY, 505 PIR, MENTIONED IN THE DIARY

BARROW, William	'Red the Medic'
BASS, Herbert	Deceased
BATCHELLER, Lt Col. Herbert F.	Killed in Action — Normandy
BLANKENSHIP, Norell	
BROWN, Pfc. James W.	Killed in Action — Ardennes
BUFFONE, Harry	
CARUSO, Mike	
CAVALLARO, Pvt. Nick A.	Killed in Action — Ardennes
CHRISTIAN, Lt. Charles R.	
CLARK, Lt. George E.	
CRINETI, Anthony	Deceased
CRUSENBERRY, Boone	Deceased
CUTLER, Pfc. Richard W.	Killed in Action — Ardennes
CZUBERNAT, Stanley	Deceased
DEGENHARDT, 2/Lt. Richard H.	Killed in Action — Ardennes
DEY, Lt. William R.	Killed in Action — Germany
DIGIRALMO, Pvt. Louis	Killed in Action — Ardennes
DIKEY	
DOLAN, Capt. John 'Red' J.	Deceased
DOWNING, Robert James 'Jim'	Deceased
DUSSEAULT, Albert 'Frenchy'	Deceased
DYLES, Morris	
EDGERTON, Gavin	
EKMAN, Col. William E.	Deceased
FEDERICO, Frank	
FISHER	
FORCE, Dennis	
GAILLARD, 1/Lt. William S.	Killed in Action — Normandy
GEARY, Pfc. Albert	Killed in Action — Normandy
GILLILAND, Pvt. Everett W.	Killed in Action — Holland
GOODSON, Howard	
GREEN, Odell 'Moe'	
HAGEN, Maj. William J.	
HALLAHAN, Cpl. William A.	Killed in Action — Ardennes
HANKS, Sergeant Harvey	Deceased
HANSON, Russell 'Doc'	Killed in Action — Germany
HARRIS, Pfc. Oscar C.	Killed in Action — Ardennes
HILE, Pvt. Arthur S.	Killed in Action — Normandy
HILL, Paul	Deceased
HOFFMAN, Lansing C.	Deceased
HOUGH, Pfc. John J. 'Scotty'	
HOWALL, Lt. James W.	
HUGHES	
JONES, Edwin. 'Old Man Jones'	
INTRIERI, Pfc. Emelio	Killed in Action — Ardennes
KAISER, Major James	
KRAUSE, Major Edward	Deceased
KROENER, Lt. Walter B.	

KRUPINSKI, Ray	
LAWS, Pfc. William H.	Killed in Action — Normandy
LEBEDNICK, Pvt. John C.	Killed in Action — Ardennes
LEONARD, Pvt. Jack R.	Killed in Action — Normandy
LEONARD, Larry	Deceased
LESTER, Glenn A.	
LOGAN, Albert	Deceased
LOPEZ, Leo F.	Deceased
LUTZ, Harry	Deceased
MAGLOTHIN, Willis	
McNARY	
McPHEETERS, Capt. Archibald A.	Killed in Action — Ardennes
MATASH, Sgt. Charles	Deceased
MELVIN, 1st Sgt. Howard	
MORRISSEY, Edward	Deceased
MULVANEY, James P 'Gil'	
PATINO, Augustine 'Ray'	
PRAGER, S/Sgt. Clarence	Killed in Action — Holland
PRZYBYLA, Pvt. Joseph J.	Killed in Action — Normandy
REYNOLDS, Sgt. William F.	Killed in Action — Ardennes
RITCHIE, James T.	Deceased
ROBINSON,S/Sgt James A.'Robbie'	Deceased
RUSSO	
SANDEFUR, Sgt. Felix C.	Killed in Action — Normandy
SMITH	
STALD, James	Deceased
SUER, Capt. Alexander P. 'Pete'	Died of Wounds — Ardennes
SUTHERLAND, Donald	Deceased
SWINGLER, Capt. Harold H.	Killed in Action — Normandy
SYNOLD, Pfc. Frederick G.	Died of Wounds — Normandy
TEPSICK, Rudy	Deceased
TERELLA, Mike	
THOMPSON, Arthur 'Tommy'	
VANDEVEGT, Lt. Joseph W.	Deceased
WALLACE, S/Sgt. Robert E.	Killed in Action — Germany
WARD, Sgt. Elmer P.	Deceased
WELSH, Norman	Deceased
WINGFIELD, Jack C.	Deceased
ZOROMSKI, Victor	Deceased

Index